D1179944

Captivity

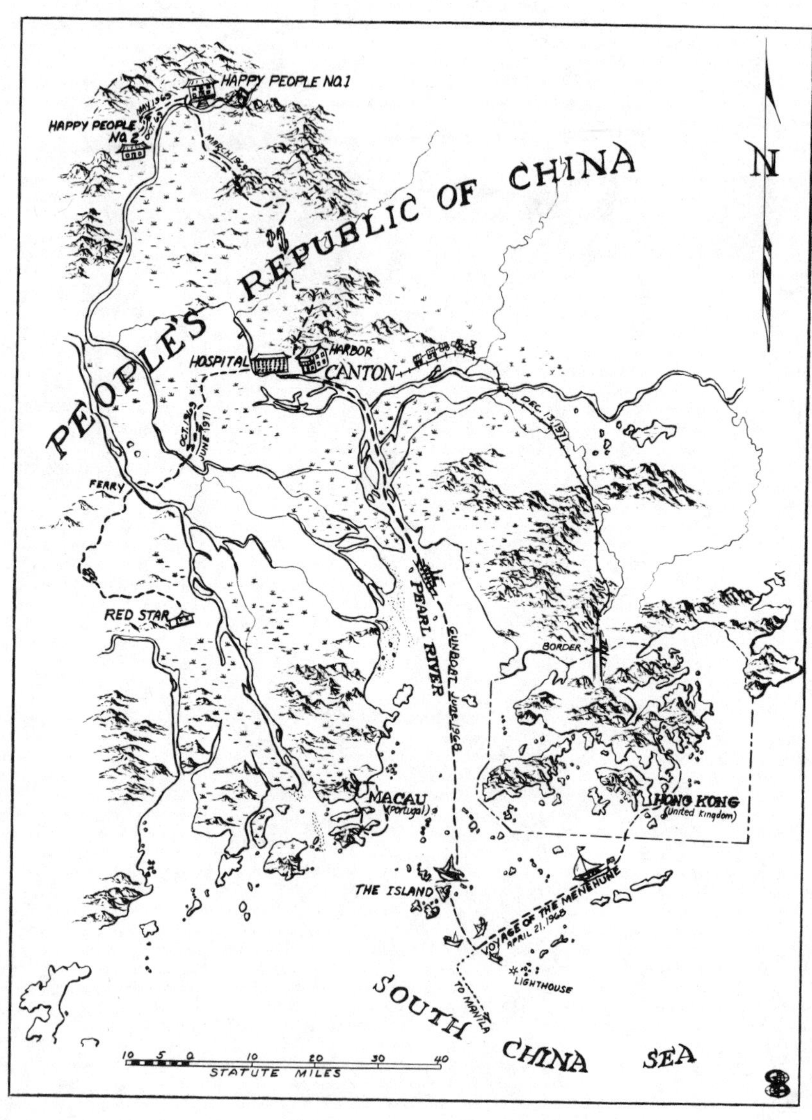

Map by Gene W. Harbert

Captivity

HOW I SURVIVED 44
MONTHS AS A PRISONER
OF THE RED CHINESE

by
Mary Ann Harbert
as told to
Charles Einstein

DELACORTE PRESS / NEW YORK

Manufactured in the United States of America
First printing—1973

Designed by Ann Spinelli

LIBRARY OF CONGRESS CATALOGING IN PUBLICATION DATA

Harbert, Mary Ann, 1945–
Captivity.

1. Political prisoners—China (People's Republic
of China, 1949–)—Personal narratives.
I. Einstein, Charles. II. Title.
DS777.55.H316 364.1'31 73-4219

TO JERRY,

AND TO ALL THOSE

WHO MADE MY HOMECOMING

A HAPPY ONE

Contents

Preface

In the course of his visits to Peking during 1971 to set the stage for President Nixon's trip to China, Dr. Henry Kissinger was reported afterwards to have negotiated specifically on behalf of two Americans imprisoned as spies.

Although it could not be foreseen, the outcome was a source of "great gratification" to the President. CHINA RELEASES AMERICAN PRISONER, REDUCES THE SENTENCE OF SECOND, said a front-page headline in the Washington Post *the morning of December 13, 1971, barely two months before Mr. Nixon's journey was to take place; and the contents of the headline were reflected in the first five paragraphs of the accompanying Associated Press story:*

HONG KONG, Dec. 13 (Monday) (AP)—One American held prisoner in Mainland China since 1952 crossed into Hong Kong Monday, and Peking announced that the sentence of another had been reduced.

Richard Fecteau crossed the border at 2 p.m., a Hong Kong government spokesman said. He was released after serving 19 years of a 20-year sentence.

Peking's New China News Agency said the life sentence of John T. Downey of New Britain, Conn., had been commuted to five years starting from the date of commutation. The agency did not give the date, but presumably it was recently.

A local newspaper had reported earlier Monday that Downey would be released with Fecteau.

Fecteau, 43, of Lynn, Mass., and Downey, 41, were captured by the Chinese in 1952, during the Korean war, when a plane on which they were passengers was shot down on a flight from Korea to Japan. The two men were listed as civilian employees of the U.S. Army, but the Chinese contended they were spies.

The same news dispatch appeared that morning in papers all across the United States, including the San Francisco Chronicle, *which did not put it on the front page and which in any event lay as yet unopened and unread on the dining room table in the apartment of Gene and Polly Harbert, in Palo Alto, California. In the kitchen, Gene Harbert, a tall, soft-voiced Oklahoman with the unexpected looks and bearing of the British colonial military, was making his breakfast. It was just past 6:30 A.M. Pacific Standard Time.*

Like President Nixon, Gene Harbert too had a momentous departure scheduled for early 1972. At fifty-nine, he was three months away from retirement from his career job with the U.S. Geological Survey. These final days, he worked out of an office in nearby Menlo Park, though his job as a civil engineer had taken him in the past as far away as Jeddah, the chief seaport of Saudi Arabia on the hot eastern shore of the Red Sea, where for diversion he might take the younger of his two daughters into the flat, inshore waters aboard a singular pleasure boat—little more than an oversize surfboard with a sail. But now he no longer wanted to think of those days.

Neither did his wife Polly, who had come to accept as reality the subsequent death of her daughter, now nearly four years ago and seven thousand miles away from Palo Alto in the opposite direction, by drowning in the South China Sea. That was the only possibility the mother could accept. The alternative, which the investigators tried to keep from her, was that her daughter had been killed by the coastal pirates who still maraud the waters from the bare granitic shoreline of ancient Kwangtung southeastward to the Philippines. The Coast Guard and other authorities had been as thorough as they could in conducting their search, as gentle as they could in reporting its failure. But they left no doubt. Polly Harbert had asked them finally what hope was left. "Ma'am," came the quiet reply, "we can't think of any."

So the younger of the Harberts' two daughters had died at the age of twenty-two. Fourteen days from now she would have been twenty-six. Time and ritual alone would heal, and by now there had been plenty of both. In the bedroom of the Palo Alto apartment, at 6:30 in the morning of December 13, 1971, Polly Harbert still slept, but no longer soundly. Any recurrent dream in which the daughter still appeared alive—and there were those dreams—had faded, and Polly was attuned instead to wake-up sounds: the buzzing of the bedside clock . . . her husband's hand to shut it off . . .water running in the bathroom and the hum of the electric shaver . . . the unlatching and opening of the door to the apartment as Gene reached out to fetch the folded morning Chronicle *. . . the clarinet effect of the kettle on the stove.*

But there was a new sound, not part of the ritual at all, nor of the comfort that came with it. There was a telephone in the kitchen and it rang. It rang only once before Gene Harbert picked it up, but already Polly was awake, listening from the bedroom down the hall. Her husband said a word or two, but as she listened it seemed a long time before he said as many as three words put together, and when those three words came it was in a voice she could not match against anything else in their thirty-five years of marriage. "Oh, my God," he said.

Polly Harbert came out of bed, and tight in her mind and throat was the certainty that her only surviving daughter, now thirty, must have been in an automobile accident on her way to work along the crowded Bay Shore Freeway. From her own apartment in nearby Mountain View, Janet Sue used the freeway to commute northward to her office job in Brisbane, just south of San Francisco.

Now Polly was in the kitchen, standing beside her husband as he put the receiver back on the hook.

What's happened to Sue?

Gene Harbert looked at his wife and shook his head. Already, he said afterwards, a numbness had come over him.

Nothing had happened to Sue. In fact she would not even be leaving her apartment for another hour. When she did reach the freeway, it would be with the radio in her Toyota turned on, and in fact she was quite close to her place of work in Brisbane, driving one of the ugliest stretches of open road in the nation—the Bay Shore just north of the San Francisco airport, a ganglia of billboards, high-tension lines, foundries, motels, furniture warehouses, and auxiliary airport parking—when she heard the news. She has a vivid memory of what happened then: "There was an open space in my lane, then four cars, then me. All of a sudden I realized I had passed the four cars. I still don't know how."

PREFACE

At that moment in time, the morning of Monday, December 13, 1971, the older sister knew more than Kissinger, more than Nixon. In Washington, they knew about the two men held all these years as spies—Fecteau and Downey. Kissinger had negotiated directly in the cases of each. Now the U.S. had been notified to expect the release of two Americans, and the AP had reported that this was taken to mean Downey as well as Fecteau.

Good to its word, China had released two Americans. Fecteau was one of them. Downey was not the other. The five paragraphs of the initial Associated Press newspaper account already quoted here did not constitute the entire story. There were two additional paragraphs:

Fecteau was accompanied across the border by a woman named Mary Harbert, described as an American citizen.

"We don't know who she is," said the government spokesman. "She just turned up."

Captivity

1

The *Menehune* from Brobdingnag

"I'm not going to prison this time," I said to Frederick. "I'm going to California."

Frederick looked at me. The look said that to him there was no difference between prison and California.

"And you're going with me," I said.

The look on Frederick's face did not change. He was a large black cat who lived with me in my small apartment in Salt Lake City, and like most cats he resented having his life planned for him. Ordinarily, we communicated easily, but today—a day in late March of 1968—was something else.

I now had my degree from the University of Utah, with a major in psychology. My field work had taken me to the women's section of the state penitentiary. My planned career lay in that same direction: guidance designed to help rehabilitate those in prison against the time when they rejoin society, and parole work afterwards. If this sounds grander than it is, I already knew that. Nothing had been gained from the group-therapy sessions another undergraduate and I tried to conduct at the Utah prison so much as proof of our own inexperience, to the point where the inmates, with a cheerful rooting interest in a young college girl's chance for a diploma, seemed often to be guiding *us*.

But skill would come with confidence, and confidence with time, and by the time I graduated I already had taken an examination for professional qualification in the field, the result of a visit to the Utah campus by a job interviewer from Wisconsin, and had finished in the top third among the applicants. That meant premium eligibility for any job opening, and now there was more news from Wisconsin: a parole worker was giving up her post because of pregnancy, so the job was there if I wanted it.

But I wanted to try California first. I prided myself on my self-reliance, my ability—which had been a fact for some years—to be on my own, living by myself; to be alone without being lonely. But to manage it successfully is not to call it an ideal state, and the fact was that California—in particular the San Francisco Bay area—is where my parents were, and many of our friends. I say "our" friends, because a number of them worked with my father for the U.S. Geological Survey, and had been with us at places ranging nearly halfway around the world. This meant too that among the friends were many who were nearer my parents' age than my own, but this had always been a factor in my life, and not an unwelcome one. Even in dating boys, I enjoyed the company of older men. The one I had come closest to marrying—I had known him in Saudi

Arabia and Lebanon—was thirty-six when I was nineteen.

Now I was less than three months past my twenty-second birthday, and in the mail delivery that morning of my last day in Salt Lake City was a postcard from another male friend, this one forty years of age. Like others, we had met through his work with the Geological Survey, and certainly my parents knew him better than I did. His name was Jerry McLaughlin. Like my father, his specialty was topographic mapping. In addition, Jerry held a degree in economics from Occidental College and had invested in the stock market regularly and carefully. He had never married, but he was at an age now where he could come to consider it.

These things I knew more from my parents' conversation than first-hand knowledge. Jerry and I had never dated. I first met him when I was fourteen, in Boise, Idaho, and saw him perhaps three times that year; then not again till I was seventeen and a senior in high school, in Salt Lake City, and saw him perhaps five times then. But it was always in the company of my parents and others, and if I knew him as a good friend it was more from hearing about him than being with him.

This day in late March of 1968 was an unbelievable day. What little snow there had been that winter already was melting from the slopes of the Wasatch Mountains, and the skies were blue and warm with early spring. My leaving Salt Lake City spelled the beginning of new adventure. The postcard from Jerry, even if I did not take it seriously, only fitted the pattern. I knew vaguely that he had been working for the Geological Survey in the Pacific—Hawaii, Guam, Micronesia. What was in the mail was far more definite than that. It was a picture postcard, dated March 17, 1968, showing a scene of Hong Kong by night.

On the message side, it said:

ALOHA MARY:

Recruiting first mate for new vessel soon to be launched in Hong Kong.

Pay—poor, itinerary subject to change, company questionable. Career opportunities exist in this service. Transp. furn. from place recruitment. Reporting date & place subject consideration.

Apply prior 4/4/68 c/o Amer. Express Hong Kong.

JERRY

I showed the postcard to Frederick the cat. Time and again the previous summer I had told him I was off to prison as I left for the 40-minute drive to the Utah penitentiary. I had discussed Wisconsin with him, and California. Now I said, "How about Hong Kong, Frederick?"

Frederick sat atop a cardboard grocery box filled with books, the weight of him keeping the top flaps down and closed. He knew that something new was going to happen. I doubt this added piece of information—the postcard—was something he took any more seriously than I did.

Later that day, my father and mother would be arriving, complete with a U-Haul trailer attached to the back of their car, to take me and Frederick and our possessions to California. For me, moving was a standard experience, as much a part of my life as my parents'. My father, Gene, was born in Arkansas, then moved to Oklahoma, where he had two years of college before he married, then went on to complete his degree in civil engineering at Oklahoma State University. My mother, Polly, was born in Texas, but met and married my father in Oklahoma.

I myself was born in Arlington, Virginia, the second of two daughters. My longest stay in any one place was a full twelve years in Denver, Colorado, from the age of six months onward. After that the cities and towns go past like signs seen from a train in an old movie—*Ver-*

non, Texas . . . Glasgow, Montana . . . Austin, Texas . . . Lampassas, Texas (it was here that my sister, Janet Sue, married a boy named Carrington, and they went to live in Vernon) . . . *Boise, Idaho* (where I first met Jerry McLaughlin) . . . *Safford, Arizona . . . Redwood City, California . . . Bend, Oregon . . . Delta, Utah . . . Carson City, Nevada . . . Salt Lake City* (where I finished high school).

There is a temptation now, in retrospect, to blow up scenes of imprisonment beyond proportion. Still, it is not incorrect to say that I can remember a certain stirring of interest, in seeing old movies on TV, and movies in theaters too, when scenes depicting captivity were shown. Most of them lacked what I sensed was a proper degree of realism: they were an imitation of life, and even without experience you could tell that. George Raft banging his tin cup against the bars of his cell in some Big House scene lacked reality. So did Charlton Heston as a galley slave in *Ben Hur.* He was too clean, his hair too neatly trimmed—or, putting it another way, too carefully uncared-for. Heston was Raft: they had everything except the element of real suffering.

But I remember seeing something else on television, now ten or fifteen years ago, which was not a movie at all. Instead it was an interview with a woman missionary who had been imprisoned in Red China for five years. She was an older woman and she said this was the reason she managed to survive the ordeal. "If I had been younger," she said, "I would have been more active. If I had been more active, I could never have lived through it. I would have torn myself apart."

She had been held in a cell without windows; and little things, she said, had begun to take on extraordinary significance. She recalled how she used to pace up and down, measuring her cell with her footsteps, then mentally computing and memorizing the distances involved. She remembered too sitting for hours on end extracting strands of thread from a towel or blanket. From these she was able to make an abacus. As I have said, there were no windows in her cell, but there was a hole—a hole filled by a nail. Through weeks and months of patience, she worked the nail free, and could pull it out for a moment, then always hastily replace it. It was a surreptitious act—it had to be, because that tiny deed kept alive the spirit of three things prohibited by her jailers: resistance, rebellion, escape—but that moment would provide a pencil-thin shaft of daylight from the outside, and that light became a clock, telling her what time of day it was.

She was observed only in captivity. This in itself made an impression upon me, and I suppose it may have contributed to my decision to try the unknown prospect of work in California against the known offer of a job in Wisconsin. Again, I don't want to make the mistake of placing extra emphasis where it isn't deserved. The choice between California and Wisconsin was decided principally because there were friends and family in one place, and only strangers in the other. What's also true is that prison work and parole work—the one conducted before, the other after, a convict's release—can be part of the same job undertaken by the same person.

But the Wisconsin job had become available because of the departure of a parole officer, and that carried with it the prospect of working after the prisoner had been released. When you do that, you work with somebody who is, essentially, free. But before release the story is different; and to me, particularly as a newcomer starting out in the field, it was important to be able to follow a case once I had begun it. In Wisconsin, this advantage might not be there. I hoped that in California it would be built-in. In short, I did not want parole work so much as I wanted prison work. The difference is that the prisoner is, in a sense not meant cruelly, a "lab animal":

when it is time to take up her case, you know she is always there.

* * *

My father and mother are beautiful people, and a handsome couple, both of them slender and tall, his steel-gray hair and trimmed mustache a counterpoint to the dark brown page-boy she often affects. They have delicious differences in temperament, too. Three years younger than my father, my mother, Polly, is the more outgoing, the more spontaneous, the more emotional; my father the more practical, the more reserved, the more, perhaps, philosophical. The main ingredient in this balance is that it is just that, a balance, and the effect of it is two people, married all these years, who enjoy doing things together.

They arrived together, complete with U-Haul trailer and a traveling crate and tranquilizers for Frederick, that day in March of 1968, and all of us, Frederick excepted, pitched in to carry my belongings to the car. In the course of things I showed my parents the postcard that had arrived that morning from Jerry McLaughlin in Hong Kong.

"You see?" I said. "I can always get a job."

"At poor pay," my father said, quoting from the postcard.

We all took it lightly. Through the Geological Survey grapevine, my parents had heard that Jerry was having a boat built to his own specifications. He had spoken, in fact, of a lifelong dream—to have his own boat and sail around the world.

"Career opportunities exist in this service," my mother said, reading from the postcard. "It sounds as though he's proposing marriage."

"He's being offhand about it if he is," my father said. "It reads more like a want ad than a proposal."

I said, "What fascinates me is that it got here today, my last day in Salt Lake City."

"They would have forwarded it," my father said. "You did leave a forwarding address with the post office, didn't you?"

I nodded. "You'll be getting my light bill."

"You'll be getting your light bill," he said. "I know how to forward mail too." I had listed my parents' place in Menlo Park, a suburb of San Francisco, as a forwarding address, but the plan was that I would be taking an apartment of my own in San Francisco. Toward this, I had about $200 in savings, which meant I would have to look for work right away.

We stopped for the night at a motel en route from Salt Lake to Menlo Park, and I smuggled Frederick out of his crate so he could spend the night on my bed. Both of us were wondering the same thing: what if I couldn't find an apartment building that permitted pets? Come to think of it, what about the postcard from Jerry? Maybe I would join him on his boat, and we would sail off into the sunset—though if you sailed into the sunset you'd be in Red China—and be married under a Tahitian moon and live a Gauguin life complete with Bob Dylan records playing on the stereo, and *then* what about Frederick?

Common sense suggested that I would find an apartment house in San Francisco that welcomed cats, and that would be that. Nevertheless, I was to answer Jerry's postcard. There were reasons enough for that. One of them consisted of curiosity itself, and find a twenty-two-year-old girl who wouldn't be curious about a postcard like the one Jerry sent me. Another was, quite simply, the act of replying. Jerry had written to me: unusual, but there it was, and it was right for me to answer. And there was a third reason: my discovery that to get a job in my chosen line of work in San Francisco I would have to wait till well into June—nearly three months—to take the county exam that would qualify me there.

I would have to get other work in the meantime, and I did almost at once as a secretary for a San Francisco firm of architects, but that didn't keep me from writing Jerry right away. It was brief—I let his postcard to me set the tone, so that no hint of overt affection, let alone intimacy, would appear. If his postcard to me was captain-to-first-mate talk, them mine in reply would be seaman-to-captain. I told him that no one could get a card like the one he sent me without being interested in further details, and I added a P.S. saying I'd been graduated from college with a degree in psychology, and sent it off. Sent it off, I should add, quite with the expectation of not hearing back from him—at least, not immediately nor responsively.

There are, as I have said, men who reach the age of forty without marrying, as Jerry had done, and then, quite suddenly, as it would appear, ready themselves for marriage. But others at that age can manage very well, if not without women, then certainly without wives. What I knew of Jerry suggested that he might well be of the type to think now of marrying, but I knew too that he had a kind of mordant strain that could be utilized, among other ways, to cloak emotion. Some people (so my college texts spelled it out) master this as a defense against rejection. The same postcard he sent me might have been sent to twenty other people. "I'm screening first mates," he could have said afterwards. "The main thing is, I just wanted my friends to know the boat was in the works." And of course, the facts would back him up.

So it had to be an offhand thing, and so I went about my normal course. Almost as soon as I got a job, I found an apartment, and it was in San Francisco—and they didn't want cats. So the decision was being made, where Frederick was concerned. I cast about among friends and found one who agreed to take him in. I was sad for the two of us but relieved for him, because his health was involved—he tended to wheeze and would value tender loving care.

From Jerry I came to expect no reply. If I regarded his postcard as offhand, as I've said, that by itself means no reflection on him. As I knew him, and as I knew about him from others, he was responsible, careful, conservative in every way even down to his politics. One of his known traits was interesting, and very much (I thought) in his favor: one thing he didn't want in life was to be in command of other people. He didn't want to be a boss. If he did take on another person when he launched his boat, it would be, despite the official language of his postcard, on the basis of needing a companion rather than an employee.

How automatically I came to expect no reply from him is measured by how fast he answered my letter.

He answered it with another postcard. The officialese was still there. This one was dated March 27, 1968, only ten days after the first. The picture on the card showed the President Hotel in Hong Kong.

The message read:

> ALOHA
>
> You are mad to consider such a venture. If you have not recovered to the extent that want to be de-selected then you should consider reporting @ convenience prior to 4/10/68 Hong Kong. Will authorize Pan Am to issue ticket.
>
> Details: Boat small, looks O.K.—hope it floats right side up.
>
> Advise.
>
> JERRY

What cold language to present such an exciting prospect! Yet I think he may still have been using the language of defense. What I know is that I still didn't believe it.

This time, though, there was a way to check it.

I called Pan American on the phone.

"My name in Mary Ann Harbert," I said into the telephone, "and I want to know if you have a ticket in my name for a flight from San Francisco to Hong Kong."

"What flight?" they asked.

"Any flight."

"You mean an open reservation?"

"If that's what you call it."

"When did you buy it?"

"I didn't buy it."

"But you say it's here."

"I don't know if it's there. I'm asking you."

"Hold on," they said. Then after a while they came back on the line: "We're holding no ticket purchased here for a Mary Ann Herbert."

"It's Harbert, not Herbert," I said, "and it wasn't purchased here. It would have been purchased in Hong Kong."

"Hold on." And after a time they came back again: "We don't have a reservation for a Mary Ann Harbert purchased in Hong Kong—"

I suppose I smiled to myself.

"—but," the voice said, "we do have a Mary Harbert."

I said, *"I'm* Mary Harbert. Mary and Mary Ann are the same thing."

"Then we're holding the ticket for you," Pan Am said. "Do you wish to make your flight reservation at this time?"

I held the phone receiver a little away from me and looked at it. After a bit, I said, "No, not just now, not at this moment. I'll have to call you back. But you're sure it's there?"

"Oh, yes. It's there. It may be a little unusual, though."

"I know it's unusual," I said.

"Then do you want us to make it a round trip?"

I puzzled over that for a moment. Obviously, when we thought of the word *unusual,* Pan Am and I had separate things in mind.

"You can't fly in to Hong Kong one way," Pan Am said. "They don't permit it. You have to show evidence you can afford to leave once you've been there. A paid round-trip ticket is your evidence."

"But," I heard myself saying with perfect logic, "I don't think I'll be coming back."

Strangely, I can recollect the spoken detail of that conversation, yet I can't remember whether it was a man or a woman I was talking to. The reason for this is not who said it but what was said. What I'm talking about here is my name.

The ticket called me Mary. Jerry called me Mary. My parents called me Mary. So did their friends.

But Mary is not my name. My name is Mary Ann. That is what I call myself and what my own friends call me, if they call me anything.

Which in some weird way they seldom do. I can be in a room for three hours with somebody and he or she will never use my name in conversation. But then their phone will ring, and in talking on the phone they will address me repeatedly by name. Maybe this is normal to some people, but I've never found it so, and the problem where I'm concerned is heightened by the business of *Mary* vs. *Mary Ann.*

Names have meanings. I can remember in college reading the notebooks of F. Scott Fitzgerald, with his observations of clumsy girls named Grace, prostitutes named Faith. Some names are no names at all, but the possessions of other people, if not the possessions of other people's possessions, such as Nately's friend's friend, I think it is, in *Catch-22,* or a hotel I heard about alongside the Dead Sea when I was in the Middle East: Lot's Wife's Inn.

To me, in any event, a Mary is one kind of person, a Mary Ann is another, and I have gone through my life so far being known as both—when I was known at all. It could almost give one the feeling of being a non-person.

* * *

There was another reason for remembering that Pan Am conversation: the business about needing a round-trip ticket. Obviously Hong Kong had a rule that you didn't arrive there without some evidence of your intention to leave. But why should that automatically mean a round trip? Why a ticket that had to promise that you'd go back where you came from?

The reason for this, as I thought about it, had a sense to it all its own. As long as I left, Hong Kong obviously wouldn't care where I was going. But suppose I had written it as a continuing ticket to Singapore. Now Singapore would take over, and they would have the same rules as Hong Kong, so *they'd* want evidence that I was going to leave. If I told them Bangkok, then Bangkok would want proof of intention to depart, and if I told Bangkok I was going to Djakarta, then Djakarta would demand to know I had arranged continuing passage, and it could take me around the world before I knew it.

On the other hand, I hadn't told Pan Am I was leaving by boat from Hong Kong. Furthermore, the continuing-passage business was not the sort of thing a meticulous person like Jerry would tend to overlook. So what Pan Am might have been giving me as a routine advisory to a typical commercial airlines passenger would not apply in this case. If I'd told them over the phone, for instance, that I didn't need a round-trip air ticket because I intended to be returning by ocean liner, naturally that would have satisfied them just as well . . . or, at least, satisfied the problem. As for any ports of call after Hong Kong, I could only suppose those regulations, if they had any, would be taken care of as they came up. After all, Jerry himself was in Hong Kong, so presumably *he'd* met their requirements for evidence of ability to leave the place. And what he'd done for himself, he would do for me, too—as soon as he learned I was coming.

And everything made me want to go: the adventure of

it, the curiosity and fascination in getting to see faraway places I had always wanted to see, the prospect of a lasting romance—certainly not excluding marriage—growing out of an old friendship. Jerry himself had alluded to that last part of it in his first postcard: *Career opportunities exist this service,* he had written.

By the same token, a *career opportunity* was just that—an opportunity. It was not a commitment. It was what it was: an interlude with no strings attached. It was to be played by ear. It could last forever. It could last for less than two months. If the decision were forever, it would be because developments suggested it. If it were for less than two months, it would put me back in San Francisco in time to take the county exams for my chosen career—with a sort of vacation-and-adventure in between. Against the dull interim job I had taken with the architectural firm in San Francisco, this had to be, as they say, no contest.

And so of course I opted for it. During the time before I left, many necessary things would be done: passport application, medical shots, the usual range of cleaning up and buttoning down. Even these things, though, didn't foreclose the final option. I was still in California, and would remain until I chose to leave. And that meant there was some time remaining.

In that period of time, I sat my father down, and my mother, too, in their apartment in Menlo Park one evening when he returned from work, and told them I intended to take Jerry up on his offer.

I expected no opposition from them—no opposition, at least, that would carry weight—on the basis that I was going off by myself. I was, after all, twenty-two years of age, and I had been going off on my own long before this. While they were in Saudi Arabia, I had lived with them for a time, but then went on by myself to Lebanon, where I enrolled in the Beirut College for Women. Obviously this was not a co-ed institution, and it had been founded originally by upright American Presbyterians. But that didn't make it a convent. I was still a single girl in the swingingest city in the Near East, and my parents knew it.

They stayed on in Saudi Arabia when I first came back to the United States, to continue my education at the University of Utah. Salt Lake may not swing the way Beirut does, but it was twenty times farther away from my parents than Beirut , and so parental control, if that ever were a factor, was no longer seriously in question. Their faith that I could be left on my own was equally pronounced in either case, and therefore they would not be expected now to oppose Hong Kong on that basis. If anything, it would be less so, because unlike the cases of Beirut or Salt Lake City, in the Hong Kong situation they knew in advance who I would be with, and they liked and approved of him.

Their opposition would have to arise instead from a different source, and we all knew what it would be. It was simply that now suddenly we were all together again in the Bay area, and the last thing anybody had planned was for me to take off. That the seed should be planted, with that first postcard from Jerry, the very day they came to Salt Lake to bring me back with them so we could all be together again—this had to strike them in a negative way.

When my father came home from work, I poured him a martini and sat him down and told him Jerry had bought a ticket for me, and so the offer was real and I wanted to take it.

I suppose the martini was to ready him for the shock of the announcement, but it may have been a kind of *pro forma* gesture—a romantic girl's fealty to the way they do things in movies and plays—because he doesn't depend that much on liquor. By the same token, I might have thought to substitute a Scotch for a martini, but it would never have occurred to me to pour him a bourbon, and that says a great deal about my father too: a man from Oklahoma who still is not first and foremost a bourbon drinker has to be a man with a mind of his own.

In any event, I poured him the drink and he sipped it and looked at me over the rim of the glass. Then I made the announcement. I told them, first off, that Jerry was serious about it: I'd called Pan Am, and in truth there was a ticket waiting there in my name, just as Jerry's first postcard had in such arch military lingo promised: *Transp. furn. from place recruitment.*

I pointed out that at the worst I could be back in San Francisco in time to take the exam and go into my career work just as though I'd never been away.

I told them I wasn't pretending it might not lead to something more lasting instead—but what if it did? At worst again, it would be with a man they liked, trusted, and knew even better than I knew him.

Their reaction was interesting though not, if you think it through, illogical. At the emotional level, it was exactly what was to be expected: my mother more vibrant, my father cool. But what they said, rather than the way they said it, became the thing of fascination, because ordinarily my father was the practical man, my mother the dreamer.

My father, the practical one, said, "It's your chance, and in my position I have to advise you not to do it." He took another sip. "I also have to say that if it were my chance, I'd jump at it and take it in two seconds flat."

And there was the dreamer talking, while my mother, suddenly, was the practical one, asking the specific questions: what was the itinerary? . . . how long a cruise did Jerry have in mind? . . . how big was the boat and what was it like? . . . would I have to perform tasks that demanded more than my experience could offer? . . . wasn't the typhoon season coming up in those waters?

I told them I had sent Jerry one postcard, accepting

the offer, and that I was writing him at once to get further details from him. And that night I did write again including every question any of us could think of, even down to the business of whether an exiting ticket from Hong Kong would be required.

Under postmark of April 7, back came a long letter from Jerry:

> Aloha Mary,
>
> Received two letters this morning and will respond with one or two little crumbs of info.
>
> Boat: sloop rig, valve diesel engine for aux., good w.c. enclosed & suitable for gentle folks, main cabin & small forward cabin, kerosene cooking and lights (elec. lights but for limited use), fiberglass & teak construction, 28 feet length which is small but perhaps adequate. Do not have shower, may rig some such but it is possible to get clean with less sophisticated appliances. Also to be considered is the considerable motion to be found in this form of transport. Boat is new & to my way of thinking reasonably well appointed. One purpose boat this size is that it can be sailed solo. "Labor" problems being what they are these days that is important.
>
> Voyage: Manila is only fixed point in itinerary but aiming Australia, New Zealand way unless astrologer comes up with veto. Duration not considered @ this point & *modus operandi* adopted is to sail as pleased till not pleasing.
>
> Crew: two people only for this boat if for extended cruise. The crew is the most important part of outfitting the boat as you can usually make out if the lantern won't work but if the crew don't fit together there is no question of an enjoyable voyage. To put it in a colloquial expression: "gonna take some kine pretty civilized people for make da kine go." Many places in our society offer opportunity for tasting of life's wares without any involvement but not so here. If you put us in "that" proximity sparks are going to be generated & the only question is what the nature of the charge is. As you know there are provisions for "career apptment." this post.

I have the feeling that your thought processes don't need my directing your attention to the aspects of human beings getting on as your pseudo science major should solve all. Going boating is but one of the many alternatives for you at this juncture so think! Think!

A bit of doing would be needed on the part of all concerned to make a meaningful & enjoyable outcome but it seems possible & worth the effort to find out (in my estimation). Give a little consideration to this crew business as it is the most vital thing for you to consider. My thought is that it is generally possible to muddle through the mechanical problems if all else is well.

Navigation: You may if you like. Not too sure I have the hang of the thing & will probably be seasick anyway. Typhoons: This is good time; you got bum dope. Clothes: off boat usual (informal mostly), on boat slacks, shorts, etc. most of the time. Anything available Hong Kong or Manila. Weather to be varied. Ocean sailing (previous): me (refuse to say how far).

Onward passage should not be necessary according to immigration people I just spoke to on phone. If it did get to that point could buy a ticket here to get through customs.

Alternate plan suggestion. Provided interest remains after this letter and your reflections you could catch boat @ Manila around 4/27. You would have to make reservation and then wait for ticket and wire or ? that I was in Manila. This would give you a little more time and if "the thing" won't float that far you could save a trip.

If you come Hong Kong: Residence: President Hotel then boat. Ask Pan Am to get reservation (always room here). Plan to move over to boat about Wednesday if all goes well. Boat is "MENEHUNE" @ Hebe Haven. Will keep in touch with Pan Am and AmEx. Will wait till I hear from you so let me know your thoughts as soon as possible. Tell Polly & Gene have been aiming to send a card ever since Nov but have not found just the right one yet.

JERRY

Planes arrive Hong Kong 10 PM, 12 PM, will be there but

if slip up go to President Hotel & remember AmEx for note.

And so it was definite, yet still entirely up to me. Warmer, too, than the postcards that had preceded it though still not exactly a love sonnet by Elizabeth Barrett Browning. The alohas and the pidgin Hawaiian, he came by through habit—he had spent a good deal of time in the Islands. And he must, I thought, have labored considerably on that part about the crew, even to the point of the gentle sarcasm about my "pseudo science major," which of course was psychology.

In terms of the size of the boat, he was saying of course what already had to be taken for granted: it was big enough for one person or two *friendly* persons. *Proximity sparks are going to be generated & the only question is what the nature of the charge is. As you know there are provisions for "career apptment." this post.*

But as obvious as that proximity would be, with all it implied, there was a touching, almost Puritanical, contrast in the sleeping arrangement he proposed for what would be our three or four days in Hong Kong before we went aboard the boat. Far from the assumption that I share his hotel room—which, considering that we would be moving from there almost at once to the cabin of a 28-foot boat, would certainly make up in logic what it lacked in innocence—and far even from saying, again in logic, that he, being there on the spot, would see to the hotel arrangements himself—he was telling me instead to make my own reservation through the airline.

He was, in truth, urging upon me not only circumspection but introspection; and the more interest I displayed, the more details he supplied, the more the admonitionary thread appeared.

Going boating is but one of the many alternatives for you at this juncture—thus Jerry had written—*so think! Think!*

* * *

Of course, other people were doing my thinking for me or, at least, giving it a good try. It would have been less than normal for my parents, after our recent years of separation, to be happy about my decision to take off like this at almost our first moment together again. And what an alien hand of fate it must have seemed to them that the self-reliance of their daughter, and their friendship and respect for Jerry—all these qualities in charge of their own nourishment over the years—could have resulted in that first postcard from him to me that very day they arrived in Salt Lake to take me home with them!

But the qualities were just as real as the postcard, and they had grown over the years, and neither they nor the U.S. mails could be shut off. I don't believe I ever showed them Jerry's long letter—they didn't even know the name of the boat was the *Menehune,* though what difference that might have made, I could not imagine. But they knew of course that I had written to him, and when his letter came, its "little crumbs of info," as he called them, enabled me to answer questions—some of them, anyway—as they came up. Those which I couldn't answer directly I could handle indirectly. "I don't know," I'd find myself saying, "but Jerry must have thought of that." And the more the questioner knew Jerry, the less comeback there would be.

As I say, they gave it a good try anyway. I remember in particular one night when my parents got me together with some friends of theirs, members of a prominent yacht club in the San Francisco area. It was a solid barrage of argument against the plan, and everything they could think of was trotted out.

The case against my going took basically three avenues of reasons: weather, health, mechanical failure. This was to be "blue-water" sailing, as they call it, and what did I know about it? Suppose the mast broke? Suppose a storm came up? Suppose there were illness or, even worse, injury?

I think I did a fairly bad job of satisfying their queries —in fact, I know I did: afterwards, I was to hear that one of them came away from that evening session "convinced we had Mary talked out of it." But given their determination to argue against it, I doubt any answers I gave would have left them serene. And in an interesting way, their strongest attack was also the weakest. For they tended to shore up their premonitions of what could go wrong with examples, and the more examples they gave of what could happen to a boat or its occupants, the more boats and occupants there had to be. The more they cited the South China Sea, the more familiar the South China Sea had to be. And so the basic point that Jerry and I would be pioneering the unknown was completely lost. What their line of argument developed was that at worst, instead, we would be sailing a well-traveled waterway with the odds against peritonitis wholly in our favor. At times, for the sake of defending myself that night, I found myself wishing I had asked Jerry more questions—just as at times the people I was with, that evening and afterwards, found themselves wishing they had thought of additional objections.

But if they were obdurate, so was I. It came down to a standoff. They didn't want me to go; I wanted to go.

And if they thought they had me talked out of it, events of the ensuing days dispensed with that notion. Now I had my passport. I had my shots. I'd done my shopping—very little of it, really. A couple of new things from J.C. Penney's, plans to pick up a few things more in Hong Kong. At one counter I hovered over a sketch pad, then decided to buy one in Hong Kong instead. My departure date was set, then reset; the second time, I misunderstood the clock factor, and the international date line. I found myself sending three consecutive cables to Jerry, each successive cable correcting my arrival time.

I would be leaving at 9:00 A.M. San Francisco time on Tuesday, April 16, but at that moment is was already one o'clock in the morning of Wednesday the 17th in Hong Kong. What a curious place the airplane has made of this world! My mother and I looked at the timetable and marveled at it. "Think of it," she said. "You leave at breakfast time one day, get there at ten o'clock the next night, and you'll see less than two hours of darkness!" Which was the way Pan American's most glamorous flight—Flight #1, westward around the world from San Francisco to New York—would make it happen. Touch down in Honolulu: before noon. Touch down at Tokyo: still daylight—only mid-afternoon. Mid-afternoon, though, of the next day, for between Honolulu and Tokyo the great Pan Am 707 would have crossed that invisible dateline.

My mind's eye told me that the final leg of my trip, from Tokyo to Hong Kong, would mean flying not into the west, but into the south. In truth Hong Kong does lie south of Tokyo, but almost twice as far west! Thus Pan Am's Flight #1 had a magic of its own, in its routing, that its Flight #2—in all other ways its equal, round the world eastward from New York to San Francisco—had no chance to claim. Each day, I learned, the two planes passed each other between San Francisco and Honolulu, and the crews would exchange special salutations, even relay the news of the moment of passing to their passengers. Flight #1 would be outward bound; Flight #2 would be coming home. But Flight #1 would be doing what Flight #2 could never do: the same thing Icarus tried with his wings in a time by now forgotten. For we would be racing the sun.

"Well," I remember saying to my mother (or words to that effect), "I suppose I won't miss losing one night in my life." The temptation now is to keep remembering things like that, things you said and did, as some sort of parade of unconscious prophecy. And there may have been more of it in my case than in most. But if so, I assign it to the quality of irony, not predestination. Even though, for example, I had chosen a career in prison work, and had an interest of long standing in it, I had not selected that originally as my college major. Instead, I had thought more of becoming a professional musician, and in transferring from college in Beirut back to the U.S., I had applied first on that basis to the University of Maryland and received a curt reply saying no. The University of Utah, where I had had a summer semester just after high school and just before leaving for the Middle East, was my second choice—and their answer was yes. So I re-enrolled there, thinking perhaps to become a musician—from childhood piano lessons I had gone on to take up the flute—and discovering, after only a few weeks of college, that my talent, though it may have contented me and pleased some others, did not seem adequate to launch me on a serious professional career.

That was when I turned to psychology as my major, accepting the switch with the same dry-eyed realism with which I can remember—remember vividly—accepting the last spanking I ever got, administered with a yardstick by my mother. Why? Because that day I had refused to practice my piano lessons. I must have been all of ten years old at the time.

From my mother, Polly, I inherit many things—surface things that people notice, such as the fact that the women in our family, my mother and sister and myself, are the ones who wear glasses—but of course far deeper and more important things as well. But not all things. For my mother wears her heart on her sleeve, and I don't.

If I would not practice the piano, I would be spanked. This I knew. I accepted the prospect only within the framework of a private added decision, and it was my decision. Ten-year-old girls do make decisions of this kind, and so I made mine. Spank me though she would, I would not cry out. No tears would come. I knew she would stop as soon as I cried. Almost as a third party viewing the scene from the outside, I wondered what would happen if I didn't.

What happened was what I think I knew had to happen: we both advanced, each in her own way, to a state of private alarm; maybe even panic. The more she hit me, the more it hurt. That was my problem. The more she hit me, the more my silence continued. That was her problem.

Pragmatically, I decided I had to be the one to end it. I uttered one small cry. The yardstick stopped instantly; was never used on me again.

In later years, I would read the existentialist works of Pascal and Søren Aabye Kierkegaard, the theists, as well as the essentially atheistic views of Sartre and Camus. I remember discussing with a friend a French movie that was shown on television, with English dubbed in for the voices, whose plot I forget, except that it began with the killing of one man's father by the father of another. The man to be killed lay helpless underneath the raised sword of his rival, and cursed him. His rival then drove his sword into the man's innards. In the French version, the victim screamed as the sword entered him.

"You see," my friend said, "that's the difference between a French movie and an American movie. In the American version, the guy wouldn't have yelled."

"No," I said, "I don't think it's a matter of French against American. I know I don't sympathize with the man for screaming, but that's not because I'm American. I think people *anywhere* exist who have it within them to control not what events do in their presence but what they do in the presence of events. Free will belongs to all of us."

"You're preaching," my friend said. "Did that guy's free will keep him from being killed?"

"No," I said.

"Then what choice did he have?"

"He could have chosen not to scream."

The reaction to pain . . . to punishment . . . to torture . . . to *danger*—the questions here of human response and the exercise of individual will—these things have long held fascination for me. Perhaps I ought to dissect that word: *fascination.* If it conveys anything of thrill, anything of deliberate desire to place myself in harm's way, anything that might suggest this sort of thing as an off way of getting one's kicks, then it is being read totally wrong. What I mean when I say *fascination* is a combination of anticipation and curiosity—nothing more than that; but nothing less either, for the combination of anticipation and curiosity can be a strong, almost governing, factor in some people, and I am one of those people.

Indeed, when it comes to the old saying: "If rape is inevitable, lie back and enjoy it," my fascination takes hold—but that doesn't mean I regard it as enjoyable.

But neither do I regard it as inevitable.

My thoughts, conditioned both by experience and observation at places as far apart as Beirut, Athens, and the women's section of the Utah State Penitentiary, have been that more females cry rape than have been raped. Once in Beirut, an Armenian girlfriend and I were walking on the street late at night when a Volkswagen with two male occupants coasted by us, then suddenly swung to a stop, blocking our way as we began to cross an intersection. The men wanted to drag us into the car with them. The Armenian girl screamed. I swung with my handbag. I'm not that hefty a customer—my normal weight is under 110 pounds, and I doubt it was more than 100 at that time—which may have added to their surprise at being attacked. Whatever it was, it drove them off. They piled back into their Volkswagen and sped away, the one on the passenger side still trying to close his door as the car careened up the street.

Another time, while on a school tour from Beirut to Athens ("Stay away from Piraeus! A girl isn't safe there!") another girl and I found ourselves, with our dates, parked in a hilltop lover's lane, amidst ruins which I'd have to suppose were 250 times older than the combined ages of the four of us in the automobile. It became clear that my date was after something equally historical, as opposed to just a session of necking, and no actions of mine seemed about to turn him off. So for actions I substituted words. One word, really. I said, "No!" And he stopped. Maybe it isn't the height of self-flattery to proclaim that when I say no, they stop. But in this case, as in others I could tell about, what I didn't want to happen was what didn't happen.

The converse did not hold true. I found myself strongly attracted to a man in his mid-thirties, whom I had met in Saudi Arabia shortly after my first airplane flight took me there the autumn following my graduation from high school. I had with me at the time an extremely unusual document, my Utah driver's license, which I had got two years before at the age of sixteen. It was unusual from a couple of standpoints, one which I will have more to say about, but its main function in Saudi Arabia was no function at all: no women can drive there.

The Saudi Arabians had "rented" the talents of the U.S. Geological Survey, my father included, to do surveying and mapmaking for them, and so it was that my father, my mother, and I found ourselves in Jeddah, the chief seaport and a place of questionable charm. For the Americans, there was a level of boredom, certainly not ameliorated by any U.S. diplomatic representation which, as I suppose is the case in many foreign countries, did not seem to touch the lives of American citizens in residence. Of all the elements involved in that existence the boredom had to be the worst. At one point my parents took me to Egypt—"to get close to civilization," we all said. The trip was meant to last two weeks. It lasted ten days, ending in an undignified rush to get back to Jeddah. The high point, as I remember it, was a train ride from Alexandria to Cairo, aboard wide coaches from Hungary running over narrow-gauge track from Russia. At least, that is how I remember it. In any event, the effect was that of Scarlett O'Hara walking a straight-line, drunk-driver test in her hoop skirt. The wide "skirts" of the train caused a swaying motion that brought upon me the only authentic case of "seasickness" I ever knew.

Following this, my parents enrolled me in the college at Beirut, where my roommate was from Cyprus—the two of us actually went there, but the Greek-Turkish warfare was exploding at the time, and I saw little of the parts of the island I wanted most to see. It was during Easter vacation from school in Beirut that I made my trip to Athens. And when the school year was over, I returned to Saudi Arabia, as a stopping place before coming back to the United States.

But the man in my life, at that time, was Joseph, a Lebanese whom I met in Saudi Arabia where he was serving as an attaché to the Swiss Embassy. I came close to marrying this man. At least, we had reached the point of talking seriously about it. What prevented it, as much as anything, was a personal situation of his own, a family-support problem he felt unable to solve.

But before we gave it up and I left to return to the U.S. and complete my college education, Joseph—and other people, too—had left a particular imprint on me. Traveling as much as I have, it has been my habit always to pick up local accents in speaking English, and the effect in this case was to increase a tendency I'd already acquired—who knows where or how?— to speak somewhat in the cadence of the Lebanese, and with over-enrichment of the vowels. People say to me, "You have an accent, but we can't place it." It does have a strange impact. It means talking faster overall, yet still pronouncing some words more slowly. Americans pronounce "Baghdad" as if it were "bag" plus "dad." But if you will say "Boch-a-dod" instead, very quickly, you will get the sound of the way the Arabians say it, and you will find you are using three syllables instead of two. Americans say "money" as though it rhymes with "funny," but as I say it there is more of the sound of "fawn" than "fun." Perhaps most characteristic and obvious of all, where an American says "want," I say "won't." Somebody in a foreign country, just starting to learn English, could, as a result, have trouble understanding mine. Perhaps a great deal of trouble. At least at first.

I quit my secretarial job in San Francisco at noon on Good Friday, April 12, 1968, to the overt irritation but perhaps private satisfaction of my immediate supervisor, a middle-aged lady who had testy theories about part-time college girls, and there was a long final weekend that came to a bleak climax the night of Monday, the 15th, my last night at home.

My parents had advanced funds to me for various purposes, primarily the purchase of a return air ticket from Hong Kong to San Francisco. Despite the assurance I told them I had got from Jerry in his long letter, the travel people continued to assert that evidence of passage out of Hong Kong was essential, and since round-trip routing was symbolic evidence that I would be coming straight home again, I found myself in possession of the return ticket.

But it was a smaller expenditure that took on the overtones. This too had its symbolism. My mother had written a check to cover the gas deposit on my apartment, and now, in so short a period of time, it would have to go through channels for refund. Add to that a misunderstanding as to when I was supposed to be at my parents' apartment for dinner that final Monday evening. Other people were coming for dinner too—friends of my parents, newly home from assignment with the U.S. Geological Survey in Hawaii—and I was the one who caused a transportation snafu, interrupted the preparation of dinner, and showed up late. It was neither typical nor intentional on my part, but it was there, and the evening, as it unfolded, was almost surrealistic. The conversation was entirely between them and their guests. I sat there ignored.

And I went to sleep in their apartment that night feeling sorry for myself. What if Jerry and I were lost in a storm at sea and they never saw me again? Ah, *that* would serve them right! I closed my eyes and feasted on the luxury of it. My mother in tears . . . my father close to them, his voice quavering . . . *"The last time we saw her we treated her like dirt, as though she wasn't even there!"*—what a marvelous way to go! Particularly because it existed in the contemplation, not the expectation.

But I was too healthy to dwell sleepless on it, and so were my parents. In the morning we were all friends again, and they drove me to the airport, and we were a family together once more, and how dearly we all loved one another! Tears from my mother, a hug from my father, and then I was passed through the modern accordion chute into the tubular wonder, complete with soft canned music, that was Pan American Flight #1.

Then the doors were shut, the engines started, and we were taxiing out for takeoff. The pilot told us we would be using Runway 19—19-Left, I think he said—which I did not connect with anything, until Jerry explained to me that runway numbers indicate compass direction. Even then I didn't see that it made all that much difference, except that it would make for small talk between us, and there might, I thought, be a lot of that. For we were two people who, when all was said and done, were not particularly known to each other. *You are mad to consider such a venture*—so Jerry had begun his second postcard. The fond counter to that, of course, was that if I was mad, what did that make him?

Flight #1 was to take twenty-two hours of elapsed time from San Francisco to Hong Kong that day, and there was little if any sleep for me the entire trip. The wakefulness was not due, I think, so much to excitement as to the absence of nightfall. In that suspended state, darkness came only at the end of the flight, well after we had taken off from Tokyo on the final leg.

One thing that did not worry me was whether I would have trouble recognizing Jerry, or he me, after the interval of five years. I have long dark-brown hair, and always wore it that way, and the main difference in me since last Jerry had seen me was that I had put on weight. Twice in my life, I had gotten to nearly 120 pounds—once after Beirut, now again after San Francisco (and for the same reason: much dining out in both cities)—and although my height of five feet five inches was certainly enough to carry it, I thought of myself both times as overweight. A nice Far Eastern adventure would be slimming, I thought.

As for Jerry, I knew there would be no mistaking him. Part of his conservatism, as I suppose it is part of anybody's, was a certain resistance to change. He had blond hair and blue eyes; at five-foot-ten he had a small-boned, but not unathletic, build. I knew him additionally as a good swimmer and a reader of books who prided himself on his vocabulary. And though I doubted he would be either swimming or reading a book when he met my plane—*if* he met it—he had one outstanding "landmark" that would bring instant recognition to anyone who knew of it: his face was Bing Crosby's face.

Not so much as to make him Crosby's double, but very much the same shape and, most important, very much, set away from the head as they were, the same ears.

I was wearing the only dress I had brought with me, and I had a feeling Jerry would be dressed in a business suit. For all the informality we had planned for the boat, it was not "appropriate" (to use one of Jerry's favorite words) to play beachcomber to the multitudes.

We dropped down over the night, the lights of Hong Kong appearing close and with suddenness after the blackness of the East China Sea. The 707 taxied to a stop, the passengers debarked, and there, waiting at the customs barrier, was Jerry—wearing his suit.

We recognized each other at once, but on my part it was with a sense of alarm. I had worried that being tired, I would look tired. What hadn't occurred to me was that *he* would look tired.

But he did. He looked terribly tired. And he had lost weight from the last time I had seen him—visibly so—and there was something else besides: the animation that once had been in his face was no longer there. It was missing . . . gone . . . even as he took me in his arms to kiss me hello.

I expect that it's easy to proclaim love at first sight. What is not so easy to proclaim is its opposite. It's handier, more convenient, certainly more powerful, to make the positive judgment: *this is it.* What, after all, is the negative counterpart? *This isn't it. . . ?*

And yet how do two negatives produce sparks? And that was the state of Jerry and me when we met at the Hong Kong airport. I had been awake, all told, for more than twenty-four hours. I had my reasons for being groggy. So, it turned out, did he. He was on the mend from a severe bacterial infection, centered in an arm but virulent enough to attack his entire system. Beyond that, it evolved that after he had given up his career with the U.S. Geological Survey, a few months earlier, he undertook a private assignment in Micronesia. There had been a distinct personality clash between him and the last man he had worked under. And this had left recent scars all their own.

In some circumstances, for a forty-year-old man to be joined at that point by a twenty-two-year-old girl could be the most positive of therapy, embodying the qualities of refreshment, replenishment, the restatement of youth. But for one practical reason I could not fit that bill. For by every measurement I was not a link to the future; to Jerry, I had to be what I was: a link to the very past he had now relinquished. By dint, innocent though it was, of his having first met me through his work, he would always connect me with it. A man whose prime purpose is to forget he ever knew the color purple doesn't begin by going out and buying a purple sweater.

I don't say I reasoned all this out on the spot, at that very moment of our coming together at the Hong Kong airport. I do say I had the moment of intuition there, of knowing this wasn't going to work out, that he planned to dump me, and the idea of me, at the first port of call, which would be Manila, a week's sail away from Hong Kong. And I'm convinced Jerry had the same feel of it that I did.

But neither of us wanted to be the one to say it, and I'm sure each of us held hope against hope. I know I did. Perhaps once we were at sea, things would change. However uncertain a prospect, it certainly was worth holding out. Jerry was overtired from his illness, I was overtired from my trip. I had made that trip at his bidding on the one hand, at his expense on the other. And by no means could it be called a commuter jaunt, to be reversed on the spot by taking the next plane home. I had, after all, come a third of the way around the world to join him.

It was around 11:00 P.M. on Wednesday, April 17, that

my plane had landed at Hong Kong, and it went without saying that we would go straight from the airport to the hotel, so I could get a night's sleep. The airport-to-hotel ride was given over, as without needing much prescience I had forecasted, to small talk.

I asked Jerry, "Did you get my cables?"

"Radiograms," he said.

"I mean radiograms. I sent three of them."

"I know. They all arrived at the same time."

"You deciphered them, though."

"It wasn't that hard. And you got my letter?"

I nodded.

He said: "No questions?"

"About what?"

"My letter."

"Why should I have questions about it?"

"I just thought you might. There may have been things I left out."

"I'm sure there were things you left out. I thought you meant questions about what you put in."

"All right, then," he said. "Questions about what I put in."

"I only have one," I said.

"Which is?"

"The part about your astrologer."

He grinned. I was playing it lightly, and he was playing it the same way.

"My astrologer?"

"You said you were aiming at Australia unless your astrologer came up with a veto."

"I see," he said. "Tell me. Do you believe in astrology?"

"No," I said.

"And you think I do?"

"I didn't say that. But I do know people who do."

"Like who?"

"Friends of mine in San Francisco," I said. "It's an interesting story. She became a hippie, and he was an astrologer, so she became interested in astrology. He worked out his own chart, and do you know what it told him? It told him he was going to wind up in prison."

"So what did he do?"

"He quit his job and went to work as a social worker in a prison. I guess he figured he'd get there that way before the stars got him there the other way."

"That is an interesting story," Jerry said.

"I know," I said.

"Tell me," he said, "have you got a lot of friends like that?"

"Like what?"

"Hippies."

"Not really," I said. "The usual number. Nothing to write home about."

He nodded, no longer playing it lightly. "The usual number?"

"I guess so."

"Including you?"

"Me?"

"I know about those campus demonstrations," Jerry said.

"I wasn't part of that," I said.

"But you had one."

"*I* had one?"

"The university where you were—Utah—they had one."

"Yes," I said. "They did. But I wasn't a part of it."

"Why not?"

"Because nobody believed in it in the first place," I said. "On that campus, it was more a holiday than a cause."

There was a silence from him, and now I said, "When do we go on the boat?"

"*Aboard* the boat," he said.

"Aboard the boat."

"Saturday," Jerry said.

"I'm dying to see it."

"You will. Saturday."

"Not before then?"

"No."

"Why not?"

"It wouldn't be appropriate."

It was my turn to fall silent, and Jerry sensed that I was puzzled. "Look," he said, "we've got things to do tomorrow and Friday. Supplies. The boat has to be outfitted. And it's not just a question of walking two blocks to the waterfront. People have the wrong impression of Hong Kong. They think it's just a tiny island where everything's right around the corner from everything else. Actually, it's eight times bigger than San Francisco."

I said, "In population?"

"Population and area both," he said. The harbor where the boat is—it could take us a couple of hours to get there from the hotel."

"Hebe Haven," I said, giving the name of the harbor he had written in his letter. "The *Menehune* from Hebe Haven. Sounds nice."

"No," he said. "Hebe Haven isn't the home port. It's just the place where the boat's anchored."

"Then what is the home port? Hong Kong?"

He shook his head. "Brobdingnag." He was watching me for the effect the name would have.

"Brobdin . . . dig . . ." I couldn't even get it right.

"Brobdingnag," he said again.

"That's the name that's painted on the boat?"

"That's the name that's painted on the boat. On her official papers, too."

"But where on earth . . .?"

"Nowhere," he said, enjoying it.

"Nowhere?"

"That's right," he said. "Don't you remember your *Gulliver's Travels?*"

Now I did remember. I said, "Oh."

"That's right. Oh. So you see the symbolism."

I began to get the feel of how tired the trip had made me. "I'm sorry," I said. "I'm not sharp tonight."

"Menehune," Jerry said, almost pedantically, "is the Hawaiian word that means little people."

I nodded. "Like fairies."

He nodded back. "Or elves. And Brobdingnag could be anywhere. So that describes you and me: little people in a big world."

I was almost asleep. "Or nobodies from nowhere," I said, or something very much like that.

Our rooms in the President Hotel—old-style British granite high rise, like every hotel you ever saw on any postcard—were, it turned out, three floors apart, for whatever difference that made. It didn't make that much. I was destined to sleep the sleep of the dead, and to tire easily—the east-to-west "jet lag" that takes a subtly different form when you have traveled long distances in the opposite direction—and it was not till noon the next day, Thursday, that I awoke, only to become sleepy again quite early Thursday evening. In a way this suited Jerry's mood; but in a way it didn't suit mine. For if I still needed to catch up on sleep, I was still a twenty-two-year-old girl seeing one of the world's most fabled cities for the first time, and I wanted to see as much of it as I could.

But Jerry discouraged that plan. So our sightseeing was limited—its high point was the ferry ride between Victoria and Kowloon. He wasn't interested in night life either: he'd already seen it, and said it wasn't all that much. And when I suggested we try a Chinese restaurant for dinner, his response was one I have had reason never to forget.

"I'm sick to death of Chinese food," he said.

So we dined, and dined well—particularly a memorable supper at the Peninsula Hotel Thursday night—but the cuisine was Western.

So was the shopping I did for the boat. Though Jerry estimated Manila to be a week's sail, I must have stocked enough food for a month: canned things mostly —meats, spaghetti, juices, soup—but some fresh things too, including bread. And filet mignon, for our first night aboard the *Menehune,* and some bourbon and Scotch; and, for me, a carton of Newports.

Jerry left the shopping list to me—*totally* to me. In strange contradiction to the pleasure he must have had in the realization of such a deep-seated ambition—a boat of his own—he seemed oddly disinterested in what to put in it.

"Buy anything you need," he said to me.

"I don't even know how big the storage space is," I said.

"Big enough," he said.

For myself I bought a couple of things—a sketch pad, some plastic foul-weather gear—all the while trying to plot out a checklist of things we would need on the boat. If I had seen the *Menehune* first, I could have had an idea not only of what the storage space was but what supplies, if any, were already aboard and therefore not necessary to purchase. Equally important, just being in the actual surroundings could have suggested certain necessities to me. But such a visit, Jerry had said, was "not appropriate," and although this statement was startlingly out of character, it wasn't worth hardening his attitude by arguing against it.

So I bought the food, and things like rubbing alcohol, witch hazel, Band Aids, toilet tissue. And if in spending Jerry's Hong Kong dollars I overlooked something—well, we would just have to put up with the deprivation. Manila, after all, was not that many days away.

On Saturday I mailed a postcard to my parents, telling them they'd hear from me again when we reached

Manila, and we drove to Hebe Haven where the *Menehune* was. Jerry had been right about the distance. It was a long, twisting, mountainous route, taking us finally to a small boat landing where a Chinese boy, who had been hired by Jerry to sleep aboard the *Menehune* as her caretaker, was waiting for us with two boats: his own large rowboat, which had been tied ashore, and the *Menehune's* own dinghy, a tiny, coracle-like craft, barely big enough for two people. For a moment, wondering how he and Jerry had managed to have both boats in the right place in their combined comings and goings, and wondering also how we would now transfer the human bodies and supplies from the shore to the *Menehune,* I had a flashback to one of those brain-twisters on the Sunday puzzle page—you know: a man has to get a fox, a chicken, and a sack of corn across a river, but if left by themselves on either shore the fox will eat the chicken or the chicken will eat the corn—but of course it worked out simply enough. Jerry would row me, with the two of us crammed into the tiny dinghy, and the caretaker would row the supplies in his much larger boat. Once we reached the *Menehune,* the supplies would be transferred to her and the little dinghy hoisted aboard—it turned out to have a cute resting place all its own, just over the forward hatch—and then the caretaker would row back to shore for the last time, in his own boat, leaving Jerry, me, the dinghy, and the supplies all snugly aboard the *Menehune.*

Snug was a word for it, too; beautiful was another, and exciting yet another. She was white and sleek, her single mast in perfectly proportioned counterpoint to the eager newness of her body line. A misting rain was just now beginning to clear, and the *Menehune* was moored a long way out in the harbor, so we came upon her almost suddenly, first in profile, then as she swung gently at her mooring, with the carefully painted lettering on her stern in full view:

CAPTIVITY

MENEHUNE

BROBDINGNAG

Jerry had not been joking.

Nor had he misled me in saying the storage capacity was "big enough." There was in fact room and a place for everything, and the fun of discovering them was the same fun of going through a mobile home or trailer or camper, where tabletops swing up and become beds instead, where not just the crowded essentials but the civilized amenities thrive almost as if by magic. At twenty-eight feet, the *Menehune* was by no exercise of the imagination a large craft, and her cabin was less than half that length, but within it were two beds, a sink, a stove, a private toilet with its own door, a closet for clothes, a cabinet for dishes, drawers for pans and utensils, even bookshelves and curtains for the windows!

Underneath the step leading to the open cockpit aft was the engine. To either side of it were the icebox and chart drawer, and leading from them back to the stern, on either side of the cockpit, were low storage cabinets topped by cushions. There were places for kerosene, fresh water; even a place, complete with mirror for the assortment of jars and tubes and bottles no American girl travels without. And to top it off, there were two beautiful sets of chopsticks—either ivory or a costly imitation—which the builder of the boat had given to Jerry as a gift upon its launching.

I could not find anything missing. My own shopping list—instant coffee, dish towels, soap—proved more complete than I had dared to hope, and I found myself thinking of Jerry's apparent disinterest in a different light. Perhaps, I told myself, it had been in fact a gesture of his to demonstrate his confidence in me and my ability to think, as a woman, of whatever it was he as a man had not already thought of. His apathy then would have been not true apathy, but a cover instead for the act of an aviation instructor's turning over the controls to a fledgling student pilot. On my "shopping solo," Jerry knew I wasn't going to crash . . . and I didn't.

In any event, my spirits were rising. "I want to learn everything!" I exclaimed. "I want to do everything! Where do I start?"

Jerry was amused. "You could start," he said, "by making supper."

"It isn't time for supper. We've been eating late every night."

"Then what do you want to do? Steer? It might be a little silly—hardly appropriate, really, seeing as we're moored at anchor."

"Then what about the radio?" I said. "Teach me about the radio."

"Nothing to teach," Jerry said. "It works like any other radio. Turn it on to the station you want, and that's it."

I said, "But I meant I could learn to be the official radio operator for the *Menehune,* and talk to other ships and boats and stations on land. Doesn't that have a language of its own? I don't even know what to say."

"Whatever you do say, it's going to be an awful one-sided conversation." He was still amused, more so probably because he saw I failed to understand. "It's a one-way radio," he said. "We receive but we can't send."

I still failed to comprehend. "Well, what good is that?"

"A hundred percent good," he said. "It gives us everything we need. Weather information. News. Music. Most of all, marine time signals. The time signal is the one really important thing. It gives the precise time to the fraction of a second."

"Why's that so important?"

"Because we navigate by it. I'll teach you navigation, starting tomorrow. We'll begin as soon as we're under way."

I said, "But you still can't talk to anybody."

"I'm talking to you now."

He was laughing, and I laughed, too: "I mean on the radio."

"Did you have somebody in mind you wanted to talk to?"

"No," I said, "but what if we needed help or something?"

"Listen," Jerry said, "the one thing I've confirmed since I last wrote you is that the *Menehune* floats. It isn't some kind of experimental raft like the *Kon-Tiki.* After that, what problem is left?"

I thought back to that session in San Francisco when people were trying to talk me out of the trip. "All kinds of different problems," I said.

"Solved by being able to talk on a radio?" Jerry said. He shook his head. "No. It's a basic thing, and the more you examine it, the more basic you realize it is. What it comes down to is this: If trouble comes, you fix it yourself. If you can't, you live with it. If you can't fix it and can't live with it, a radio's not going to do you that much good. Help just doesn't come that fast."

It had a kind of logic to it, the logic of extra persuasion because we were where we were, aboard the *Menehune,* surrounded by obvious evidence of workmanship and care. As reassuring as Jerry's words was the boat itself; and not just the boat, but the big things and little things that went with it—the wealth of charts and nautical books, for example, that Jerry was now stacking into place. I thought back to the self-deprecatory remarks about his seamanship in his long letter to me. Now, at this moment, it seemed to me he was far more qualified than he had chosen to let on.

The negative time of it we had had in Hong Kong might be behind us. Both of us were tired. Both of us needed a change. It occurred to me that having gone directly from college in Salt Lake to work in San Francisco, I myself had been a long time without a vacation. Yesterday and the day before, the prospect had not seemed agreeable. It was a matter of *You've come this far, we both know you've got to last it out at least till Manila.* But there was always a whisper of other hope behind that. That hope—and it was only a hope, and a faint one at that—was the breath of the sea change: *Things will be different once we're on the boat.*

The rain had gone by now, and darkness came and with it the stars. Moored far out in Hebe Haven, we rode gently at anchor, and ate filet mignon under a canopy that seemed the dome of a planetarium. We could see some lights on land, some lights from other boats, but nothing close enough to cut the silence. They were simply there, to remind us that other people were there, too.

And after dinner we went to bed. The proximity that had to generate sparks, as Jerry had put it in his letter, was there without question. To give decent space for sleeping, one of the two beds in the cabin had to be slid out against the other. I suppose there was a symbolism to it: an effort to recapture something that had never existed—the *Menehune* from Brobdingnag—the nobodies from nowhere.

At dawn the next day, Sunday, April 21, 1968, we weighed anchor and were under way. The day was going to be clear, and the seas were fairly calm for the fact that a fair wind was blowing, snapping the nautical pennant on its flagpole at the stern. The stripes on the flag were red and white, as always, but instead of 50 white stars in a box of blue in the upper corner, there were 13 blue stars instead, forming a circle at the center: a pattern Jerry said dated back to U.S. colonial times.

We were under engine power at the start, but soon after we cleared the harbor Jerry began to set us under sail instead, and my "education" was under way. He brought out a sextant and explained its use, began to show me how the sails worked, let me trail the "odometer" in the boat's wake—it was a bullet-shaped object with a little propellor, and if you checked the revolutions of the propellor against the clock, you knew how fast you were going.

The *Menehune* did have considerable sea-motion to it, as Jerry had forecast in his letter, but I wasn't physically upset by it. I ate very little in the first hours—only a roll—but for lunch we finished off the rest of the steak from the night before, and once again it was a case of the instructor turning over the controls to the student.

"I'm going below for a nap," Jerry said easily. "You're in command."

"What does that mean?"

"Just hold the wheel," he said, "so it stays between those numbers."

"That's all?"

"That's all."

It seemed simple enough and it was. Our course seemed simple enough, too—or had seemed that way from the handy map I'd looked at back in San Francisco: from Hong Kong to Manila looked to be open water all the way, straight out away from land through the South China Sea.

But once Hong Kong had been left behind and was no longer in sight, it still turned out to be not the way it had seemed on the map, for on that first day there was never a time when we were completely away from land. An island would appear in the distance in one direction; then the shape of another island in another; then a third. And so there was land—some kind of land—always, one way or another, in view.

Jerry came up from the cabin about two in the afternoon. He yawned a time or two, and reflexively I yawned back.

"All right," he said. "Nap time for you. I'll take over. Did you stay between the numbers?"

I nodded, and he cast a look about us and was satisfied. I went into the cabin, but I found it was uncomfortably hot . . . hotter, and of course more confined, than the outside, where the temperature, which may have been close to eighty degrees at that point, was gentled by the sea breeze.

So I went outside again and lay down on one of the long side-cushions that outlined the cockpit. As I've said, these cushions were placed atop areas for storage and other functions. Mine was right above the starting switch for the engine.

Before I knew it, I was asleep. I have no pinpoint memory of how long I slept. It must have been over an hour. When I awakened, it was to a sound I couldn't imagine existing where we were. It was the sound of many voices.

They were all saying one word:

Hello!

In a final sleep-confused moment, I wondered if Jerry had turned on the radio, with the volume up loud, but he was standing beside me, and he was one of the ones doing the shouting.

But at the same time his hand was urgently on my shoulder, and in a low, tense voice he was saying, "Get up! Get up!"

I sat up, rubbing my eyes. "Why? What is it?"

"I've got to get to that switch! Get up! Wave to them. Smile. Say hello!"

I saw them then: up ahead of us on the left, a large fishing junk . . . and behind us, also on the left and even closer to us, another one.

Fishing junk is the word for them, but if you expect what you see on a picture postcard from Hong Kong, then what I saw would leave you as uncertain as it did me. One thinks first of colorful sails and a vessel somehow graceful in contour despite its functional purpose. I saw no sails. I saw no color. What I saw was a floating shantytown, its "rooms" piled askew and against each other four floors high. Crop the picture—take away the outline of ocean and hull—and you would be staring at a slum.

And an overcrowded slum at that, tenanted not only by men who fished for a living but an equal number of women and an equal number, at least, of children, some of them so small they were tethered by a leash to any handy fixed object, lest they wander and fall overboard.

How many families there were aboard each of the junks, I could not estimate—my guess is they'd hold a minimum of forty people apiece, all told—but families they were, for the junks wore the badge of family life anywhere that washing machines and dryers have not yet arrived: over what seemed every available inch of open space aboard the two junks, you saw one thing—laundry hung out to dry.

And if that is the emblem of those societies, then what I heard, directly behind me, had to be the emblem of our own: the engine that won't start when you want it to. Jerry was fuming with the key of the ignition switch. I heard the engine cough and sputter, but refuse to catch. Perhaps by the fourth or fifth try it had become flooded, but whatever had happened meant nothing anyway. Obviously, if the junks were not under sail they must be powered by engines instead. Obviously, from their size and the way they had come upon us, they must be capable of speeds more than double our own, which was not much more than eight knots per hour.

But as I turned to look at Jerry, as he bent over the switch, I looked past him, out to starboard, and there was a third junk, possibly the largest of the three. And so in reciting the obvious, I need to add another "obviously": obviously, we were surrounded.

I said to Jerry, "What do they want?"

"I don't know."

"Who are they?"

"I don't know."

"But they're *friendly!*" I said.

Jerry nodded grimly. "As Winston Churchill once said, it costs nothing to be polite. Come on, wave at them. Look happy!"

I waved and shouted hello. They waved back and shouted "hay-o."

"Well," I said, "they must want *something.*"

"That's the most profound comment of this century," Jerry said.

I let the sarcasm pass. "But if they're not pirates . . ."

"Pirates?" Jerry said.

"Well they certainly aren't anybody's regular navy," I said. "And they don't *look* like pirates."

"Not out of *Treasure Island,* anyway."

"But all they're doing is waving at us."

"And they've got us boxed in," Jerry said. "Have you noticed that?" He looked around us. "And some of that waving is saying hello, but some of it's telling us they want us stopped dead in the water."

"So they can board us?"

"I don't know." He seemed defeated, knowing we could neither fight nor run. He laughed a kind of gallows-humor laugh. "Look at that guy."

I looked. On the junk closest to us, astern to port, a man was busily at work at the base of the mainmast.

"He'll run up the skull and crossbones," Jerry said. "Watch and see."

He was right in one way. The man was preparing to hoist a flag. *Through darkest Asia with gun and camera* . . . we had no gun aboard; no camera either. We did have binoculars, though.

We didn't need them. Though the flag now running up the mast of the junk was small, its pattern was unmistakable. It was solid red. Beside its inner border was a large gold star, semicircled by a crescent of four small gold stars.

The flag of the People's Republic of China has a main star for the Communist Party. The four smaller stars represent the proletariat, the peasants, the national bourgeoisie, the petty bourgeoisie. . . .

2

On the Island

It was not in any sense a classic boarding-at-sea. No pieces of eight. No cutlasses held between teeth. No Virginia Mayo lashed to a mast. The junk in front of us simply hove to, attached a line to our bow, and took us in tow, its engines making at least twice the speed the *Menehune* could do, so that we seemed at times to be leaping over the waves. The other two junks accompanied us, witness to the procedure from either side.

In the process, the symbolism of the *Menehune* from Brobdingnag may have lost something in the translation, for all of us. The flag we flew was the American flag, and so we were not people from nowhere. But our efforts to point this out to our captors, by shouting and pointing, had no effect.

"I don't even think they *recognize* our flag," Jerry said.

I said, "Why should they?"

His eyes flashed hard at me. "If you're saying they don't respect the sovereign flag of the United States of America . . ."

"We weren't talking about respect," I said. "We were talking about recognition."

"What's the difference?"

I said, "The difference is that 'recognition' has two different meanings. One can be the same as respect. The other is they just don't know what the flag stands for, period."

"Well, if they don't know that," Jerry said, "they're going to find out damn soon enough."

His voice had a convincing ring to it, and I said, "Then what is it that's happening now?"

"They'll take us someplace and question us for ten minutes and let us go. That's what's happening. It happens all the time."

Later, I was to discover that he was right. It did happen all the time.

Which was not fortunate for us.

My feelings as we were placed under tow were a mixture of things. The least of them—but I confess it was there—was a sensation of petty, self-centered annoyance: barely had I started on my long-delayed vacation when these people were, for no good reason, interrupting it.

There was a second feeling, by far the larger. It was the feeling of fear itself. Fear of torture, fear of death, fear of the unknown. One would have to be stupid to assert that the adrenalin did not flow in the presence of these things. And yet this fear did blend into other sensations. One, as I have just said, was the silly irritation of having my vacation interrupted. But that was there. And something else was there, and this has to be confessed to, because it formed a major element all its own: I found myself beset by the same sense of *fascination* I have already mentioned.

And so my feeling of fright was real, yet no less real for the fact that it was something less than 100 percent fright; yet no less did the other elements—irritation on the one hand, challenge (or, if you prefer, "thrill") on the other—enter into it too.

I am sure that at the same time Jerry had his own private index of feelings about what was happening. He could have shared each one of my feelings, yet added some extras of his own and those extras in his case could only be hurtful. For it was his boat and his idea, and so he would feel guilt on that account. Guilt, and responsibility too. There are various levels of guilt and responsibility, I know, and if you feel them when you have a passenger, then will you not feel them more when that passenger is a female half your age?

In that way, I had an additional sensation of my own: I felt sorry for Jerry. In subtle fashion, the realization that his range of problems probably exceeded mine—*guilt and responsibility*—I found myself "taking command," in a way that saw me thinking of things before he thought of them.

"Jerry," I said to him, "we're going to have to talk about our stories."

"What stories?"

"Yours and mine."

He stared at me. "Mine and yours?"

"You said they were going to question us."

"For ten minutes, that's what I said."

"Will they question us together?"

"How do I know?"

"Then if they question us separately we'd better have the same answers."

He thought about that. "You're right," he said. Then he thought about it some more. "No, you're not right."

I said—this was what we were reduced to, under tow —"If I'm right, how can I not be right?"

"Because," he said, "we both have the same answers anyway. What do we have to hide?"

"I just wanted to make sure," I said.

"But," he said, "if they question us separately, who knows whether they'll ask the same questions to each of us?"

"That was exactly my point."

"Ah," Jerry said, "then it won't work."

"Won't work?"

"Of course not."

"Talking about it beforehand won't work?"

"No," he said. "There's something you don't understand, Mary."

"What's that?"

"You don't know anything about me," he said.

What shall I say now? That Jerry was telling me he was a spy and I was being used as his "cover" companion? If so, he was some spy. No gun with which to defend himself. No camera with which to take pictures. Equipped with no more than a set of binoculars and sea charts you could buy openly on any downtown street in Hong Kong or any other major city? Captured the first day of his voyage by people with their laundry hanging out?

No, it was not intrigue—*You don't know anything about me*—but something, I could only suppose, far more complex . . . related in some way to the loss of weight and fatigue of spirit I found when I arrived in Hong Kong. *Maybe the sea change will help,* I had been thinking, but with the junks surrounding us it didn't help.

The question was whether the people in the junks understood what I understood. The answer had to be an absolute no, because even if they did understand, they were taking us somewhere, and the eventual judgment would be not up to them but up to that somewhere.

Where that place might be, there was no way of telling. As before, there still were islands on the horizon, and we seemed to be headed for one of them. But it was still too far off to tell.

Jerry a spy, using me as his "cover"? Why then would he, in writing to me while I was on the U.S. mainland, have left it up to me whether I would join him at Hong Kong or Manila or at all?

I knew nothing at all, really, about the theory and practice of espionage, but it did occur to me that if this was what the CIA called spying, our country might be in worse shape than we thought. And so, when it came to convincing me, there was no problem.

Convincing our new-found maritime friends might be something else. *"They'll take us someplace and question us for ten minutes and let us go,"* Jerry had said. I wondered, and as I wondered I looked at him. His face was thin and sad. Then an idea came to me. He had reassured me. Now I could reassure him.

While I had been shopping for the boat in Hong Kong, Jerry had been off by himself—"seeing to details," he said. One of those details obviously would come to our rescue now.

"Jerry," I said, "you saw to it that we both have visas for the Philippines."

He looked at me, but not with any real interest. "So?"

"So they'll know we were bound for there."

"Why? Anybody can get a visa."

"But *Hong Kong* knows it."

"How?"

True, the positions had reversed themselves. I was now convincing *him.*

"Because of the flight plan you filed, or . . ."

"You don't file a flight plan for a boat."

"I was going to say, or whatever you call it. When you

filed for permission to exit or whatever it is, then the harbormaster or whoever it is *knows* where we are, *knows* what the boat looks like, *knows* we only left this morning . . . and we've got a paper to show it!"

"That doesn't mean they know we've been picked up."

"It doesn't have to," I said. "Don't you see?" I gestured toward the junk that was towing us. "These people don't know they don't know. All we have to do is show them the piece of paper. It's the same as what you said—it happens all the time. And why does it happen all the time?" In convincing Jerry, I was, I found, convincing myself. The logic of it was impeccable. "Because Hong Kong and Red China live side by side. They have to do business with each other and they know it."

Jerry smiled. "So all we have to do is show them the piece of paper." The smile became a rueful laugh.

I said, "What's so funny?"

"The piece of paper," he said.

"And what's so funny about *that?"* I said. "Don't tell me they don't exist. I don't know what you call them—exit permits, or whatever—but I know you get them, and they have all the information written on them, and that's why people only get questioned for ten minutes."

Jerry nodded. "You're right," he said. "They do exist."

"And they must be a standard form," I said. "These people must have seen them before. They probably do this all the time."

"Right again," Jerry said. "But we're going to have to hope for something else."

"What else would we need? I thought you said it was a standard piece of paper."

"It may be," he said. "But we don't have one."

At that point, I reached for a cigarette. The gesture had no dramatic implications. My effort to show Jerry that we had nothing to worry about had failed. His news that we were sailing without the usual permit had spoiled that, but it did not really ruin my own expectation that we were destined to be released almost at once. The first thrill of fear had been reduced by an anticipation colored by common sense. Perhaps we had trespassed into Red Chinese waters—and perhaps not. But we meant them no harm, and they had to know this, piece of paper or no piece of paper. Our worst fate would be—what? Temporary detention, a fine, something like that.

That was my mood as I lit the cigarette, and as if the action were a signal of confirmation, men on all three of the junks escorting us began to wave at me, smile—and light cigarettes of their own! *Look at us,* they were saying to me with pride: *We have cigarettes, too!*

So I had reached for a cigarette and the smoking lamp was lit. So much for an ordinary act on my part. There followed now an ordinary act on Jerry's part. The sun was beginning to go down, and he felt cold, and started for the cabin to get himself a sweater. Another ordinary act, and once again one that produced a reaction:

As Jerry moved toward the cabin, the closest man on the closest junk pulled out a gun and pointed it at him.

You've got a radio down there, the gun said, *and we don't want you using that radio.*

They didn't know at that stage, of course, that it was a one-way radio, that we couldn't send on it. If Jerry had told them, as he'd told me, why we didn't *need* to send, my guess is they'd never have believed him.

Ahead of us, ever closer under our rapid tow, loomed an island. I'm not good on directions and distances, but the island was not a small one. I'd guess it ran well over a mile from left to right as we headed toward it, but we were not approaching it straight on.

I started in with Jerry again, urging that we go over our stories to make sure they were the same, but he was basically spiritless, just as I was basically uninformed, and the "rehearsal" lasted but briefly, and went very badly indeed. How uninformed I really was had just started to dawn on me. Given the background of the entire situation, there was nothing really illogical about my presence on the *Menehune.* The worst that could have been said was that I acted on impulse, although even there it had in truth been something far more considered and drawn-out than just some spur-of-the-moment decision. But try to tell that to the people who, I could only suppose, were going to be questioning me. What would *they,* not knowing the background, think of the surface details of my story?

The surface details were just lovely, was my ironic thought: young girl gets postcard from older man she hardly knows, thereupon flies 7,000 miles to join him, without any seagoing experience of her own, on a deep-water ocean voyage aboard a tiny boat never tested at sea.

That would be hard enough to explain to somebody on Main Street, U.S.A., much less a Chinese Communist whose own background was totally different and whose knowledge of English, let alone English spoken with unconscious Lebanese cadence and sounds, would be severely limited to begin with.

Surely no one aboard the junks knew English or, if they did, they weren't trying it on us. We could hear them talking back and forth among themselves, but aside from their shouted "hay-o" imitations of "hello" at the outset, all of their communication with us had been by gesture rather than voice.

In my mind, I cast about for ways to simplify my story . . . to make it more understandable. One thought came to me: this was, after all, my vacation. Perhaps they could relate to that.

I said to Jerry, "Do these people go on vacation?"

He blinked at me. "What kind of a question is that?"

"I need to know," I said. "Do they know what a vacation is?"

"Know what a *vacation* is?" he repeated. "You think they're like the folks back home?" He gestured toward the junks. "Let me tell you something. You know the biggest thing that ever happened in these people's lives?"

"No," I said. "What?"

"Us," he said.

You could see why he said that. The junks were alive with eyes of all ages, simply staring at us. The act of lighting the cigarettes had been for our benefit—a display. And now another display began to take place. With great and unnecessary show, the women aboard the junks began to pile firewood on the decks. An open fire on the deck of a boat at sea—this was something no "civilized" American could ever have known about. But these women had the skill for it, grown out of practical considerations and necessities. If they and their families lived aboard the junks, they ate aboard the junks. And the fires were to cook the food.

By now we had almost reached the island. We were by-passing it at one end, and I could see that it stretched about as long in its side presentation as it had from the front. Then we were past it, and now almost at once we commenced a great sweeping turn and found ourselves headed back toward the island, approaching the very center of it as we had first seen it, but from the rear instead of the original front. The setting sun was directly behind us now, so our line of final approach was from west to east. Behind us, barely visible in the great distance, were sunset shapes that could have been another body of land, one that seemed to stretch infinitely from left to right. I had brought contact lenses and prescription sunglasses with me and I was wearing the sunglasses now. In indistinct imagining, the outline of extra-dark purple where sea and sun came together behind us would have been mainland China.

Looking frontwards, I saw now that the island was not the solid square mass it had seemed up to now to be.

Instead, it was a huge crescent, into whose heart we now were headed, with a harbor the shape of a quarter-moon. Hills ending in a jagged outline of mini-mountaintops rose steeply from all points along the shoreline, so precipitously that you wondered how any port, with any level shoreline accommodations, could exist. But as we got nearer, we could see that a port town did exist, at the very inner center of the half-moon, within two inner crescents formed by two piers standing far out into the harbor.

We were taken to neither of the piers. Instead, a distance off shore we were signaled to drop our anchor. Jerry did so. The lead junk now was even with us in the water, and the men aboard it dropped a second anchor, this one attached to our bow.

From the village at the base of the port, there now came a rowboat, worked by two gray-haired women in shapeless tunics. It came alongside, and everyone gestured at Jerry. He had a fixed smile on his face. Without protest, he got into the boat, and the two old women rowed him ashore.

The most prominent building of the port, a long, low concrete structure painted yellow, was on a hillside elevation above the harbor on the left-hand side of what was acutely more a V than a simple crescent. There was a spiral pathway leading up to it from the rowboat landing, and it was up this pathway that Jerry was led. Viewed from the *Menehune* at anchor, the pathway was visible only at intervals. I saw Jerry start up the path. Then he disappeared from sight, then reappeared. Ever climbing, he would disappear again, reappear again. It was like the backdrop in *The Sound of Music*—a stage cut-out to provide the illusion of climbing a distant height, first from left to right, then from right to left.

But this was no illusion, and as I watched, the second time Jerry came into view his hands were locked behind him.

He's been handcuffed, my mind told me.

* * *

My mind told me wrong. Jerry had not been handcuffed; instead, he had clasped his hands behind him during his climb. He told me that when they rowed him back to the boat after a short period of time.

During that period, I had not been alone aboard the *Menehune.* People kept boarding, searching. One of the men pointed to the stove in the cabin, then to his mouth, then to me. Was I hungry? I nodded. With a smile and spread palm he made the charming universal gesture that says "Be my guest," and so, with half a dozen of them watching me, I prepared and ate my supper.

Jerry's return to the boat was a brief one. Now it was made clear to us that we would be expected to sleep ashore. In obedience to hand signals we took our blankets, descended to the rowboat, and were taken to the big yellow building up the hill. Obviously, this building was the headquarters for the commune that embraced this island and, I was to surmise afterwards, the floating population of the fishing junks in the area and perhaps other neighboring islands as well. The building was fronted by an austere but nevertheless pleasant-looking concrete terrace, dotted with chairs and concrete tables in a sort of "sidewalk-café" configuration, running the length of the structure's long side. Inside the one-story building, viewed from its center entrance, the left-hand half was given over to two rows of rooms, half of them facing the front, and across the bisecting corridor the other half looking out on the back, which had very little outside space before an embankment that renewed the continuing rise of the hill. To the right as you came in there was an auditorium, complete with movie screen and projector.

Jerry and I were assigned separate beds in the same room—the first front room down the hall of the "bedroom wing." But we were not destined for any immediate sleep.

First there were questions, a comic-opera kind of interrogation best remembered for its lack of believability. One of the men—apparently a cadre, or minor local administrator—led the questioning. In slow and almost indecipherable tones, he made it known that he had been teaching English to himself, and he displayed two books as proof. One of the books was little more than a pamphlet—a phrase book, obviously printed for use by Chinese businessmen or visitors to Hong Kong—that had all sorts of Chinese-to-English questions and phrases, none of them of the slightest possible application to the present circumstances. I mean, it is fine to be able to say, "Where is the post office?" or "How much does that cost?," but things like that have limited usefulness in a situation like ours.

The second book, of which the self-appointed "interpreter" was even more proud, was a large and quite complete English-Chinese dictionary, but in its own way it was almost as useless as the phrase book, because to say it was an English-Chinese dictionary is to say *exactly* what it was: a book printed for English-speaking people. All translations were from English to Chinese, with the English words listed in alphabetical order. Thus if our interrogator wanted the English equivalent of a Chinese word, he couldn't find the Chinese word to begin with, for he wouldn't know where to look.

Jerry and I could cooperate in a makeshift way by finding a word *we* wanted to use in the dictionary, then pointing to its Chinese equivalent, but that made for one-sided conversation, and very slow-paced at that.

The best we could do in that session was to make use of what few words of English the cadre already knew, and pantomime or search out a handful of others. We did give our names. "Miss Harbert," Jerry said, pointing to me. "Ah," said the cadre, "Miss Hobbitah." And, said Jerry, "McLaughlin," pointing to himself. The cadre beamed. "Muckaluck," he repeated.

We established, or tried to, that we were Americans,

bound from Hong Kong to Manila, and a few other facts, one of which seemed painful and embarrassing to the cadre.

"Not wife," he said to me.

"No," I said. He already knew we had different last names. Even in view of that, he tried hopefully again:

"Maybe sister."

But he was shaking his head even before I shook mine. Jerry reached for the dictionary. "Companion," he said.

"Companion?"

"Here:" Jerry found the word, and pointed to the Chinese characters running alongside.

"Ah," the cadre said. He turned and spoke in a rapid flow of Chinese to the other people in the room. They in turn began talking among themselves. At last, one of them said to me, "Ee-tay?"

I said, "Ee-tay?"

The cadre said, "You like to eat?"

He was not asking me if I enjoyed eating; instead, it was an offer of food. I shook my head again. He turned to Jerry, who shook his head too.

"Drink?" the cadre said.

"Water," I said. "I'd like some water."

"Ah," he said, and turned and said something in Chinese, and one of the other men left the room and came back with a thermos jug. "You like this water," the cadre said. "From spring."

It was water, but it was also what I have come to believe is the national beverage of China: *hot* water. I tried one taste and refused any more, which proved to be just as well. We were to discover that the spring water was not safe unless it had been boiled first, and this, while hot, may not have been boiled.

What it did, however, was to signal the end of our first interrogation. Or perhaps I had signaled it first, by yawning as the questioning wore on.

Was I taking the whole thing too informally? Was I playing it too cool? I know I had been frowning while the others were smiling—something within me told me I'd have to cure myself of that, be more prepared to suit my mood to theirs—but somehow the situation, as menacing as it could be, seemed devoid of the trappings of menace, and that quieted my sense of alarm. The terror of the inquisition is not served by a man with a phrase book and the wrong dictionary, whose only badge of office is the same badge everyone wore, even the little children on the junks—a badge showing the smiling, benign face of Chairman Mao.

Without even undressing, Jerry and I rolled ourselves into our blankets on our beds.

"Good night, Miss Hobbitah," he said.

It was good-night-Chet, good-night-David.

"Good night, Muckaluck," I said.

The first thing in the morning was the face of a little girl pressed against the outside of our windowscreen, staring in at us. She was perhaps eleven years of age.

"Hello," Jerry said to her.

"Hello," she said, mimicking him perfectly. Then she laughed.

Jerry said, "How are you?"

"How are you?" she repeated, and laughed again.

"You're Giggle Gertie," he said.

"Giggle Gertie," she said.

"Listen to that," Jerry said to me. "She talks better English than they do."

They were of course the adults who had surrounded us the night before, and now *they* appeared again. This time they made it clear they wanted us to return to the *Menehune.*

"Ee-tay," they explained.

We were escorted down the path to the shoreline, and there awaited our transportation: the same rowboat with the same two silent, white-haired old ladies, seated at the oars in their black tunics.

"Twin Charons in drag," Jerry said to me.

In silence, we were rowed to the *Menehune,* which in barely more than a full day's time had taken on the appearance of home.

"Breakfast, woman!" Jerry said to me, as soon as we were aboard.

"Not till I brush my teeth," I said, for we had been shown no washroom facilities in the building where we were housed overnight. The only thing that seemed to be provided there was an old-fashioned red-brick privy, a little way down the winding path from the building's front terrace, which Jerry immediately dubbed Mao Primitive. Its waste-disposal system consisted of an open trench-like sluice running down the face of the hill and emptying into the waters of the little harbor.

We washed and changed to clean underthings, and then I prepared our breakfast.

"Jerry," I said, *"did* we?"

"Did we what?"

"Trespass?"

He looked at me blankly. "Whoever said that?"

"Well, we're being charged with it."

"Charge? I haven't heard any charge."

"Then why are we being held?"

"Why anything?" He said it almost amiably. "Who's going to be captured like this in the first place? A bunch of fishing junks staffed with whole families, women with babies strapped to their backs, and then what? Interrogated? You call last night an interrogation? Nobody even knows our language."

"But they went through your papers."

"So?"

"So they know you don't have an exit permit from Hong Kong."

"How do they know that?" He laughed. "Here we've got Emerson's essays in our little library, and they can't even read."

"But they'll find out," I said.

"Suppose they do?"

"Then they'll know."

"Know what?"

"That if we didn't tell anybody we were going, then nobody will be thinking to look for us."

"Miss Harbert," he said to me, "I've told you before—I'll tell you again: As soon as they find out we're not spies, they'll let us go."

"But how *will* they find out we're not spies?"

"Because we don't have any spy equipment. No guns, no cameras—remember? Worst weapon we own is a set of binoculars."

"And a one-way radio," I said.

"And a one-way radio," he said. "That they already *do* know. So. You see?" He was looking at me carefully. "I know what you're thinking. If it had been a two-way radio, we could have called for help. But then, I say, no, we couldn't have called for help, because if I'd gone down into the cabin while we were under tow, they would have shot you. Did you ever think of that? And if we'd had a two-way radio, then, you say, I could have called for help before that, while you were still having your nap. But why would I have done that? Sure, I saw them, a long ways off, before they surrounded us. But why would I have been alarmed enough to radio for help because of a sight like that? Three fishing junks? They didn't even seem to be together. It was only at the end that they converged on us."

I said, "I'm not blaming you."

"Yes, you are," he said. "And you have every right to. I'm the one who got you into this. You're thinking, *We know we didn't have a two-way radio, but they didn't. And they weren't about to mess with people who hadn't done anything wrong, so close to help from Hong Kong."*

"I don't know," I said. "If we *did* have things most people have—a radio we could send on, official papers giving a record of our trip—maybe somebody could say they wouldn't have bothered with us. But they didn't know we didn't have those things, and they *did* bother with us."

"Exactly," he said. His smile now was tight. "Which could make me something else, couldn't it?"

"Make you something else?"

"Well," he said—his voice was light but tense—"we both know *you're* not a spy. But what about me?"

I said, "Jerry, this doesn't make any sense. You're not a spy."

"I *know* that," he said. "But do you?"

"Of course I know it."

"You say that. But do you believe it?"

"But you're the one who said they'd be letting us go," I said. "You're the one who said we didn't have any spying equipment with us."

"Ah," he said. "And doesn't that make me the perfect spy?"

"The perfect spy?"

"The one who doesn't behave like a spy," he said.

I stared at him. "But what would you be spying *on?* Fishing boats? The outhouse on the side of the hill?"

"Me?" he said. "I wouldn't be spying on anything. *You're* the one who might think it, not me."

After breakfast, our bleak lady oarsmen came and got us and took us back to the island. The process was repeated again for lunch, again for supper. Once again we were to sleep overnight in the headquarters building. This time, Jerry took his battery-operated electric shaver with him. They confiscated it.

"You see?" he said to me. "They don't even know what

the hell it is. I show them how it takes my whiskers off, and they think that must be a cover for something else it does."

On our supper trip out to the boat, the same children we had seen earlier that morning marching off to school with their books strapped to their backs, were fishing from the rowboat dock. Some had bait and hooks and lines. Others were equipped simply with a piece of string, which they would cast into the water, hoping its wriggling tip might attract a fish. Then suddenly they would jerk it back out again. From time to time, we were to learn, that seemingly futile action actually would land a fish, his own trajectory flipping him up on shore even after he had let go.

And side by side with the children doing the fishing were their mothers and grandmothers, resolutely emptying chamberpots into the water.

And side by side with them were great mounds of fish—the catch of the fishing junks—set out to dry in the sun and be salted, then transported to the mainland and the canning factories there that would market them in tins for people to eat. They were not boned. They were not de-gutted. People walked over them, and swarms of flies settled upon them.

"I'll never eat another can of fish as long as I live," Jerry said to me.

"Neither will I," I said.

We saw children as young as eleven and twelve years of age working on the fish piles, alongside their grandparents.

"You know what the glorious thing about that is?" Jerry asked.

I said, "What?"

"The equality of it," he said.

"You call children and adults equality?"

"Of course," he said.

"I don't understand," I said. "Why is it equal?"

"Because," he said, "None of them pays any taxes. Do you know what that makes this place? A hippie haven, that's what. Write postcards to all your friends, Miss Harbert: *Un-named island, somewhere off the city of Canton to the southwest of Hong Kong, all modern conveniences, no taxes. I, Mary Harbert, resident hippie, recommend to all free-loaders this discovery of this tax-free haven. After one day here, I have noticed that even the young women are bow-legged, due to malnutrition, but vitamin supplements contained in food packages from home should cure . . .*"

I said, *"Resident hippie?"*

"What else would you call yourself?"

"But you said we're going to be released."

"So we are," he said. "So we are."

So that was his brand of humor, and it seemed he was right. The following morning, when it was time for us to be rowed out to the *Menehune* for breakfast, the cadre came and said to us, "Take blankets. Probably leave today."

But we did not leave that day, nor the next, nor the day after that. The cadre had mastered one phrase in colloquial English: *"Any minute now."* We were transporting our blankets back to the boat from the island each morning on the breakfast trip—*Any minute now*—then resignedly bringing them back with us after the trip for supper, with the signaling reappearance of our convoy, the two silent old women in the rowboat.

But still the litany kept up: *Any minute now, Muckaluck . . . Any minute now, Miss Hobbitah.* My initial insistence that Jerry and I get our stories straight, so we would not contradict each other, had lost force since there were no more interrogations. Dimly we perceived that our release was but a matter of hours, maybe minutes away, at any time, awaiting only a bureaucratic signal from somewhere.

At last, a signal did come, but it was more real than bureaucratic. It came in the form of a destroyer that tied up at one of the piers. Off it stepped a man in his fifties, wearing a navy uniform, short of stature and with his hair cut even shorter, down almost to a crew cut. There were many wrinkles around his eyes and lips produced perhaps by smiles, for all he did was smile: a perpetual, frozen grin. He had served in the past aboard a British warship, and there he had learned English.

He came directly to our building, and for the first time we heard our language spoken in a way that made basic conversation possible. No more the "Where from you?" or "What name you?" that had punctuated our first night ashore with the cadre.

His first question was disarming.

"Are you being fed well?"

Jerry said, *"Being fed?"*

The grin. "No, no. I understand. You are eating aboard your own boat from your own supplies. But we can make up for this. There are fresh vegetables, and water . . ."

Jerry cut him off: "We'll pay for anything."

The grin was still there, but a film seemed momentarily to form over the eyes. The navy man turned to one of the Chinese who flanked him and said something. I said to myself, *Was Jerry too quick to offer to pay? Is he making it sound as though he expects us to be here a longer time?*

The film disappeared as quickly as it had come. The grin remained. "You will have tomatoes, cucumbers, onions, fresh fish. You will have fresh pork."

Jerry kept it up. "We insist on paying."

"This is China. You cannot pay."

For the first time, when he said that, I knew a feeling akin to terror. *This is China—You cannot pay: This is San Quentin—You cannot pay.*

The new man even got our names right. "You are McLaughlin? You are Miss Harbert?"

We nodded, and asked him his name.

"It does not matter," he said.

"But we want to know your name."

The grin, if anything, widened. "Why?"

"So we can know what to call you."

"It isn't necessary," he said. "Meanwhile, see what it is I have brought you."

From his uniform pocket, he extracted two small but identical books, bound in red leather or some close facsimile of same. Stamped in gold on the front cover, in English, at the top over a centered gold star, was the small lettering:

QUOTATIONS FROM

And underneath, in larger letters:

CHAIRMAN
MAO TSE-TUNG

I opened mine, and at the front, inside, it said:

Study Chairman Mao's writings, follow his teachings and act according to his instructions.

LIN PIAO

A directive from Lin Piao, I knew, was as important at that time as a directive from Premier Chou En-lai . . . the next thing to a summons from Chairman Mao himself.

"To begin," said the navy man, "we will select a saying of Chairman Mao's and discuss it."

I guess Jerry and I both blinked at him. This was real and unreal, all at once and the same time.

"All reactionaries are paper tigers," the navy man said, reading from the book. "You see, you can relate to this—that is why I begin with it—because this is quoted from the sayings of your own Anna Louise Strong."

Jerry looked at him carefully. "What makes you think we know Anna Louise Strong?"

The grin. "Ah, but you know *of* her."

"Yes," Jerry said. "As a matter of fact we do. And it might interest you to know she never said what this book says she said." And he tossed the little red book onto the floor.

The navy man nodded at him, smiling. "Please," he said. "Pick up the book." The smile widened. "For your own well-being, never throw it on the floor again."

Jerry reached down and picked up the book. He covered it well, I thought. "The point is," he said, "what Anna Louise Strong said was that all reactionaries are *scarecrows,* not paper tigers. There's a difference."

"Yes," the navy man said, nodding happily. "And I am glad you appreciate the distinction."

"Why?" Jerry challenged. "Why are you 'glad'?"

"Because it forms the basis for discussion," the navy man said. "If we both were to agree on everything, what would there be left to discuss?"

I said, "Why have any discussion at all? Aren't there more important . . ."

The smile cut me off. "The entire purpose is discussion."

I said, "But how can foreigners . . ."

"Foreigners? Look here"—he reached again into his pocket and drew out another red book, this one in Chinese—"I have my own book. Everyone you have met and will meet has this book. You think it was written for foreigners? You think our beloved Chairman Mao intended his sayings should *not* be discussed?"

This was unreal. Part of the unreality was Jerry, who now said: "All right—then we have before us the question of paper tigers against scarecrows."

"Exactly," the navy man said.

"So then," Jerry said, "if Anna Louise Strong said scarecrows and Mao said paper tigers, it can only mean one of two things: either Mao knew what she meant by scarecrows but decided she meant paper tigers instead, or he knew English and used "paper tigers" to prove a knowledge of colloquial English."

I could see what he was doing here. He was threatening—dominating—scaring the navy man off by means of his own superior command of the English language. And in its way it worked.

"Yes, exactly," the navy man said. "And if you like we can postpone the discussion, for it's easy to see you want to think about it further."

He had been backed into a corner, and I thought that wasn't good.

I said, "Jerry . . ."

"Be quiet!" he said to me.

I turned to the navy man. "I was only going to get back to what we said at the beginning: What should we call you?"

"I already told you. It is not necessary."

"You heard him, Miss Harbert," Jerry said to me. "It isn't necessary."

"But we have to call him *something.*"

"You heard what he said." Jerry was angry.

I persisted, clumsily. "But everybody has a name."

"Sure," Jerry said. "Like our boat. Like its home port."

"That's just it," I said. "Suddenly we get here and names disappear."

The navy man said, "Names disappear?"

"Forget it," Jerry told him. "She's upset. It's my fault. I take the blame for everything."

The navy man smiled at me. "It would make you glad to have a name to call me?"

I nodded.

The grin was at its widest yet. "Then you can call me Comrade."

True to Comrade's words, supplies started coming to the *Menehune.* "My God," Jerry said to me, "don't ever make another meal using our own stuff. Save it. Use theirs. They're not charging us a cent for it."

The politest thing to say is that what they gave us, we weren't used to. They showed up with a "supply" of rice —for Americans, it would have been a year's supply: an overflowing bucketful—but it had no meaning for us or our diets. At first they gave us honey and sugar, but in small amounts. Obviously they wanted us to have food, but not at the expense of any existing consumers on the island, so when we got squash, it was rotten. When we got eggs, the black spots of decay were already upon them. They gave us pork that had a strange taste, and day-old fish, and one day, for lunch aboard the *Menehune,* I attempted a casserole of day-old fish, rotten squash, and rice. I tasted it while I was cooking it and spat it out.

"We can't eat this," I said.

"What do you mean, we can't eat it?" Jerry said. And so he ate my portion and his too, and the next day he ate what was left of it. And became terribly sick to his stomach. So sick, our Chinese hosts were alarmed. There was a doctor on the other side of the island. They took him there. "Listen," he told them, "I am eating the bad food deliberately, so Miss Harbert won't have any of it to eat."

On the other side of the island, they dosed him with a laxative and sent him back. Maybe this is the standard treatment for those accustomed to this diet to begin with, but in Jerry's case it only weakened him further.

We went back to using our own basic supply of food aboard the boat. In addition, we did our laundry there, and bathed, and (of course) washed our dishes. Our only means of doing that was to hang a bucket overboard and collect the water of the harbor, a procedure hardly conducive to our well-being.

Then there was the haircut.

"It's not a question of *must.*"

"Of course it's a question of *must.* Because you requested it, I have brought you somebody." Comrade gestured to an equally smiling man standing next to him. "I have brought you a barber."

Jerry turned to me. "So I'm not going to turn hippie after all."

"Hippie?" Comrade said.

"It's nothing," Jerry said to him. He waved the barber on. "Come on, doll. Make me beautiful."

But in between times, there was interrogation. Comrade was in charge, translating what we said into Chinese to two male stenographers, who were writing as fast as they could. The sessions would be short—first Jerry, then me—and the whole thing was obviously unsatisfactory. Not only had Jerry and I failed to square our stories with each other, but there were basic discrepancies—or so the Chinese found them to be—from the word go.

My end of the questioning would be something like this:

Q. Knowing navigation as you do . . .
A. I don't.
Q. This is hard to believe.
A. It is the truth.
Q. Then why were you on the boat?
A. As McLaughlin's companion.
Q. You had a definite intent to be married?
A. No.
Q. You had a definite love relationship?
A. No.
Q. Then why did you trespass?
A. If we did, it was a mistake.
Q. Then you admit to this mistake?
A. Yes.
Q. Then you *do* know navigation!
A. No.
Q. Nothing about it?
A. Nothing about it.
Q. Then how do you know it was a mistake?

A. I'm willing to assume it.
Q. You've been comparing stories with McLaughlin.
A. No.
Q. Then you *do* know navigation.
A. You've asked me that before. The answer is no.
Q. Then why are you willing to assume it was a mistake?
A. Because it couldn't have been anything else.
Q. Do you know McLaughlin's version of this?
A. No.
Q. Do you know he told us once you left Hong Kong intending to sail to Manila, then told us another time you intended to return to Hong Kong?
A. No.
Q. Does it bother you he told two different stories?
A. No.
Q. Why?
A. Why what?
Q. Why doesn't it bother you he told two different stories?
A. Because I don't know how many stories he told. I know there was only one story. We were on our way to Manila, from Hong Kong.
Q. Do you know how many hundreds of boats have sailed to Manila from Hong Kong?
A. No.
Q. And among those hundreds of boats, do you know how many have trespassed?
A. No. I'd assume quite a few.
Q. Quite a few? How many?
A. Maybe half of them.
Q. *Half* of them? You assume that many boats suddenly lose their bearings?
A. No.
Q. Then how do you account for what you have just said?
A. Because "trespass" is your word, not mine. Who

knows how many boats you've arrested in international waters?

Q. Then you think we were behaving criminally.
A. I didn't say that.
Q. Then what *did* you think?
A. I thought we weren't doing anything wrong.

Where Comrade may have found it hard to believe I didn't understand navigation, Mr. Wang found it even harder. Mr. Wang was a strange stereotype. All at once, Comrade was gone from the scene and Mr. Wang had taken his place. Mr. Wang was exactly what in your mind's eye you would imagine Mr. Wang to be, if you can believe that what came after Comrade had to be more Comrade than Comrade. And so Wang was.

Although Chinese, Mr. Wang was the prototype of every Japanese villain in every World War II movie you ever saw. He was young, fanatic, short, had buck teeth, and wore glasses with heavy plastic frames. He even hissed.

My introduction to him was on my terms, not his. That is to say, I had an initial request to put to him. By now, more than two weeks had gone by, and both Jerry and I had got the feeling that our promised release: *You leave any minute now, take your blankets*—was something we could no longer depend upon. In unfortunate fact, we had no sense of unity about it. Mine was the part of the aggravated citizen—*what right do they have . . .* ? And his was the old martyr's cliché—*Do anything you want to me but let the girl go . . .*

There was no plus in that combination. Indeed, it took Comrade only a day or so, once he arrived on the scene, to issue the lasting order that Jerry and I be separated.

He did this for three reasons. The first was at the same time the most logical, yet the most mysterious. They wanted us kept apart so they could interrogate us separately, without our having "compared notes" beforehand. Time and again, when they saw us talking together on the island, they would wag their fingers and place them to their lips: *silence, no talking.* Yet at the same time, religiously—three times a day—our two old women would row us out to the *Menehune* and leave us totally alone, so we could talk to our heart's content.

"No sane person is going to believe this," Jerry said to me aboard the boat one day. Whereupon, methodically, he began to take the cabin apart, hunting for a tape recorder.

I said, "Maybe they don't think the way we do."

"That's not the point," he said. "The point is, either they're crazy or we are."

"But this isn't the only thing that doesn't make sense," I said.

"It's good enough for me," he said. "There's got to be a recorder here some place. Help me look. I know they're listening."

There was no recorder, of course. Instead there was another episode, this one along the same lines and even more contradictory than the business of communication between us. We had run out of the kerosene I used for cooking on the *Menehune,* so the Chinese gave us a new supply. But it was of an inferior grade, and gave off a black smoke that dirtied the curtains that had hung so starched and clean against the cabin windows. I wanted privacy—this was, after all, where I bathed and changed. But at the same time this was home, and I was not able to put up with dirty curtains. So I took the curtains down and substituted in their place the pages of an English-language Hong Kong newspaper we had brought with us when we first boarded the *Menehune* at Hebe Haven.

Within five minutes, a motorboat manned by four men pulled alongside. They stomped aboard the *Menehune,* ripped away the newspaper "curtains," confiscated what was left of the newspaper, and departed.

I said to Jerry, "What do you suppose *that* was all about?"

"They wanted to be able to see in," he said, "It's as simple as that."

"But they never objected to the curtains."

"The curtains weren't in English."

I thought about that. It made a wild kind of sense, yet at the same time no sense at all. "But the newspaper was lying here all the time."

"Not where everybody could see it," Jerry said. "Don't you see? That newspaper is a symbol of the free world. They don't want us displaying it."

"Why not?"

"Because," he explained, patiently, "they're afraid it could corrupt people."

"How?"

"It's in English, isn't it?"

"But they can't *read* English."

"How do you know?"

"I suppose I don't. But even if they could, we're out here in the middle of the water. Who could come close enough to read what it said to begin with?"

"It only takes one," he said. "Don't you see? They think it's a signal."

"Horse racing and brassiere ads?" I said. "A signal?"

He shook his head. "You'll never learn, Miss Harbert. Don't you see what it was?"

"No."

"It was the *act,*" he said. "The *act* of taking down the curtains and putting the newspapers up. *That* was the signal."

"Then why did they take the rest of the paper with them, too? And why didn't they make us put the curtains back up?"

"Because they're out-thinking us," he said. "They don't want us to have a back-up plan. They think we thought that putting the curtains back up after the newspapers were taken away could be something we might have expected. Then maybe we'd take the curtains down again and put up more newspapers. So they left the curtains down and took all the newspapers away."

I said, "But how did they know we were going to run out of kerosene to begin with?"

"They didn't."

"And how did they know their kerosene would make our curtains dirty?"

"They didn't." Jerry laughed. "But they don't know what we know. For all they know, this was part of our plan." Again he laughed. "Maybe you don't strike them as the perfect little hippie housewife. After all, *is* there such a thing as a perfect hippie housewife? Aren't the terms mutually exclusive? You didn't tell *them* you don't like dirty curtains . . . you just took them down. Most hippie housewives would just have let the curtains stay where they were, dirty or not. Wouldn't they? So the minute they saw the curtains come down and the newspapers go up, what'd you expect them to think?"

I suppose there's a good deal of irony to it: we were being separated, no longer to share the same room in our sleeping quarters on the island because our hosts did not want us talking together. Yet they gave us all these occasions to do so aboard the boat. When we did talk together, though, conversations like the foregoing were the result.

But as I have said, that was only one of three reasons they had for putting us into separate rooms. Another reason was as clear to them as it would have been to anyone. It was no secret that we weren't getting along. The conflict was obvious, and to say whose "fault" it was is to beg the question. For it was, at the same time, Jerry's fault and his burden. I hadn't invited him on this trip. He had invited me. And this, coming in the wake as it did of his low state at Hong Kong, his poor physical condition, the person-to-person conflict that triggered his decision to retire, and now the interruption, if not the shattering, of his life's dream to cruise the world aboard a boat built for him alone—all these things weighed upon him, I knew. What I knew also, and what I think he knew, was the real reason he had never married. I simply don't think he liked women that much. It was not a case of his being in any way not heterosexual. Rather, it was a case of priorities, and leading his own life came first.

And so I hung around his neck like not one albatross, but three. First, I was a link to a career, a reminder that he had departed under unpleasant, if not forced, circumstances. Second, I was a woman, and—not to re-explore old ground—let it be said that it was evident that if he had had that first postcard to send over again, it would never have been sent. And third, I was his responsibility, and here we had wound up as—what?—Communist captives? Who knew? *Modus operandi adopted* he had written me *is to sail as pleased till not pleasing.*

There might have been more I could have done—me, a graduate in psychology. In fact, he invited it. "Come on, psychoanalyze me," he challenged, more than once. But I had no plan, no schedule of reactions. Through trial and error, I was to discover ways—some of them curious—to get through to him. In truth, I "discovered" one way that's one of the oldest in the book: I would snap at him, shout at him, toss his dirty laundry in his face. And that would relieve him.

Not that it would happen every day. Not that it happened by plan. But when it did happen, the effect, if not the intent, was to make me an adversary instead of a responsibility, and responsibility was what he found most crushing, so that anything that alleviated it—anything that would make him fight back instead of brood—had to be on the plus side.

Still speaking of why Comrade ordered us separated at the island, there was, as I've said, a third reason. This reason concerned morality.

Q. You had a definite intent to be married?

A. No.

Q. You had a definite love relationship?

A. No.

Those were honest answers, given without hesitation to questions hesitatingly asked. There was an overriding prim quality in the Chinese approach, and it was accompanied by embarrassment. (At first—this is by way of an example—Jerry and I thought we should ask permission to visit the privy from the headquarters building on the island. *Don't ask about it,* we were told, *just go.* This primness did not seem so apparent in their

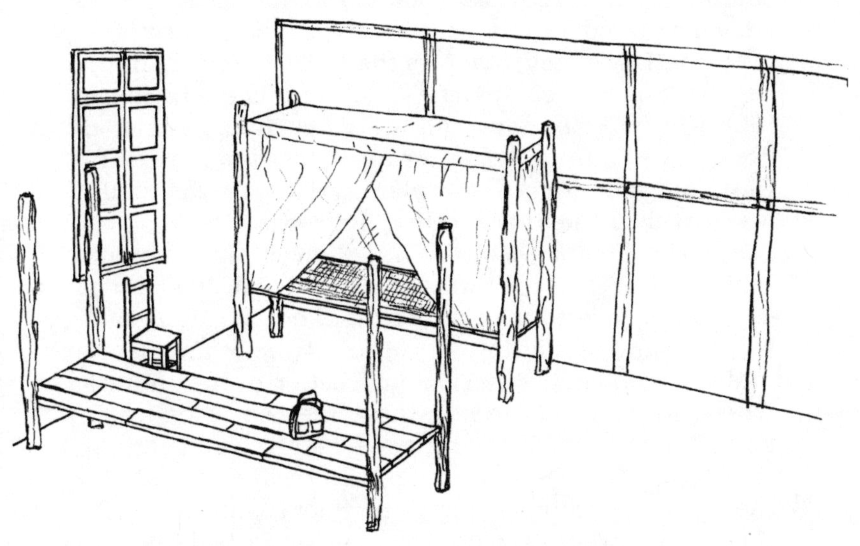

My room on the island.

conduct, but we were foreigners, and foreigners are treated with circumspection everywhere.) I did not know then, nor do I now, exactly what Comrade meant when he said "love relationship." He, on one hand, could not bring himself to ask whether Jerry and I had slept together. I, on the other, was not about to concede a "love relationship" without knowing Comrade's definition of that term. It was hardly what you would call an impasse. From the way we acted on the island, it was clear that we weren't in love. So the question in effect answered itself, and in so doing suited the Chinese purpose entire. They knew we weren't married and they could see we weren't getting along. So they separated us.

I have thought back since and realized once again, because in essence I knew it at the time, that even if we had been billing and cooing, even if there was no attempt, however silly in its execution, to keep us from communicating with each other, we still would have been separated simply because we weren't married.

And so I was moved across the hall, to a room on the back side of the headquarters building. There had been four beds in it, but now there were two. It had a broken-down chair, a bucket that obviously used to have paint in it, and a poster with Chinese writing on the wall. I asked what it meant, and they told me: *Mao has said, sweep the floor every day.* They showed me the broom that was stored in the hallway outside. But they had no dustpan to go with it, or anything like it. I started making a mound of dirt in one corner of the room.

Meanwhile, in the auditorium section of the building where we were quartered, there seemed to be a perpetual floor covering of orange and other fruit peelings, these from the audiences that congregated weekly for the showing of movies. Jerry and I never saw any of the films. They would have let us, but he forbade it. "We stay in our rooms," he said.

"Why can't we watch the movie?"

"It wouldn't be appropriate."

But it scarcely bothered me that I was expected to sweep while others didn't. I had more basic problems. The only ventilation for my room was from a back window, leading directly onto a small outdoor kitchen where the same woman came to cook every day. To leave the window open was to let in not only the smoke and fumes, but mosquitoes as well. My bed had mosquito netting with holes in it. And if I closed the window I got no air at all.

"How long is this going to go on?" I asked Jerry.

"It doesn't matter any more," he said.

"What do you mean, it doesn't matter?"

"I mean we've been here long enough. I'm through cooperating."

I didn't blame him. But the next question persisted: "Then what are we going to do now?"

"Escape," he said.

"Escape?" I said. "How?"

"You'll notice," he said, "I've never taken down the sails on the boat."

"You mean we're just going to *sail* out of the harbor?"

"Can you think of a quieter way to go?"

"I'm trying to think of a way to *start,* not go."

"The *Menehune* has an engine, Miss Harbert," Jerry said. "Had you forgotten that?"

"But an engine makes noise."

"Only for the time it takes to get under way." He smiled. "We know we're all charged up."

We did know we were all charged up. This had been demonstrated in a weird and almost frightening way, and it illustrated, more than anything else, the difficulties we were having with language. Talking to Comrade was no problem at all, so long as you were talking—what shall I say? dialectic?—and in fact he was perhaps the most literate translator we would ever encounter. His English was perfect, and it was *English* English—you know, where they say "missile" and it comes out "missile", with the "sile" pronounced as in "silo." But more than that, he knew how to manage contractions. With other interpreters, contractions were everything, so that instead of saying, for example, "What is the name of this place?" it would come out "What's this place?"

But one thing Comrade lacked, as they all did, was a vocabulary. Use words like *trespass, destination, nationality,* and he was fully equipped. But say *paper clip, can opener, eraser*—and he was lost.

And so a dilemma came into being. To keep the *Menehune* from being struck by some other boat at night, Jerry wanted her running lights lit. So did the Chinese. Jerry knew that for the boat's batteries to be able to supply that power, they would have to be charged by running the engine. So did the Chinese. But what he couldn't get across was that the engine could be revved up by running it while the boat was stationary. The Chinese understood the principle, but they didn't understand him, and since he knew the boat best they relied on him to say how it should be done. He tried to make it clear the boat could stay in one place, but it came out, in their interpretation, that it had to be in motion. So two of them took charge of the boat, switched on the engine, and in a kind of Fatty Arbuckle scene careened through the harbor, missing half a dozen other boats and objects by half an inch, if that. They didn't even bring it back to its original mooring, which turned out to be just as well. A work crew was blasting a road out of the mountain, and rocks and stones dislodged by the dynamite were flying through the air and landing in the water directly where the *Menehune* would have been, had it stayed at rest in its original location.

But its point of mooring made no difference to Jerry. What was important to him now was that the engine and sails were both at the ready.

"The escape is foolproof," he told me.

I said, "What about that destroyer tied up at the pier?"

"Simple," he said. "I've already taken it into consideration."

"But it can go five times faster than we do."

"By the time we're away, it won't make any difference."

"They'll know we're leaving."

"Why? How stupid do you think I am? We'll do it at night . . . no, I know what you're going to say: our running lights will give us away. Ah, Miss Harbert, but there won't *be* any running lights. That's the one time we won't use them. You see?"

"But the noise of the engine. As we get under way."

"You think they'll hear that?"

"I *know* they'll hear that. So will our two old ladies in the rowboat."

"And what will they do? Row after us?"

"I'm only saying," I said, "that everybody will know."

"Suppose they do?"

"Then they'll come and catch us."

"Who?"

"The destroyer."

"Not," Jerry said, "if we hang a chain on their propeller first."

"How are you going to do that?"

"You forget," he said. "I'm a good swimmer."

* * *

I need not say that the plan for escape was fanciful, and never came off, but neither part of that implies any criticism for Jerry. Had his physical condition been better, I do believe he would have been capable of it. And as for the concept of escape itself, it was never far from our minds—though it would last longer for me. This doesn't mean we could have escaped successfully. But I like to think (I know it's a luxury now) that we might have tried.

Instead, enter Mr. Wang.

The destroyer that had brought Comrade to the island weighed anchor and left. As it was leaving the harbor, a gunboat was coming in. I have already described Mr. Wang, the quintessential "Jap villain" in any post-Pearl Harbor movie you ever saw. To describe him thus is to describe the gunboat that brought him into port. No archetype such as Wang would arrive on any other kind of ship.

And he was Comrade with a cutting edge.

At first he talked only to Jerry. But then he came across the hall to me, sputtering.

"Your friend is sick," he said. "A nurse came—there is always a nurse here, this is China—but he sent her away. He has already had medical care. We will give him more. But he must cooperate! He must tell us the nature of his illness!"

I said, "I don't understand. I know he's been having stomach trouble. Didn't he tell you that?"

Almost spitting, Wang said, "He told me to guess!"

I said, "Well, maybe it's a trouble with language."

"You thought of that?" Wang said to me. He pointed violently at himself, at his own stomach, almost in a hara-kiri gesture. "*I* thought of that before you did. I said to him, if it is a language barrier, then you write it down. I said to him, you can not have it two ways, being a yachtsman and having stomach trouble at the same time. And so, I said, if you are a yachtsman and if you have stomach trouble, then at the very least you will be the one to prescribe for yourself—in writing. Give me your written prescription, I said to him, and I will see to it. This I promised him!" His hands were shaking. They clutched a piece of paper. "And this—*this*—is what he wrote!"

Mr. Wang showed me the piece of paper. On it, in Jerry's handwriting, it said:

Sodium Acetylsalicylate, Calcium-Sodium Phosphates, Sodium Bicarbonate, Sodium Citrate.

I don't pretend to swear from memory that was exactly what it said, but it was close enough. I know that because I have had an easy way to check my memory since then, and because of what Jerry said to me at the time.

"Does he take me for a dispensary?" Mr. Wang said. "Or does he take me for a fool, to be put off by medical terms he thinks I have no way of understanding?"

I said, "I don't know, Mr. Wang. I do know there's something I want to talk to you about."

"You will talk to me when I talk to you," he said. "Our beloved leader Chairman Mao says one may not remain mute when there is something to be said. I will teach you Chinese by using the sayings of our beloved Chairman Mao. You will like that, I think."

I said, "But for now—"

"For now," he said, "I am going to respond to this insult in writing." He waved the paper. "It will receive the reply it deserves."

He left my room and as I followed him to the doorway, I saw Jerry opening his door across the hall: he now occupied by himself the room the two of us had shared at the beginning.

He said, "Did he show you what I wrote?"

"Did he?!" I said. "He's gone off to make a reply for you. In writing."

He nodded. "I thought it would be appropriate for him to understand what kind of people he was dealing with. From the very start."

I said, "Is it wise?"

"Is what wise?"

"To make fun of him? Obviously, he's someone in authority. And he does talk English."

"I'm just testing him," Jerry said easily.

"I'd say it was a pretty tough test."

"What's the matter, college girl? You don't know your basic chemistry?"

"It isn't a question of what I know," I said. "It's a question of what he knows. How is he expected to know those long words?"

"Well, I wasn't asking for much," Jerry said.

I didn't understand that, and it seemed to amuse him.

"You see," he said—appearing to enjoy me now as much as he had enjoyed Wang—"all I was putting down in writing there was something very simple, actually. A nice little formula, native to the great state of Indiana."

I said, "Jerry, I don't know what you're doing."

"I'm doing what he asked me to do," he said. "It's as simple as that. He asked me to set down in writing a formula for what I needed."

"But they don't have all those things."

"Maybe not," he said. "It's really not that complicated."

"He seemed to think it was complicated."

"He's a Chinaman. What do you expect?"

"But you're using long words on him."

"Am I?"

"You know you are. You're having fun at his expense."

At this moment, Mr. Wang reappeared, coming along the corridor that separated Jerry's room from mine. Once again he had a piece of paper in his hands, a different piece of paper.

"Here," he said, thrusting it at Jerry, "is my reply to you."

Jerry took it from him and smiled and tore the paper gently but methodically into little pieces, and scattered them over the floor. "You have to understand, Mr. Wang," he said, "I'm not a doctor. So I really can't prescribe medicine, can I?"

"But you said . . ." Wang started it, then broke off. Without a further word, he turned and left.

"Say good night to Muckaluck, Miss Hobbitah," Jerry said to me, from his doorway.

"What did you accomplish by that?" I asked him.

He shrugged. "He asked for it in writing. He got it."

"He got what? What did those words say?"

"Alka Seltzer," Jerry said.

"He is being difficult," Mr. Wang said to me. *He* was Jerry. "He is attributing a saying of our beloved leader Chairman Mao to Anna Louise Strong."

"I know," I said. *"All reactionaries are paper tigers.* But what Mao thought she meant was . . ."

"You do not say Mao," Mr. Wang, said. "He is Chairman Mao, our beloved head." He seemed agitated, his talk disjointed. "He says he wants to talk to me, then when I arrive he has nothing to say." Once again the *he* meant Jerry. I said to myself, *Wang complains to me about Jerry, Jerry complains to me about Wang. They're like two little boys, running to me and tattling on each other.*

I said now, "But Comrade said—"

"Comrade?"

"The man who came before you. He said Anna Louise Strong—"

"He didn't say that. Nobody in China would say that. Look in your book of the sayings of Chairman Mao. That is what the book is for. You will find that *Mao* said it, *in conversation* with Anna Louise Strong."

I said to myself, *Why is he carrying on like this?*—and then, in self-reproach as part of the same thought, *And why are you arguing with him?*

"Everything reactionary is the same," Mr. Wang said now. "That is what *he* does not understand. You will find it in your book of the sayings. *Everything reactionary is the same; if you don't hit it, it won't fall. This is also like sweeping the floor; as a rule, where the broom does not reach, the dust will not vanish of itself.* You understand?"

"Yes," I said, with a side look at the Mao quote hanging on the wall of my room.

"But *he* doesn't understand," Mr. Wang said, with a wave toward Jerry's room. "He thinks somehow he is superior. But Chairman Mao has said: *It is my opinion that the international situation has now reached a new turning point. There are two winds in the world today, the East Wind and the West Wind. There is a Chinese saying, 'Either the East Wind prevails over the West Wind or the West Wind prevails over the East Wind.'* You will find it in your book of sayings. And then, Chairman Mao concludes: *I believe it is characteristic of the situation today that the East Wind is prevailing over the West Wind. That is to say, the forces of socialism have become overwhelmingly superior to the forces of imperialism.* This is what your companion Muckalucking"—even Wang could not master *McLaughlin*—"fails to comprehend. And why? Because we gave him the book of sayings but he refuses to read it. Do you want a further example? Then I'll give you the tobacco and the alcohol."

Still disjointed, with relation to the overall feel of the things we were talking about, but on this specific I could at least follow him. By now my carton of Newports aboard the *Menehune* had been used up. As for whiskey, I drank very little—and what I did take would be totally diluted in water, taken more to be sociable than anything else. And I had picked up a cigarette cough and told myself it was just as well I had run out of them in these circumstances. What better excuse to quit smoking?

But at the same time I ran out of cigarettes, so did the rest of the island. You could see people busily rolling their own, making do with substitutes till a new supply came in.

The new supply did come in aboard Wang's gunboat. Jerry and I were aboard the *Menehune* at the time. A rowboat came directly from the gunboat to us, and one of the men in it solemnly handed me a pack of Chinese cigarettes. I forget which brand it was, for the Chinese manufactured several brands. There was a brand called De Taen Mein, another called Glory, with a star on one side of the package, a picture of a carnation on the other. And there were Flying Horse, and Flying Eagle. All were old-time style, old-time cigarettes. None came with filters. And so my resolve to give up smoking was destroyed, for from that time on, I was presented every other day with a new package of cigarettes.

But we had run out of whiskey, too, and in this direction the Chinese offered no replenishment. I don't think that was the end of the world for Jerry. Just as I could do without cigarettes, he could do without alcohol. I didn't depend that much on smoking and he didn't depend that much on drinking.

But although I was practically a non-drinker, he was absolutely a non-smoker. And on that account it appears he had raised holy hell with Mr. Wang.

"He is lecturing to *me* about equality!" Wang shouted at me now. I sat in the broken-down chair in my room, my feet propped up on the rough-hewn wooden bed, watching him as he marched up and down. "He says he must have alcohol. Why? Because *you* are getting cigarettes! He charges discrimination. He said to me, 'Miss Harbert is your pet.' " He wheeled and stared at me. "What's that mean, *pet?"*

I said, "It's like a dog or a cat."

Mr. Wang frowned. "You're a dog? You're a cat?"

"No. Someone you like. Someone you favor. That's what it means."

"I don't understand. What is our word for this?"

"I don't know your word for it. But let me show you something." I got up and fetched, from underneath the pillow of my bed, a poem I had written. I had seen two kittens on the island. The friendliest had a fluffy tail; the other had had its tail cut off.

I said to Wang: "Have you ever heard of Bob Dylan?"

"Heard of what?"

"I'm influenced by him, I think," I said.

"Don't talk to me the way Muckaluckding talks to me," Mr. Wang said. "Don't be superior. Remember what I have told you about the East Wind and the West Wind."

I found myself laughing. When I cited Bob Dylan to Mr. Wang, he thought I was being superior. When I had cited Bob Dylan to Jerry, he thought that was proof positive I was some kind of left-wing hippie. Given the choice of reactions, I had to prefer Mr. Wang's.

"Here," I said, and showed him the poem I had written:

The cat with the big fluffy tail
Cries loudly for entrance.
The cat with no tail
Mews quietly.

Mr. Wang read it. His nostrils flared. He read it again. He began to hiss. He fixed me with a stare. He said, "You know the penalties for this?"

"The penalties?"

"What would you have called this, that you have written? Would you call it art? Art for art's sake?"

"I don't know. I suppose so. A try at it, anyway."

"Don't you know there's no such thing as art for art's sake?"

"Who said that?"

"Our beloved leader. Chairman Mao. *There is in fact no such thing as art for art's sake, art that stands above classes, art that is detached from or independent of politics.* Now—" he seemed to subside "—tell me again about this word."

"What word?"

"The word you used for cat."

"Pet," I said.

"Pet," he said. "And you said it means a dog or a cat?"

"Or anyone you love," I said.

"Ah. Then Muckaluckding is your pet?"

"No."

"Ah. Because you do not love him." He nodded. "Then your boat. That is your pet."

"No."

"You don't love your boat?"

"Only in a way. Not in any way that would make me call it a pet. A pet has to be alive."

"Ah. And that is why you wrote the poem?"

Unwittingly, he was leading me into a strange, almost enchanting entrapment. Would I call poetry one of my pet hobbies? If then, I would be using the word *pet.* But I had said a pet had to be alive. Is a poem alive? There flashed before me in that moment the memory of the daughters and wives of U.S. survey and oil men in Saudi Arabia, some of whom had undertaken to teach English to groups of Saudi Arabian children. There were already teachers there who understood both languages. Yet, invariably, it seemed that the pupils of the untrained Americans, who themselves spoke no Arabic, seemed to progress faster than than those whose teachers spoke the students' own language. Had Wang known no English, I could have taught him the meaning of "pet." But he knew just enough English to make this impossible. And in this he was typical of all the interpreters I was yet to meet.

I say this now, but I had a sense of it then. A sense, that is to say, that I was going to be in China for a long time. The feckless business of trailing our blankets to and from the boat, the "any minute now" business of our being released, things like those were no longer there. Unlike Jerry, I could see no practical means for escape. But like Jerry, I was searching my mind for such means.

And so, for the meantime, I made my request to Mr. Wang:

"You've known I wanted to talk to you."

"Certainly," he said. "It's only right and proper. Our revered head Chairman Mao says one may not remain mute when there is something to be said."

"I know that," I said. "But what I have to talk to you about is just a simple request."

He stopped pacing, and glared at me. "All of us have a position to perform," he said. "I asked you why you trespassed, and you said it was maybe because you had to tack. I know this word *tack.* Believe me, it counts against you. Over here you tell me you know nothing about navigation. Over there you use the words of navigation."

"It's just a word I've heard," I said. "I didn't give it to you as a fact. I gave it to you as a possibility. I *don't* know that much about navigation."

"And you are asking me now to believe this."

"Yes," I said.

"And therefore you wish me to stop questioning you, even though it's my duty to do so."

"No," I said. "That isn't what I wanted."

"Then what do you want?"

"To send a letter to my parents."

"Why? To tell them you're being ill-treated?"

"No. To tell them I'm all right."

"I don't understand that request." Again the wave toward Jerry's room. "Muckaluckding has made no such request."

"He's older than I am. The situation isn't the same."

"But you are healthy. You are well." He laughed. "Muckaluckding is sick. The healthy one wants to write letters to the outside world. The sick one doesn't."

He argues like Jerry, I thought. *It isn't appropriate.* Aloud, I said, "You mean I can't write a letter?"

"Exactly. I could not permit it."

"Why not?"

"Because things are done the way things are done."

"But you could be mistaken."

"No. I am guided by the principles set forth in the book of the sayings of our adored leader, Chairman Mao. If you had bothered to open your book, you would know."

"But I have bothered to open my book." I reached for it. "See here—page 265. *If we have shortcomings, we are not afraid to have them pointed out and criticized, because we serve the people. Anyone, no matter who, may point out our shortcomings. If he is right, we will correct them.*"

Mr. Wang looked at me narrowly. "I've noticed," he said, "that you and your associate Muckaluckding share one thing in common. You twist your language. In this, you seek to deceive us. I say proudly that I am a citizen of China, and therefore I take responsibility for China's policy. You say you are a citizen of the United States, but you take no responsibility for its policies. You talk in generalities. You think I don't know what that word means *generalities?* Always you seek means to excuse your country. You know the guilt is there, and yet you—"

I said, "All I wanted was to write a letter home. You said no, and you told me to look in the book, and the book says that you may have shortcomings and anyone can point them out."

"Then write your letter," he said.

I wrote the letter. Sensing that to have any chance at all it would have to be as short as possible, I made it as short as possible:

> DEAR PEOPLE,
>
> Don't worry. We are being detained in Red China. They said we had trespassed. I don't know how long we will be here. Don't worry. I'm all right.
>
> LOVE,
>
> MARY ANN

Mr. Wang read it.

"Who is 'People'?"

"My mother and father. I always write "Dear People" because it takes so long to write 'Dear Mother and Father.' "

"What are their names?"

"Mr. and Mrs. Gene W. Harbert."

"What is their address?"

"I put it there on the envelope."

"You must write it on the letter."

"Okay."

"You can not insult China. This is new China, not old China. This is the People's Republic of China, led by the Chinese Communist Party with our great leader Chairman Mao Tse-tung at the head. You must write People's Republic of China, not Red China."

"Okay. Okay. I'll do what you say."

"It doesn't matter," Mr. Wang said.

"It doesn't matter?"

"No. Just as I told you before you wrote the letter, you cannot send it."

"Why?"

"It is the policy of the government. I didn't think you could send it."

"Could I contact the American Consulate in Hong Kong? The British Consulate? The Swiss Consulate? Somebody?"

"No."

"I know my parents are worried. They think I've drowned at sea. Couldn't I just write them a short note telling them I'm alive?"

"No."

Mr. Wang left the room. He took my letter with him. For a moment, I wondered what would have happened if I had pleaded with him, gone into long entreaty, broken down and wept. But I knew nothing different would have happened, other than whatever satisfaction he might have derived from seeing me cry.

The sense that came over me now was a sense of too many tomorrows. We had been on the island for less than a month, yet there was a feeling of forever to it. Today's Chinese have accomplished many things in a remarkably short period of time, but even here in the midst of an epochal event, the Cultural Revolution, the entire setting was one of infinite, plodding patience.

I opened my little red book of quotations from Chairman Mao. "There is an ancient Chinese fable," he had written in 1946, "called 'The Foolish Old Man Who Removed the Mountains.' It tells of an old man who lived in northern China long, long ago and was known as the Foolish Old Man of North Mountain. His house faced south and beyond his doorway stood the two great peaks, Taihang and Wangwu, obstructing the way. With great determination, he led his sons in digging up these mountains, hoe in hand. Another greybeard, known as the Wise Old Man, saw them and said derisively, 'How silly of you to do this! It is quite impossible for you few to dig up these two huge mountains.' The Foolish Old Man replied, 'When I die, my sons will carry on; when they die, there will be my grandsons and then their sons and grandsons and so on to infinity. High as they are, the mountains cannot grow any higher and with every bit we dig, they will be that much lower. Why can't we clear them away?' Having refuted the Wise Old Man's wrong view, he went on digging every day, unshaken in his convictions."

3

The Inn of the Fifth Happiness

There were many mistakes that I made, and one of them was to use the phrase "Red China" in the letter I tried to have sent to my parents. Mr. Wang had recoiled at that, turned almost into a serpent in his anger.

What affected him of course was the word "Red." Had I written "Communist China" instead, I realized, too late, it would have affected him the same way. It was not that they did not like or want to be called Red or Communist. And there was certainly no lack of accuracy in those words.

But when "Red" was used by me, I came to see that this was, to Mr. Wang, the same as it might be if I introduced my mother as my "real mother." She is that, of course. But the implication is left that there's somebody else. Thus my use of "Red China" allowing for the presence—and surely it was there—of what westerners knew was a "somebody else": the China of Taiwan, Chiang Kai-shek, and the Kuomintang. If I had set out deliberately to make sure my brief letter to my mother and father contained the most viciously sarcastic reference to mainland China (there I go again!), I could not have succeeded any better than in fact I did.

But there were other manifestations of my "mistakes." I found it hard to anticipate the mood of the moment, the way they would expect me to be. When it should have been right to smile, I would be frowning. But when I smiled, I discovered they were not smiling at all . . .

This applied not only to my interrogators, but to whatever I did. I remember two different episodes, each happening at the same place—the rowboat landing at the base of the path and the fact that Jerry's physical condition had deteriorated. By now he was a full-scale victim of dysentery, able to get back and forth from his room to the privy, but lacking the real strength or will to go to the *Menehune* three times a day. By contrast, I found it important never to miss one of those trips. Even the clock became important. If they delayed the breakfast trip because it was raining, I'd find myself saying to them: "People starve before they melt. Since when did a little rain hurt anybody?"

As a result, there were those two lunchtime visits to the boat and each time I descended the pathway alone. One of the times I was in a kind of Jesus-freak mood, and as I reached the boat landing I saw an old woman there, a very dirty old woman, squatting in the mud as she went about the task of plucking a chicken. I watched her. She looked up at me, and I beamed: a beam of love from one stranger to another, containing in that certain smile all of the universal beatitude practiced and preached by the most radical arm of the hippie cult at the University of Utah.

The old woman returned a look of such utter loathing as I can not remember before or since. Then she went back to plucking her chicken.

The next time, as I arrived at the bottom of the path, a pair of men's undershorts arrived with me. They had been hanging on a clothesline next to the village cafeteria. But where the Chinese have clotheslines they don't have clothespins, and a gust of wind had taken the shorts off the line and wafted them down toward the water. They landed a short space away, then another gust of wind brought them to my feet. Another gust, and they would end up in the harbor.

One side of me said *Pick them up. Save them.* Another side said *Touch them and you'll be accused of stealing.* And so my decision: I would not touch them. And now, looking up, I saw a thin Chinese man, sprinting out of the building to chase his shorts. Here came the man and here came the next gust of wind. He passed me as I stood there and in one final grasp snatched his shorts out of mid-air, inches away from the water at the landing where the old ladies emptied their chamberpots. Then, fighting for breath, he turned to me. I had been doing exactly what I had been doing: standing there, my face impassive.

And now he turned on the Jesus-freak smile. He gave me a smile of total love, total gratitude. The smile of warmth, the smile of affection, the smile of polite thanks.

Either way—with the woman plucking the chicken or the man chasing his shorts—I had to come out the same: the Ugly American.

It was even worse than that. I knew I had infuriated Mr. Wang by mentioning Bob Dylan, a name he could not have known, in the course of conversation. What Mr. Wang would never understand was that the part of conversation in which Dylan's name arose was conversation primarily intended for myself. For I had begun to daydream, not as an abandonment of sanity, but to protect it. Does that sound too dramatic? Perhaps it is. "You were very lucky to be captured in a Communist country," Comrade had told me, and I'm sure he believed it, but I wasn't feeling very lucky.

In a way I was not without friends, for there were people I'd come to like—the island nurse, a little boy, a sympathetic woman from the village—but the language barrier was always there. As for Jerry, by now the separation between us was nearly complete. His physical condition was worsening, and in its own way that made his hostility increase, for he could not take solicitude from one whose plight he felt he had caused.

Therefore, I was, for all practical purposes, alone. And so I began to write poems. I began to compose songs. And the one person with whom I could hold an enjoyable conversation was myself.

The daydreams were the best part, because they were free of limits. The most satisfying was the one about the chocolates. As our own stock of food had decreased, to be replaced by local fare—strange, rancid, often inedible—the notion came to me, when I became hungry, that I would go to the candy store, with its bright candy-striped awning and wondrous candy-box smell, and there I would buy, each day, a large, two-pound box of chocolates, each separately wrapped in gold foil. The box would be gift-wrapped and tied with bright red ribbon and a fancy bow. And I would take it home with me, unwrap it slowly, saving the bow and the ribbon and the pretty wrapping paper. Then, slowly, I'd take each individually wrapped chocolate, remove the protective gold foil, and eat it.

I would finish the whole box. Ordinarily, I knew, such gluttony would make me sick. But I didn't feel sick. I felt wonderful. Strangest of all, as the dream receded, I found I was no longer hungry.

* * *

The bed in which I slept did not have a mattress. It had a straw mat instead, and a quilt, which the Chinese would use as a cover for warmth, but which I used as a mattress instead. As a cover, I used a blanket from the boat. As for sleepwear, it had more circumstance to it than choice. Usually I would go to bed dressed in a sweatshirt and a pair of underpants. To a certain degree, it upset me that this might make me something of a peep show—there was no private place to dress or undress, except for the *Menehune*—but I could have been wearing a Mother Hubbard, instead of delicate panties, and I would have been a peep show anyway. At six o'clock each evening, they would set out a radio on the terrace of our building, point its speaker toward the harbor below, and turn it on full blast, for music and news. The men playing chess at the tables on the terrace wouldn't even look up. But if I came into view, all heads snapped in curiosity. I could have attracted it for being an American. I could have attracted it for being a young woman. What I did get was the full combined force of both those factors. I didn't like it but I quickly got used to it, just as I became accustomed to the parade of peeking faces at my back window.

I let it bother me as little as possible, and, unlike Jerry, I had no trouble falling asleep. Each night I would "daydream" myself into sleep, not with the chocolates but with a menu for a full meal. Having heard or read somewhere that people do not dream in color, I forced color into the dream. I was a young housewife, planning a dinner: shopping for it, cooking it, laying out the decor of the table. And if at any point I made a single mistake —in ordering at the store, in setting out the ingredients, in placing a floral centerpiece on the dining room table, in allocating the correct silverware for each child (of course I had children)—I would go back to the beginning and start over. And soon I would be asleep, and no longer dreaming.

But in the middle of the night, one time, I was awakened out of that sleep, and I saw Mr. Wang standing there, flanked by one of the male stenographers who held a kerosene lantern toward my eyes.

"Sign this!" Wang commanded, and thrust a piece of paper and a pen at me.

I sat up in bed. "What is it?"

"Your confession."

Of course it was not "my" confession—it was Jerry's, for both of us.

"Read it first," Mr. Wang ordered.

"Why?" I said.

He blinked. The sense of it had gone through to him: actually, what difference did it make if I read it? Jerry had already discussed with me his "draft" of the "confession." And what position was I in to disagree?

"Very well," Wang said, and reached for my hand. Against my thumb, he pressed a red, waxy substance, made warm and pliable by the heat from the lamp. And then he pressed my thumbprint next to my signature.

As I've said, Jerry had already told me what the paper would say.

"I want you to know," he had said earlier, "that I take full blame for everything."

"Everything?"

"In what I'm writing down on paper, yes. I'm going to admit that we trespassed. But I'm saying it was *my fault.* Do you understand?"

We had been alone on the boat at the time: it was one of his last visits there. Before then a small Chinese fishing boat had come alongside the *Menehune,* circling her at close range while a man on board took endless pictures of our boat from every angle.

I said, "What are they doing?"

"They want to give us snapshots for our album," Jerry said. The sarcasm hung heavy. "And I suppose you haven't noticed the women at the dock."

"Not really. What was I supposed to notice?"

"The way they talk together any time we pass them."

"They talk together when we're *not* there. They're no different from women anywhere. They get together and gossip."

Jerry shook his head. "You say that because you want to believe it. Either that, or you want *me* to believe it." He nodded heavily. "If that's your game, it's all right."

I said, "I have no 'game.'"

"Have it your way," he said. "You have to save yourself. Here. You'd better have these, too." And he gave me his own booklet of traveler's checks. It was more gesture than reality, for the checks could only be cashed in his possession, not mine, since they required his presence and counter-signature. "You have to save yourself," he said to me. "Remember, I'm going to be taking full and single responsibility for trespassing. And that's the only thing they've got against us."

I said, "But they haven't actually *charged* us with anything."

"What difference does that make?"

"Well," I said, "they haven't put us in jail, have they?"

"With bars on the windows? No, not quite that."

"It's not just a question of bars on the windows," I said. "The point is, there's a difference between a confession and an apology."

"If there is, they don't see it." He covered his eyes with his hand. "Neither do I."

"All right," I said, "maybe there isn't a difference. But you can say *if I trespassed, I apologize,* instead of just *I trespassed.* And if they won't accept that, then say if *we* trespassed *we* apologize. They already know I don't know anything about navigation."

"Do they?"

"And," I said, "if you include me, then it sounds that much more accidental."

"Do they?" he said again.

"Do they what?"

"Know you don't know that much about navigation?"

I stared at him. "What are you trying to—"

He looked at me, half mockingly, half in affection, interrupting, "Save yourself, Miss Harbert," he said. "There's nothing else to be saved."

I said, "What are you talking about? You know we didn't do anything wrong. We could be released any day now. Any hour."

"Sure, we could," he said, "and go sailing off together in the *Menehune,* as though nothing ever happened. But something has happened, Miss Harbert." His voice was spiritless. "Have you looked at the *Menehune*? Have you seen the moss on her sides? Do you know what she's getting ready to do? She's getting ready to rot."

"You talk to him," Mr. Wang said to me. "We brought him a doctor and he refused to see him."

"What can I say to him?" I said.

"Tell him that now we're bringing him *two* doctors."

"He won't listen to me," I said. "He thinks I'm on your side. That you and I are together, against him."

"You can tell him to take the pills they ask him to take."

"He has no confidence in physicians." (Three weeks before that, I would have said "He has no confidence in *your* physicians," but slowly I was learning.)

Learning what? "Our doctors are better than your doctors," Wang said. "He must be made to understand this."

So we were back where we started. I could not spell out for Mr. Wang, any more than I had, the fact that part of Jerry's rebellion against any show of concern on my part was because he thought the Chinese were using me to "get secret information" out of him. To say that would have been to imply he had some secret information to give.

Yet at the same time he obviously needed medical attention.

I was allowed to go into his room. "Look," I said to

him, "at least *see* the doctors. You don't have to do what they say. You don't have to take what they give you."

He shook his head. "It wouldn't be appropriate."

"What isn't appropriate," I said, "is to be sick and refuse to have a doctor. It isn't reasonable."

"I haven't been unreasonable," he said. "I just don't think it will do any good."

"Then seeing them can't hurt you."

"Fine. I'll see them."

The two doctors came, and Mr. Wang insisted I join the party in Jerry's room to witness the examination. It was a strange tableau. "We are ready to begin," Wang said, whereupon he took out his little red book, gesturing to Jerry that he should do the same and follow along in English, so we could all discuss a saying from Chairman Mao. This one, as I recall, had to do with how the Communists inevitably treated Kuomintang prisoners with sincerity and kindness.

This ritual performed, the two doctors took over. One of them was small, thin, and reedy; the other, obviously the senior member of the team, was tall and fat, with a bloated face and a tunic whose main event was a pair of huge dirty pants, whose enormous pockets turned out to be his "doctor's bag." Out of these gaping recesses came his instruments, including a small bottle of alcohol and a tiny piece of cotton. With this, he washed his hands over and over; then one by one he "sterilized" his instruments with the same alcohol-soaked cotton swab, itself by now gray with the dirt from his hands.

He and I had been sitting on the bed across from Jerry's as this process unfolded. Then he rose, bent over Jerry and, with a sharp pointed tool, "clipped" his ear lobe, then immediately took a dirty glass slide from one of his pockets and ran it over the little bubble of blood that appeared. He handed the slide to his sallow partner, left the room, and returned shortly with a microscope. He passed the slide into the microscope, "read it," then spoke to his fellow doctor in rapid Chinese.

"There are certain pills to be prescribed," Mr. Wang said to me. "In addition, some further treatment and other doctors may be in order."

I said, "How many doctors do you have on this island?"

"It doesn't matter," Mr. Wang said.

"What do you mean, it doesn't matter?"

His eyes invited me to stand up and come out into the hall with him. Once we were there, he said, "I do not wish to annoy Muckaluckding. If you must know, I don't even like to speak with him. Lately I have been going to him only because he demanded to talk with me. The talks turn into nothing."

I said, "That doesn't answer my question."

"Ah," he said. "Your question."

"I was asking about this island and how many—"

"China does not consist of this island," Mr. Wang said. "There are other places. The main land." He said it that way, as if "mainland" were two separate words.

A cold feeling of fear came upon me. The island was part of Red China—no one could dispute that. But still it was an island, in known proximity to Hong Kong and the West, a place that symbolized temporary detention and therefore the great hope we had.

I said, "You're taking him to the mainland?"

"Yes. For his own sake. For his health."

"But how long will he be there?"

Wang looked at me quixotically. "He should be prepared for a long stay," he said. "His health requires it. Also, there are further questions that must be asked." He smiled. "I know you feel concern for him. And I can see something else. You wonder what will happen to yourself once the two of you are separated." The smile broadened. "It's a legitimate concern. But I assure you, you're not going to see your friend disappear."

"But if you take him—"

"No, no," the Wang smile said. "What I mean is this: you're going, too."

* * *

They came for us at five o'clock in the morning. It was mid-June by now—we had been captive how long? two months?—and the weather had begun to get hot. This day I knew, the instant they awakened me, would be not just hot, but oppressively so. It was still dark, yet the feeling of a baking, tropical sun already was there.

"You must take your things to the boat," they said.

"What things?"

"Your blankets."

"What else?"

"Nothing. The rest you can take with you."

"I don't understand."

"The blankets go back to your own boat," they explained.

And so they took me on my last visit to the *Menehune,* to deposit the blankets, mine and Jerry's.

Jerry's strength that day was sufficient to go to the *Menehune* with me, but he refused. Whether he did so out of some sense of martyrdom—("I won't make any detours I don't have to make")—or disconsolation ("I'll never see my boat again")—or practical foresight ("I have to show them a man as weak as I am can't even make a side trip like that") . . . these questions I couldn't answer then and can't answer now. But I do know that he was taken straight to the gunboat in the harbor for the trip to the mainland. I was rowed first to the *Menehune,* with our blankets, then over to join Jerry on the gunboat.

My last memory of the *Menehune* is prosaic, I suppose. It consists of the sight of a batch of Jerry's shirts, washed but never wrung out or hung out to dry, already beginning to mildew as a result. We were to see the shirts again, as we were to see other articles that had been aboard the *Menehune,* delivered piecemeal afterwards, but as for the *Menehune* herself, I can only suppose she fell victim to total destruction. I say this through the process of post-reasoning: what other fate could have befallen her? Essentially she was a pleasure craft, for which the Chinese have no use. Worse than that, from the Chinese standpoint, she could be telltale, if ever photographed from a low- or even high-flying aircraft. If people occupy a boat it is one thing. If non-people occupy it, it had better be a non-boat.

I can only suppose they sank the *Menehune* without a trace. I don't know what Jerry thought. Though I had no way of knowing it at the moment, after today's trip to the mainland in the gunboat, he and I would talk with each other face-to-face on only one other future occasion.

"How long will we be aboard?" I asked Mr. Wang.

"Till noon," he said. "No longer."

He was a liar and he knew it. The trip was to last a full fifteen hours, and all the time we were in the stinking, oppressive, heat-locked hold of a gunboat—probably of Russian make, Jerry supposed—the paint peeling, the equipment rundown, the portholes closed.

For breakfast we were given a cup of warm milk, laced with sugar, into which had been dropped a whole raw egg; and little, tasteless sawdust cookies. For lunch—you remember unusual meals in unusual circumstances; I say this because under questioning I couldn't remember usual meals in usual circumstances, and that seemed to make the Chinese think I was obstructing their inquiry—for lunch was one of the strangest meals I ever had.

There in the bowels of a rotting gunboat, with the temperature well up over a hundred degrees, with instructions that we could sit down or lie down (there were low chain-slung bunks along the wall) but we could never stand up, with nothing to drink but hot water (and even that they took away from us the last four hours)—there we were fed for lunch one of the most delicious meals I can ever remember: a beautiful omelette with rice and something else that had the taste of bacon rinds, but may have been some kind of native root instead.

For supper, which was served in late afternoon, there was another cup of hot water, containing a whole raw egg. And that was the last of the water, if also the last of the eggs.

We had an armed guard with us in the hold, though from time to time he would disappear up the ladder and through the hatchway above to get some air. From time to time, too, a smiling Mr. Wang would let himself down the ladder, to make sure we weren't standing up.

For if we had stood up, we could have seen out through the portholes.

But if we were not permitted to look out, others were permitted to look in. Not just permitted—*invited* might be a better word. For in the course of that slow gunboat journey, we must have pulled up alongside different docks five or six times, and each time the procedure was the same: people would come aboard and stare down at us through the hatch.

I don't know how much this affected Jerry, given his condition, but to me it was next to intolerable.

"Where are we?" I said to him. "In a zoo?"

"No, Miss Harbert," he said. "I'd judge we're in the Pearl estuary."

"The Pearl estuary?"

"The Pearl River," he said. "Splits the city of Canton pretty much in half on its way to the sea."

"Why have we made this many stops?"

"Canton's a big place," Jerry said. It was more observation than explanation, but it was to turn out he was correct. I took it at the time to be a guess, stemming from nothing more or less than Jerry's common-sense knowledge of geography. A day or so later it was to occur to me not to say *Canton* to anybody till they said it first. I don't know if Jerry said it or not. Maybe it doesn't sound important now, but I wish I had thought to bring it up while we were together in the hold of the gunboat. For if either of us had said *Canton* in front of the Chinese, they would have taken it not as a guess but as a known fact. And if Jerry "knew" where we were without even being able to look out the window, why then could he not have "known" where we were when we were picked up that April Sunday aboard the *Menehune?*

It was well after dark, at least nine o'clock at night, when we tied up for the last time. They brought us up the ladder then, and we had to walk across three or four other ships before we reached the dock where a jeep was waiting. Into that jeep, six of us were crammed, together with what luggage we had been permitted to bring. There were Jerry and me, a driver, Mr. Wang, an army guard, a navy man from the gunboat. The soldier and sailor wore identical-looking uniforms, save the soldier's was brown, the sailor's light blue, now faded into gray.

The trip was a short one, but I remember saying to myself, *Canton? Canton? Canton is a huge city. This is no city.* For we were aware of no buildings, no lights. Instead there were signs only of vegetation, giving off a sweet and not unpleasant smell. Here and there, there would be a house with people seated outside in front in the warm night air, eating and talking. Following the gunboat, it was so good to breathe the outside air that everything seemed serene and pleasant, even the severe two-story concrete building in front of which the jeep came to a stop.

Jerry was taken inside to a first-floor bedroom facing the front. I was taken to the second floor, to a room also facing the front, but not directly over Jerry's: we were separated by a stairway hall.

Indeed, we were separated by more than that: "Hello," the girl said to me. She was smiling and friendly. She was short and thin, with cropped hair and a big nose, wearing loose charcoal pants and a blue blouse, in the style of the 1920s or Pearl Buck's *The Good Earth.* "You must be tired," she said. "They want to talk to your friend, but you can go to sleep if you wish." She spoke excellent English—yet again here, where the specific names for things were concerned, her vocabulary was terribly limited.

"I'd like some water to drink, and I want to know where the bathroom is," I said.

"You have your own bathroom," she said, pointing to a door at the back of the room. "Unfortunately the door doesn't open for now. We'll fix it as soon as we can. But for now"—she pointed to a side door—"you can go through that bedroom, which also has a bathroom attached to it. And while you're there, I'll bring you water."

I went through what turned out to be an empty bedroom, into a conglomerate of old-style plumbing that I will have more to say about. But it was my "private bath," and it had running water. And when I returned to my room, the girl was there, with a glass of hot water to drink.

I thanked her, and said, "What is your name?"

"You don't have to ask that," she said.

I said, "But I want to know."

"It isn't necessary."

"Why are you afraid to give me your name?"

"I'm not afraid," she said. "It's just that it isn't done."

I said, "I don't understand. Mr. Wang gave *his* name."

"Mr. Wang is unusual," she said. "But perhaps you find all of us unusual."

"I find it unusual not to be able to use somebody's name."

"Very well," she said. "Then you can call me Lee."

"Lee," I said. "And will you be here?"

"Will I be here? I am here."

"I mean all the time."

"As long as either of us stays," she said. "You can leave before I do. Or I can leave before you do. It depends on what we're permitted to do. Please don't worry yourself about it. I know you're tired."

I liked her instantly, immensely. From downstairs I could hear male voices, Jerry's among them. His interrogation had begun.

I said to my new interpreter, "They shouldn't be doing that. He's tired. He's sick. Don't they understand? He needs rest and medical care."

"He'll get excellent medical care," she said. "That's why you've been brought here."

"But if he's in that kind of physical condition, how can he answer questions? How do you know he won't say things just because he's sick?"

"I don't know," she said. "I just don't."

It was interesting. She knew how to use the word *just* in *I just don't,* yet *ashtray* or *pencil sharpener* she would not know.

"But we have to do something about it," I said now.

"We?" she said. "*We* are here together. I'm assigned to you, not to him."

"But they should understand," I said. "He doesn't have the right kind of physical health. They should take that into consideration."

"I agree with you," she said. "I'll try to talk to them. But all I can promise is that some of them must understand this, too. For now, I'm not assigned to him. I'm assigned to you. Miss Harbert. Did I say the name correctly?"

"Yes," I said. "It's Mary Ann Harbert. And you're Lee."

"And you're Mary Ann Harbert," she said. "Then I will call you Mary."

"Why not?" I said. "Everybody else does."

* * *

But in the middle of the night, they woke me up. Lee was not there, but Mr. Wang was. *Does he keep appearing in the night?* I asked myself.

This time it was not the Dracula's-castle performance of wanting a thumbprint sealed in wax by the light of a kerosene lamp. It was a methodical search of my luggage instead.

They took away one of my nail files, first off, and I said to myself, *They think I'm going to commit suicide.* But they left a sharper nail file, my razor, and my scissors. They took away the drawings and poems I had done on the island. But they left paper and pencil.

"We are here," Wang hissed, "to tell you the rules. You are confined to this room."

I said, "How will I get to the bathroom? The doorknob's stuck."

"Doorknob?" Wang said.

"The door," I said. "The door won't open."

He raised a finger, like a debate in counter-rebuttal. "For that temporary purpose, you will use the next bathroom through the next bedroom." He smiled. "A mechanic will come to fix the door of your own bathroom. We have many such mechanics."

I said, "Why are you taking away my nail files?" I gestured at them.

"The reason," Mr. Wang said, "is that the decision has been made."

"Then how will I do my nails?" (I realize now how silly that must have sounded, or do I realize it? Some day perhaps I may be able to make a contribution to research into the subject that now is called most loosely, in my opinion, brainwashing. Leave a girl everything, but take her nail file away from her: an interesting result. Particularly if it is the first step in a series of steps.)

"You must not be angry," Mr. Wang said to me. "What we are doing is the correct thing, I can assure you."

"You mean it's correct to search my things?"

"Of course. Why do you think we're here?"

"But you already searched them."

"One never knows what one may find."

"Who said that? Chairman Mao?"

The smile stopped. "You could be in prison behind iron bars at this moment," Mr. Wang said to me. "Do not forget that. All we're doing is what's necessary and what's right."

"But you're taking away—"

"We are taking away nothing that you need. Here." And he threw two papers on the bed beside me. "These documents we leave with you."

I looked at the documents. One was my Pan Am ticket from Hong Kong back to San Francisco. The other was my Utah driver's license.

There were three doors in my room at the Harbor. (I was to come to call it the Harbor, just as I called the island the Island. Once again, this was a form of dormitory building within a commune, whose real name, unlike those of others to come, I never learned. I called it the Harbor because of the nearby sounds of moaning whistles from ocean-going steamers.)

The three doors occupied three different walls. One of them led to the stairway hall; the back one, which didn't work, to what was supposed to be my bathroom; and the front one, flanked by casement windows that had no screens, to the front balcony.

I awoke in the morning to the sound of music. Early morning: six o'clock. The music blaring from a loudspeaker ("The East Is Red" was the name of it, one of the most familiar marches in all China). I got out of bed and walked onto the balcony.

Off to my left I could see the rising sun of China. So that must be the east, and therefore my balcony must face south. I could see some houses, too, and some people up and about, and beyond them a rise of hills caught and swirled in the mists of morning. I knew it was China, but I didn't have to know that, for it *said* China. You could have imprinted it on a postcard, and you would have, if you'd been in the postcard business, for it was a scene of beauty. *Of course they love it here,* my mind said to me, *and this is why.*

The scene out to my left, to the east, was the one that gripped my attention. Closer at hand, I could see a truck passing by on a road, a great stand of banana trees, a mother goat assiduously teaching her kid to butt his head against her. Which was going about it the more earnestly? The mother or child? The kid exhibited more glee, but not that much more. He could weary, too. But his mother, in her patience, roused him to it time and again.

Across the road was a ditch, and here is another reason I called this place the Harbor, for already at this time of day there were people there fishing for mud crabs, so salt water could likely be at hand.

One of the fishermen, a clean-cut teen-age boy, stood up and turned, and saw me standing on the balcony. His look said: *My first American.* But he wasn't shy about it. Far from it, he was polite; more than polite, he was eager. He moved toward me as I looked down from the balcony. Obviously, he wanted to tell me something.

And the something was that he knew English.

Forty paces away he stopped, and looked up, and then, in his breaking teen-to-adult voice, he began to sing. Sing? Yes, sing—the most familiar song, perhaps, that any of us know:

"A-B-C-D-E-F-G," he sang, "H-I-J-K-LMNOP."

I stared down at him. "LMNOP-Q-R-S-T," I sang back.

"U-V-W. . . ." he sang.

"Tomma!" For the first time, in reflex response to that sound, the sound of an epithet—a command—a dirty word, I looked in that direction, to my right. There stood four fully armed soldiers, with machineguns, bayonets, grenades.

I looked back at the boy who had been singing the alphabet song. But he was no longer there. Now I looked back at the guns. They were pointed at me.

* * *

Lee and I were to talk of many things. We could discuss reasonably the sayings of Chairman Mao. (*Power comes from the barrel of a gun*— it may sound like an absolute, but it has interesting byways: when, for instance, does the power that comes from the barrel of a gun cease to need a gun for the sake of its continuing existence, and why?) We could talk, to some extent at least, of love and marriage, and of things that actually rate up or down as being nothing more than girl-talk.

Among other things, she was "liberated," in the sense that China was ahead of the United States, with respect to equal rights. She showed me the sayings of Chairman Mao:

> Enable every woman who can work to take her place on the labour front, under the principle of equal pay for equal work.

That had been written by Mao in 1955.

And as long ago as 1927 he had written:

> As to the authority of the husband, this has always been weaker among the poor peasants because, out of economic necessity, their women folk have to do more manual labour than the women of the richer classes and therefore have more say and greater power of decision in family matters. With the increasing bankruptcy of the rural economy in recent years, the basis for men's domination over women has already been undermined. With the rise of the peasant movement, the women in many places have now begun to organize rural women's associations; the opportunity has come for them to lift up their heads, and the authority of the husband is getting shakier every day. In a word, the whole feudal-patriarchal ideology and system is tottering with the growth of the peasants' power.

Lee lived in Canton, and periodically, every two weeks or so, would go home for two or three days. When she returned, she would bring me things: watercolors and brushes, a pencil sharpener, an eraser. She brought a crocheting hook for me and taught me to use it, but the yarn was very cheap and poor and I never got to complete anything. Most Chinese yarn that I saw was of that same low quality: they would never wash their sweaters, wearing them for a full year while holes formed and widened; then at the end of the year they would unravel the yarn and make a new sweater.

If I said we did things differently in America, Lee, unlike so many of the others, would not be offended, and she was quite current on western events. The male long-haired business intrigued her. "How do you tell the boys from the girls?" she asked.

We did have something of a language problem, of course, despite her excellent grammar and enunciation. Once, I told her I needed new razor blades. I gestured to my face, in a shaving motion. She looked at me curiously. She could tell it was razor blades I was after, but why on earth would I want to shave my face? Only then, having established what it was I needed, I explained I wanted to shave my legs instead. "Ah," she said, "there are some women in Canton who do that. I shaved my hair here once—" she pointed to her armpit "—but it only grew back worse."

"You don't do it only once," I said.

Lee must have been past twenty-five , and she told me that in China that was the age most girls waited till before they married; the men, she said, tended to wait to the age of thirty and beyond. But she was reticient to discuss her personal life. She was from a family of six, she said, but that was about as much as she wished to reveal.

I could talk to her about my life, however, and to a certain extent I did so. I felt safe with her, yet by the same token she was assigned to me by the government, and supposedly would be required to report about my actions and what it was I said.

The rules were I could not leave my room, except to go onto the balcony, and then only to hang out my laundry. Always beneath my balcony there were the guards, positioned at an angle so they could see through my windows and observe me in my room. They may even have thought they could see my reflection in the full-length mirror that hung on a tall wardrobe chest whose contents were quilts and other bedding.

"Why do I have to be guarded?" I asked Lee.

"They're there to protect you," she replied.

"From what?"

"I don't know," she said. In the heat, the humidity and the confinement of that summer at the Harbor, I had broken out into a rash, and I lay on the bed while she swabbed my back with "alcohol ointment". "After all," she said, "you're very adventurous, aren't you? To go on this kind of a cruise?" She sighed. "Wasn't it rather foolish, Mary?"

"Well, anybody can say that now," I said.

But that wasn't the point she was trying to make. The prospects she envisioned had nothing to do with being captured by a foreign power. "Think," she said, "just think what could happen to you on a boat like that, alone with a man."

San Francisco,
July 30, 1968

Dear Commodore:

. . . We are interested in tracing the whereabouts of the daughter of a good friend. The young lady in question flew to Hong Kong in late April with the intention of sailing back to the United States with a friend in his recently purchased boat. The family here received a letter from the girl dated April 28, stating her intention to sail the following morning, bound for Manila.

Since then there has been no word, and all of us have

become quite concerned. The U.S. Coast Guard has been contacted and is conducting inquiries through channels, but often a personal inquiry by a local resident can accomplish far more than official efforts.

The information I can supply is very meager. It consists of the following:

BOAT: *Sail auxiliary-length about 30 feet. Color-May be red, white and blue but we are not certain.*

SKIPPER: *Jerry McLaughlin, U.S. Citizen, arrived in Hong Kong in mid-April and purchased boat after arrival.*

CREW: *Mary Herbert, U.S. Citizen, arrived in Hong Kong on April 27 or 28.*

I realize that this is very scanty information indeed, but if any of your members can give us any word of these young people, I will be most grateful. I know I should write directly to Hong Kong instead of to you in Singapore, but I do not have either their address or the name of their Commodore.

Sincerely,

Hong Kong
16th August, 1968

Dear Commodore:

I have received a copy of your letter of 30th July addressed to . . . Singapore.

The case was not unknown to me as our Club received Press enquiries regarding the yacht reported to be missing on passage from here to Manila, a week or two back.

Most people who contemplate a voyage from Hong Kong such as this usually contact our Club at some stage but, as far as I can ascertain, Mr. McLaughlin did not do so. His name is not remembered by anyone.

I have myself made enquiries of both our Immigration and Marine Departments with the following result:

1. If the boat did depart from here she did not clear either Marine Department or Immigration.

2. Mr. McLaughlin is recorded as having arrived in the Colony on the 12th April 1968 by Immigration. There is no record of his departure which tends to confirm that he may have sailed without clearance.

3. Immigration have no record of the arrival of Mary Herbert on or about the dates you mention. This is unusual as all persons arriving in the Colony are required to complete an official "Arrival Card." All of which do not take us much further ahead.

Immigration Department will be pleased to go into the case of Mary Herbert more deeply if we can provide, if possible, details of the means she used to travel to the Colony, i.e. name of boat or airline (with Flight Number, if possible), where she was travelling from and her U.S. Passport Number, or some of this information.

As regards the purchase of the boat by Mr. McLaughlin—is the name known? All I could do would be to make enquiries of the usual shipyards or put an advertisement in the Press in case it was a purchase from a private individual. The name of the boat, if a second-hand purchase, would be of great help for, as it apparently has an engine, it should be registered with Marine Department and I could get in touch with the former owner through them.

I hope I can be of further assistance.

Yours sincerely,

This was one exchange of letters, in this case between two yacht club commodores, and it serves interestingly to illustrate the fringe extent, rather than the core thrust, of the search. In so doing, it illustrates also that the more hopeless the search, then the more rapidly a law of diminishing returns sets in. With the best of intentions, the two commodores of the two yacht clubs found themselves dealers in bits and pieces of the facts, compounded by inaccuracy. The San Francisco commodore had received his information second-hand: through no fault of his own, he had his dates wrong, for Mary Ann had arrived in Hong Kong April 17, not "April 27 or 28" as his letter supposed. Added to this was that most common of mistakes, the spelling of "Harbert" as "Herbert." Of course a record of her arrival in Hong Kong existed, but between those two mistakes it is small wonder an immigration clerk failed to locate it.

If the records were kept by date, then ten days is a long time. If they were kept by alphabetical order, a clerk in all ways ready to check "Herbert" when he sees "Harbert" will be far less likely to check "Harbert" when he sees "Herbert," for the flow of suggestibility, growing out of familiar spellings, here runs the wrong way. Put together the factors of wrong date and wrong spelling, and the chance for confirmation shifts itself from likely toward impossible.

Less readily understandable is the assertion that McLaughlin was not recorded as having arrived in Hong Kong till April 12, and by now it is conjectural whether any inquiry, even should it be undertaken, could uncover the reason for it. One guess is that the April 12 date given in the letter from the yacht club in Hong Kong is of itself an error, pure and simple. The first postcard from McLaughlin to Mary Ann is postmarked Hong Kong, March 17, 1968. It calls for a reply prior to April 4. His second postcard to her is dated March 27, and suggests she join him in Hong Kong prior to April 10. His long letter to her is dated April 7. All of these dates serve obviously in common to place him in Hong Kong well before his recorded date of arrival there.

It invites only speculation also to question McLaughlin's reasons for not circulating notification of the Menehune's *intended departure through the normal channels. It is not illogical, but by no means wholly explanatory either, to observe that it would not have been inconsistent for him not to wish to broadcast among strangers his planned sea voyage with a young woman whose role was that neither of relative nor wife, but conjecture on this point, like the others, has to be unrewarding.*

At that point in time marked by the letter from the yacht club in Hong Kong—August 16, 1968— one might regard as very half-hearted indeed a missing-person search that could turn up, three months after the disappearance, nothing more illuminating in Mary Ann's case than official doubt as to whether she ever even set foot in Hong Kong to begin with. Such supposition is not always justified. The very gaps and inaccuracies in the query from the yacht club in the San Francisco area could in fact be viewed as a plus, not a minus, in the narrow sense at least that the less information an investigator has to go on, the more avenues he is likely to explore.

And of course others had been working on it, too. On August 22, six days after his first letter to the commodore in San Francisco, the commodore in Hong Kong was writing him again, this time enclosing a copy of a letter he had received in the interim from Marine Department, 102 Connaught Road, Central, Hong Kong:

> *Further to our conversation regarding Mr. McLauchlain who was presumed to have sailed from Hong Kong in a small boat for Manila sometime in April this year. The only information which we have regarding the boat and the persons on board was that received by the Supervisor Kai Tak in a cable from Clark Field, Philippines. His information is as follows:*
>
> NAME OF VESSEL: "V.L. MENEHUNE" or "BRODINGHAM"
> RIG: Sloop
> TONNAGE: 3.5 tons
> LENGTH: 28 feet
> BREADTH: 7 feet
> DEPTH: 5 feet
> ENGINE: Single propellor
> MAST: One
> HULL: Fiberglass
> COLOUR: White
> REGISTERED?: Not registered
> OWNER & OPERATOR: A.G.P. McLauchlain
> PASSENGER: Miss Mary Hubert

DATE OF DEPARTURE: Stated to be 19th or 20th April 1968

DESTINATION: Australia with a stopover at Manila.

Officers of this Department have already checked with boat builders who build fiberglass vessels in Hong Kong but none of these builders had heard the name of the vessel, neither did they recognise the description. Finally I would confirm that Mr. McLauchlain made no approach to this Department at any time and consequently a sailing notice has never been completed by him.

The facts had been put together from the very first queries, emanating separately and jointly both from those in the U.S. concerned with the fate of the two people aboard the Menehune.

"Mary was never a great letter writer," her father, Gene Harbert, has recalled. "We got a postcard from her from Hong Kong, and she said to expect another one when she got to Manila. But we didn't know when that would be, and Polly and I said to each other that when she did write next, it would probably come by slow boat. So we allowed, say, two weeks from Hong Kong to Manila, another two weeks after that for a new card to reach us. It just wasn't the kind of a situation where a bell goes off and suddenly panic takes hold. It goes in stages instead: first disappointment at not hearing from her that day, then uneasiness, then worry and anxiety, and finally alarm."

At that point, the investigation set in. The Harberts did everything they could possibly do. They went to the news media, the Coast Guard, the Department of State. The last avenue was of interest, for it turns out that Jerry McLaughlin had written from Hong Kong to a friend whose son was attending school in Manila, asking him to notify the son he'd be showing up there and would contact him. The notice was too casual to be of any direct benefit, but in due course the young man visited the U.S. Embassy in Manila, and reacting not just by itself but through the military at Clark Field, it began a search operation that was nothing if not thorough. It was late in the game, though, and distracted by the very familiarity of U.S. Far Eastern personnel with a specific danger to small boats in the South China Sea. They could not ignore the possibility that the Menehune *had been captured by pirates.*

Putting together the bits and pieces, the U.S. authorities were able to assemble at last a workably detailed profile of the Menehune *and her crew. Thus the bulkiest file on the search that exists today is not in Washington, not in San Francisco, not in Hong Kong, but in Manila. The attempt to seek out the pirates involved four governments: those of the United States, Great Britain, the Philippines, and, through British intercession in Hong Kong, the People's Republic of China. None of them had any tolerance for the coastal pirates, Red China least of all, because Red China was not in the murder business, and the pirates were murderers. True, they killed not by preference, but they killed anyway. They had to. For they could not afford to let their captives survive. They could not afford this because of the one thing of value they treasured the most—the one thing that would be worthless if its owner were permitted to live: his passport.*

And so the pirates that in this case did not exist were being sought out by four governments, including the one that knew they didn't exist, since it had committed the piracy itself. No one ever thought of that. There was no reason to. During the most intensive period of the search, two other American boats, manned by American crews, had been picked up by Chinese fishing junks, in the waters off Hong Kong, then released almost immediately. Of course, they held all the tickets. Their occupants were not an unmarried man and woman (not that this was a moral question so much as it suggested they might not, from a practical standpoint, be the objects of an all-out immediate search). Add to that, they had all their papers in order, and two-way radios to notify Hong Kong of their arrest.

Under such circumstances their release was routine. In the delicate orchestration of East-West relationships, pivoted in its location upon the "open city" of Hong Kong, it was not to Red China's advantage at that time to capture innocent parties and detain them indefinitely. At the worst, even if the Chinese could claim to justify such an act, they would notify the West, simply because no convenient way existed to hide what they had done.

In the single case of McLaughlin and Mary Ann, however, they came upon the realization (possibly to their private amusement) that there was no need to notify anybody of anything. There was no need to make non-persons out of the two people aboard the Menehune: *as far as any record existed of their presence in that place on that boat at that time, they were non-persons already. The only soul in the Eastern Hemisphere with any inkling of their voyage was the young man in Manila, but he still had not learned of it; when he did, his information would be so vague as to be useless; and Mary Ann does not know if McLaughlin ever even mentioned his name to their captors. She does know he never mentioned it to her.*

It was never assumed by anyone, of course, that no one would be looking for them. But the critical element in any such search—immediacy—was absent here. And so the Chinese found themselves possessors of a unique human prize: two pawns in the international chess game that could be held in private reserve, to be used, offered, withheld, dangled as bait in any given future situation. As valuable a commodity as an American citizen's passport to a coastal pirate was the citizen himself to the mainland Chinese.

And finally, if through some unforeseeable means the outside world were to discover that two innocent

Americans had been taken captive by Red China, then Red China had an answer to that one, too: namely, that they were not innocent at all. For even before the search for them was fully under way, McLaughlin had written his confession, a document that not only admitted guilt but represented of itself an excuse for further detention and additional questioning.

But such chance discovery by the outside world was not to come about. No one was thinking along those lines, not only because there was no precedent for the Chinese to do this kind of thing, but indeed because of recurring evidence that they didn't.

Instead, all lines failed, and all that was left was the presumption, correctly guessed by Mary Ann when she tried to write to her parents from the Island, that the Menehune *had been lost at sea. Gene Harbert and others knew the talk about the pirates, but they did everything they could to shield Polly from such thoughts. Better to lose a daughter by drowning, than by cold-blooded murder.*

The parents, Gene and Polly, had to learn to live with the fact of her death. The father was bringing himself to cope with it; to the mother, it came more slowly. Once she and her daughter Sue were together with a third woman, a mutual friend and yachting enthusiast who had done all she could to help with the search. The friend does not know to this day whether Sue, Mary Ann's older sister, was expressing true belief or merely trying to help her mother over a trying moment. But what Sue said was: "I think we can count on one thing: some day that door's going to open, and Mary Ann's going to walk into the room."

Regardless of Sue's motive, the friend could not see what gainful effect this kind of talk might have.

"Look, Polly," the friend said, "Mary Ann is dead. And life goes on. Sooner or later, you've got to come to grips with this and accept it."

Polly Harbert said nothing.

San Francisco,
August 28, 1968

Dear Commodore:

I am very appreciative of the efforts you have made to investigate the circumstances concerning the possible departure from Hong Kong of Mr. McLaughlin. Your reports which were included in your letters of August 16, and August 22, were very complete. We see no further need to make any future investigation at this time.

It is my hope that I may be of service to you or your members as you have been to us. All of those concerned join me in expressing our thanks for all you have done.

Please consider our club your headquarters should you visit the Pacific Coast at any time. I hope that I may have the opportunity to meet you in person.

Sincerely,

The black fan moved slowly back and forth before the dark-rimmed lenses of his glasses. He was never without the fan. He sat across a desk from me in a room directly beneath the bedroom that adjoined mine. Beside him on one side was Mr. Wang; on the other, a man dressed in what I later learned was the uniform of the Kwangtung Security Police. Black Fan was an official too, but I never saw him in uniform. His dress instead was close to western: open-throated white shirt, the top of a white undershirt showing.

Directly to my right, at right angles to the desk, was a table at which the interpreters sat. Beside them was a large tape recorder of Chinese manufacture. Before each two-hour session, which occupied my mornings—not every day, but at frequent intervals—during the first two months at the Harbor, there would be a great scurry and clamor to make sure the electricity, which was available but not always reliable, was turned on so the tape recorder could operate.

The questions were far more detailed than any I had heard on the Island; it was almost as if they were trying to investigate two wholly separate things: first, the facts relating to the voyage of the *Menehune;* but second, an insight into social and economic customs in the U.S.

They wanted to know, for example, how I got my passport, how much it cost, what questions the passport people asked, how long the process took, how many people were denied passports. They asked about the life style of my parents, my friends; they wanted names and addresses. They took me back to my trip from San Francisco to Hong Kong aboard Pan American Flight #1 and asked what food was served on the plane. They went into detail about the difference between first-class and economy accommodations in air travel. (What social class distinctions were they attempting to perceive, I wondered, between those who fly first-class and coach?!)

The questioning was directed mainly by the man from the Security Police. He had a large birthmark on his face and a memory for past contradictions—what he viewed, anyway, as contradictions. If at one point I had said I didn't know what direction we headed in when we left Hong Kong, and at another I said "maybe south," that was taken to mean I was covering up, refusing to cooperate. In one sense he was right: I had far less information to give on certain topics than anyone logically would have thought. They asked me repeatedly about Jerry, and I can understand how skeptical they were of my replies (true though they were) that I just didn't know that much about him.

"You had not seen this man for all these years yet you flew all that distance to go aboard his boat?"

I tried to explain the special circumstances, but inevitably they would then press me to explain my explanation.

"You must simplify," one of the interpreters said to me.

"You can simplify to the point where things don't mean anything at all," I said.

But there would be times too when I would ask *them* to simplify—or at least, to clarify:

Q. What did you have on the boat?
A. You mean equipment or facilities?
Q. Yes.
A. I don't understand which you mean.
Q. Stop being uncooperative.
A. Well, is it the equipment?
Q. That wasn't the question, but if you want to, go ahead.
A. But why ask me about the equipment? You know better than I about it. What equipment can I describe to you?
Q. What charts did you have?
A. They're on the boat. Why don't you look?

Or:

Q. You say you slept on the boat?
A. Yes. The night before we left.
Q. We're not talking about the night. We're talking about the day. Did you enjoy sailing?
A. That day? Not particularly.

If one thing was wasted on them at best, counter-productive at worst, it was sarcasm. I knew that. But I was also *me,* and merely to "cooperate" at every single turn and moment was not in my makeup. I don't think it would be in most Americans' makeup under similar circumstances. Even if I'd wanted to be meek, to accede to every twist and turn of their rules and questions and orders (themselves contradicting one another as often as not), I still would have been accused of resistance and failure to cooperate. For they could not believe I could have known so little about my companion, and about the boat and sailing in general, and still wound up where I was. And therefore no matter how I acted, I had to be hiding something.

I tried to get something of this across to one of the

interpreters, a young man who seemed to pride himself on his masculinity and self-discipline. "The answer to your question," he said, "lies in the sayings of Chairman Mao."

"How can that be?" I asked.

His reply was simple enough: the answer to *anything* lay in the sayings of Chairman Mao. "When you have studied them properly, you'll understand," the interpreter said to me. "Everyone in China knows the story of the truck driver in the army whose truck stopped running. He didn't know how to go about repairing it. So for three days and three nights he sat in his truck, studying the sayings of our great chairman Mao Tse-tung. And at the end of the third day and the third night, his state of mind was such that he went directly to the faulty part of the truck and repaired it."

At his insistence, I read from my little red book into the tape recorder. Then he would play back the tapes. I would hear my voice mouthing the words of Mao. And then we would discuss it.

The discussions were of only limited usefulness, for to worship the sayings of the chairman, one would best have had to pre-worship the chairman himself. "In a time forty years ago," the interpreter told me, "Chiang Kai-shek's soldiers came to Mao's village to suppress the communists there. They tortured Mao's first wife. Mao had a son killed in Korea. When Mao says sacrifice yourself and family, this is what he intends."

It occurred to me then for the first time that this was why none of them wanted to give me their names. For in preaching sacrifice, Mao was even the more preaching selflessness, and to suppress one's own name was in a small way to exemplify the teaching. Mao himself was of course an understandable exception to the rule, as were other public figures, for the people must know their leaders. I asked the interpreter what the name Mao meant in English. "Hair on arms," he said, and then added, "Repeat after me three times: Mao Tse-tung Wan Swui! Mao Tse-tung Wan Swui! Mao Tse-tung Wan Swui!"

I said, "Mao Tse-tung Wan Swui! Mao Tse-tung Wan Swui! Mao Tse-tung Wan Swui!"

"Good," the interpreter said. "You have just said long live Chairman Mao three times."

I began to laugh, and he frowned. "You think it's a joke?" he said.

"No," I said. "It's not that. It's just that what I just said was Chinese, but it had some kind of a wild English sound to it. Almost like something you'd expect to hear from the cheering section at a football game."

He looked at me, puzzled. I sighed. "It can't be explained." And it couldn't. But time and again I would be in my room, and hear the voices of Chinese speaking with one another, both inside and outside the building and somehow it would come across as being perfect English except, of course, it made no sense. *Now out Des Moines worry why* somebody would say. And time and again, I felt that impact—that the "hear" of the two languages was almost identical.

My "study sessions" with this interpreter did not keep up for too long a time. They were doing nothing in the way of making progress, and both of us realized it. He wasn't unkind about it. Knowing that I smoked, he would suggest a cigarette break in mid-session. "I would have a cigarette with you," he said, "but Chairman Mao advises against it. I used to smoke, but I subordinated my will to his."

"Well," I said, "we could discuss that saying of Chairman Mao's if you wish. I don't believe he was setting down any rule against smoking. There are too many other people here who do smoke. I think he was just cautioning against excessive use of tobacco, don't you?"

"I must confess," he said, "I haven't given proper study to it."

"Then why not have a cigarette with me?"

"You're very kind," he said. "Perhaps I will. Just this once."

At times it was not just the two of us alone together. Another interpreter, a timid little man, would accompany him now and again, remaining silent while the "study sessions" progressed. His expression was always the same: no expression at all. Once, in the course of discussion, we were arguing over Mao's contention that war can be shown to be necessary. "Today," I said, "the atom bomb blows up the whole world. How can anyone argue for war?" For some reason, the main interpreter found that to be excruciatingly funny. He slapped his knees, then threw his hands into the air, graphically illustrating the *whoosh* with which a nuclear bomb would blow up the world. He would not stop laughing.

I turned to the timid little man beside him. "What is he laughing at? What's so funny?"

The timid one said, deadpan, "It's well known that Chairman Mao says the spiritual atom bomb is bigger than the real one. After each war, Communism has had more support."

I first met the timid one the day Black Fan—the power in charge, behind the desk at the interrogation sessions—arrived at the Harbor. Together he and the timid one mounted the steps to my room to summon me to the first session of questioning.

"Don't come in!" I called. "I have no clothes on!"

I could hear voices in Chinese just beyond my door. One of them, Black Fan's, was angry.

"Miss Harbert?" the voice of the timid one came through the door.

"I'm getting dressed. I told you don't come in."

"But you must never be undressed," the timid voice said, "unless you are alone."

"I *am* alone. Who do you think's in here with me? John Wayne?

There was more discussion behind the door. I heard the words *John Wayne.*

Then the timid voice again: "But you were told to expect to be questioned."

"Nobody said when."

"But Mr. Wang said you promised to be prepared."

"I'm not even speaking to Mr. Wang," I said, and that was true.

Another day, after my "study sessions" with the "heman" interpreter were over I heard a very gentle tapping on my door. I went to open it, and it was the timid little interpreter who had sat in on the sessions.

He said, "I have a question that has to be asked."

"Come in," I said. Inwardly I felt the thrill of fear. Why would they be sending *him?*

He came and stood in the middle of my room. He shifted his feet. "I must ask you something very seriously."

I sat back resignedly on the bed.

"It's not really a question I can ask of anyone else," he said. "It has to be you who will answer it."

By "anyone else," I automatically thought he meant Jerry. *What question was there that I could answer but he couldn't?*

"In our discussions of the sayings of Chairman Mao," the timid one said now, "I saw there was something I could learn. I could learn how to smoke a cigarette. Will you teach me?"

The first morning after our arrival at the Harbor, it was Wang who brought me my first meal. It consisted of three hard-boiled eggs.

His appearance during the night, to search my luggage—luggage that had already been searched—had been infuriating. His appearance now, bearing a meal consisting totally of eggs (as if the eggs on the gunboat had not been enough), made me rebel. The rebellion might be understandable in and of itself—enough eggs are enough eggs—but behind it there was a feeling I had (which proved to be correct; not all my "feelings" had that accurate a result) that in Wang's case, the shift from the Island to the Harbor had caused a subtle but perceptible reduction of his authority. The appearance of the girl Lee, and the way she talked, made it evident that henceforth no one would play the combined role of interpreter and inquisitor both. There would be some of one kind, others of the other, but Wang, having up till now played the dual role, was in the process of being phased out. Among other things, he had, in a way, failed in his task: if his job was to deliver the two Americans to the mainland, surely he had not been asked to deliver one of them sick.

That was his point now, and in a way it was ingeniously contrived. "You don't like the eggs?" he said. "Then you blame your friend, not me. Already this morning a doctor has come to see him. He has prescribed a special diet for him. Eggs, he says, are the best thing."

"So if he gets eggs, I get eggs?"

"Exactly."

"Why?"

"Because," he aspirated buck-toothed, "there is the rule of equality! Do I have to remind you what Muckaluckding said when tobacco came but alcohol did not?"

I said, "You make him sound like a heavy drinker. He doesn't need alcohol all that much."

"Of course not. You have said it. He wasn't demanding alcohol so much as he was demanding the signs of equal treatment. Therefore the rule has gone forward: equal treatment. If he will be given eggs, you will be given eggs."

"But I won't eat mine," I said. "How do you expect me to live on a diet a doctor prescribed for somebody else?"

"Perhaps you should have thought of that earlier than this," Wang said. "As for now, you have asked for equality, and you will receive equality!"

A few days later, I asked Lee whether it would be possible to let me have a hand-fan, something that, like Black Fan himself, I could move back and forth in front of my face, to stir the hot sticky air of my room. She said she'd see what she could do, and some time later she obtained one for me. And in its wake came Mr. Wang, sputtering as ever.

"If Muckaluckding knows what's good for him, he will cease his insulting behavior! Do you know where we found his copy of the sayings of Chairman Mao?" He pointed at the foot of my bed. "On his bed, down here, where the feet go! Closer to his feet than to his head!"

One part of my mind said *Oh, now this I don't believe!* but another part warned: *Don't argue! This is one subject that's off limits!*

Aloud, I murmured: "I'm sure he didn't mean it as an insult. Maybe he just put it there for a minute, while he was rearranging himself or something."

"He did not just put it there. He *keeps* it there!" The perspiration shone on Mr. Wang's forehead. "And that's not all. Do you know what he did with the fan we gave him?"

I said, "I didn't know he asked for a fan."

"He didn't. And when we gave it to him, he threw it on the floor."

"But if he didn't ask for it, why did you give him one in the first place?"

"Because you had asked for one," Mr. Wang said.

Equality.

It applied even to the schedule that was brought to me one morning. I can reconstruct it word-for-word in my mind's eye:

> 6:00—wake up.
> 6:05—get up. wash.

6:15—dress.
6:30—exercises.
7:30—breakfast.
8-noon—study sayings of Chairman Mao.
noon—lunch.
noon-2—nap.
2-6—study.
6—dinner.
6:25—rest.
6:30—study till bed.

I remember that the electricity was working that morning, so I had a light to read by. My contact lenses having been spoiled by the sea water at the Island, I had to wear my prescription dark glasses all the time, for without them I couldn't read. But with them, I had to have light in addition to the daylight from my window.

I read the timetable carefully, then turned to Lee. "I don't understand this."

She said, "He said you had to have it."

"Who's he? Wang?"

She shook her head, and made a waving motion in front of her face.

I said, "Black Fan?"

She nodded.

"I see," I said. "And what happens if I don't do what this says?"

"It might be a better idea," Lee said gently, "to try to follow it."

"How follow it?" I asked. "It says I eat breakfast at seven-thirty, but breakfast doesn't come till after eight o'clock. It says I must study, but where are all the study materials?"

"Perhaps it means the sayings of Chairman Mao," Lee said.

"But I've *studied* the sayings of Chairman Mao."

"Yes, but they don't think your companion has studied them. They aren't satisfied with the answers he gives when they question him."

"They aren't satisfied with the answers *I* give when they question *me.* That doesn't mean I haven't read the sayings."

"Perhaps they expect more from his answers than from yours," Lee suggested.

I got the feeling that she would not report me if I failed to adhere completely to this newest demonstration of equal treatment. But I didn't plan to complain publicly about it, and when I next saw Mr. Wang I said nothing. In fact, I'd been saying as little as possible to Mr. Wang.

He had something on *his* mind, though, when he came to the doorway of the room.

He squinted at me and said, "Maybe you will enjoy it better in prison."

I said, "What have I done now?"

"You know very well."

I tried to think: *What prison offense have I committed?*

"No," I said. "I don't know."

"There was a man," he said, raising his finger like a debater making a point, "who had the will to give up smoking cigarettes. And after exposure to you, here he is now smoking again. His headaches have returned. Worse than that, there was another man, who'd never smoked in his life. Now he smokes. Don't tell me you didn't show him how! You can tell from the way he holds a cigarette—" he made a pincer of his hand "—way down at the end here, like a woman! And you want to know what prisons are for. Prisons are for people who corrupt other people, that's what prisons are for!"

* * *

A mouse came to live with me. I named him Freddie. He searched about for a home, investigating first the sagging underside of the cushions on a broken-down couch in my room, but confirmed my opinion there was no softness there, not even enough for him, and so

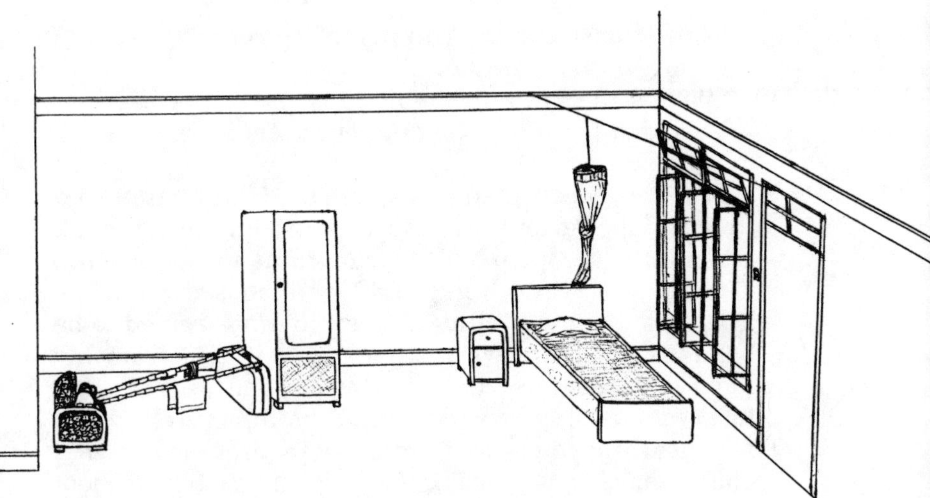

My room at the harbor.

looked elsewhere. He found a residence to his taste in the base of the tall wardrobe, amid the quilting and stuffing in there. He also found an abundance of food and water. The water trickled and puddled perpetually over the floor of the bathroom and on into my room, the result of a faulty plumbing connection, a water line that appears to have been run for the sake of providing a continuous gravity flow to a flock of pigeons being raised—perhaps to be eaten; I could not think of another reason—along the side and back of the building. And as for Freddie's food, he could share mine.

It didn't occur to me that food I found distasteful, Freddie would find distasteful too. It didn't occur to Freddie either. One night the supper was so bad I couldn't eat it at all. But I gave Freddie his usual portion. The next morning he was dead.

I brought the case before the interpreters. It was not a successful argument.

"The food here is poisonous," I said.

They looked at me. "You insult our food?"

"I tell you it's poisonous."

"We eat the same food you do."

I decided not to tell them about Freddie.

From my constricted viewpoint, the Harbor appeared to accent the agricultural aspects of a commune, though communes are primarily agricultural to begin with. The building where Jerry and I were housed was some kind of a lodging facility. The main crop seemed to be bananas but there were others as well, and from my window I could see the housing for the workers and hear sounds of construction and manufacture. I could also hear the voices of children, sometimes raised in a chorus of singing, so I knew there must be a school nearby.

And I could see lines of irrigation ditches, and telltale stretches of "too green" grass leading to them from what could only be the cesspools of the buildings. Obviously there were leaks in the cesspools, but I am not sure they were planned that way. On the one hand, the pattern was too regular to suppose the leaks just happened. But on the other hand, such leaks would not contribute all that much. The Chinese certainly believed that humans could fertilize their own food with their own waste, but they didn't depend on leaks alone: far from that, they hauled it up in buckets to make sure the earth was saturated with what they euphemistically called "night soil."

The food that was served to me varied widely, not so much in content as in preparation and, as often as not, in stages of decay. For that matter, the food was not the only thing that varied. So did the cooks and you could tell from the menu, even from the way the dishes were stacked on the tray when a meal was brought to your room, when there had been a change in chefs.

On occasion, there would be that same strange kind of

meal we had been served in the oppressive hold of the gunboat—out of nowhere, a magnificent repast: lovely fish, beautiful prawns cooked in butter, mysterious Cantonese specialties of magnificent taste and texture. One of the most attractive offerings of all, and one of the rarest, would be an obviously expensive serving of tinned fish. It was just as well that this came only at the most widespread intervals, for I could never bring myself to eat it: the memory was too new of what went into tinned fish along the shoreline at the Island.

Day in and day out, though, it required no memory to turn away from what was served or, if it was to be eaten at all, to do so with the utmost care. Bread—not bad-tasting, but already moldy at the edges—would be eaten as one might cut out a paper doll: the center part only, leaving a flimsy square hollow; but on some days the bread had worms in it, and thus could not be eaten at all.

There would be a variety of soups—egg and tomato and mushroom—and much rice and noodles, and pork, liver, and spinach. But there would be a layer of grease, a different-tasting grease, indicating your cooking had been done in a pot already used for something else. Too often the butter would be rancid, or what you got to eat would be someone else's leftovers. Sometimes the food would be infested by weevils. Once I was served steamed rolls with pork inside, and something else inside too, the straws of a whiskbroom.

My food would be brought to me in a tin box. Maybe a meal would consist of a bowl of soup in enamel-ware, like a casserole dish, then another dish of something else on top, and then another.

"But I need a cover," I said to one of the interpreters.

"Cabbage?" he said. "You want cabbage?"

"No. A cover." I demonstrated with my hands, passing them over a glass. "To keep out the insects."

"Ah." He nodded and went away and came back with a saucer, which he placed over the glass.

There was milk to drink, but often it was specked with coal dust from the kitchen. "If you have any objections to the food," I was told, "all you have to do is ask for what you want. We will try to bring it to you."

I took the interpreters at their offer, and asked for certain things: fresh fruit, cleaner dishes, meat that had not turned bad. They would nod; one of them even took notes. Then like as not would come a lunch and dinner both consisting of the same thing: fried noodles with bread, greasy vegetables on top. They would beam as they brought them: "Now you have no excuse not to eat!" At one point I learned the cook was on vacation and my interpreters were doing the cooking.

Again my daydreams of food returned. Interestingly, my fantasies had become more simple. No longer was I planning elaborate gourmet meals. Instead, I found myself in a hotel in Hong Kong, ordering a beef sandwich and a chocolate malted. That was all I wanted, really. Afterwards, I would smoke an American cigarette and go shopping. A new dress—that would be nice. But I wondered whether my money would hold out.

In my daydream, I planned to have pancakes for breakfast the morning after I bought my dress. I knew I would have to describe the pancakes to the chef, so they would turn out just right. But he was very accommodating. They were accommodating at the Harbor, too. Once, I described pancakes to Lee, and she did her best. For breakfast next day came two little square cakes with some sugar sprinkled on top.

"Not everyone has eaten what you have eaten," the masculine-type interpreter—the one I'd corrupted by putting him back on cigarettes—said to me at one point. "So there's a difficulty some times, getting to understand what it is you want."

"And not everyone has eaten what *you* have eaten," I said. "You say you eat the same things you bring to me. How can you do it without throwing up?"

"Throwing up?"

"I've been sick," I said. "The food has made me sick. I'm losing weight."

"Losing weight?"

"Getting thin." I placed my hand against my stomach, then made an arch with my hands for "fat," then put my hands against my stomach again.

"Ah," he said. "Yes. Yes. And the same with your companion in the room down the stairs." He nodded dolefully. "He's in the middle of a hunger strike."

Jerry's hunger strike was to last fifteen days, or so I was told, for I was never permitted to see him. Once in a great while I could hear him whistling—"Some Enchanted Evening" was what he liked—in his room; and from time to time I could catch a view of him in the front yard, hanging his wash on the line. But each time that happened, an armed guard would move forward, his rifle pointing, and I dared not try to talk with him from my balcony *(balcony,* I thought: *Romeo and Juliet).*

Interpreters would bring me news of him from time to time. The masculine smoker, who had laughed so hysterically when I said the atom bomb could blow up the world, reported that Jerry had given him an equal fit of laughter by telling him, in a long discussion of indoctrination and education, that basically the American and Communist Chinese views were the same. Lee told me that Jerry swept his room every day, just as I swept mine. But one thing the two of us did differently: I had learned that the best chance of getting something I wanted was to ask for it; Jerry, in contrast, was determined to ask for nothing.

"If he'll only tell us what he wants—write it out if he wants to—we'll try to see if we can get it for him," Lee said to me. "But he won't do it."

I remembered the Alka Seltzer prescription on the Island. I said, "Does he want to see me?"

"That isn't allowed," Lee said, not unkindly. "You know that, Mary."

"But has he asked to see me?"

"I told you: he hasn't asked for anything."

"But the doctor prescribed special food for him. Why isn't he eating?"

"His hunger strike has nothing to do with his refusal to eat. He was spoken to about showing better cooperation during questioning. Perhaps this is his signal that he doesn't intend to cooperate."

"You mean he won't answer questions?"

"Oh, he answers questions," Lee said. "He enjoys talking. But the answers aren't satisfactory, or so I've been told."

"Then you've got to let me see him," I said. "You can't just let him go without food. He'll die."

"I don't know," she said doubtfully. "I think it wouldn't be permitted. The entire purpose of questioning each of you separately would be defeated if you talked with him. Surely you can understand that."

"But I won't talk to him about the questions. I'll just be the one to urge him to take better care of himself."

Lee looked thoughtful. "Perhaps," she said, "we could arrange for you to see him with someone else there."

I said, "That would be better than nothing. But it might not be the right way." I remembered how it was at the Island, and the things Jerry had said. "If he sees me with your people, he'll be convinced I've gone over to your side."

"And if you talk to him alone?" Lee said. "Wouldn't it really be the same result?" She knew what had happened on the Island too.

"I don't know," I said. "But I *want* to talk to him. He's my friend. My companion. We came here together. At least on the Island we were allowed to spend time together. Why should it be so different here?"

"Because all things are different here," Lee said. "Different people are in charge of the investigation."

"But you agreed, when we first got here, that they shouldn't be hard on him."

"They're not being hard on him."

"They're not letting me see him."

"He hasn't asked to see you."

We were going round and round. And within me I knew she might be closer to the truth than I liked to think. It was the same old reminder: that *I* was a reminder, the reminder that he was the one responsible for my being here in the first place, the reminder that any contact between us might make things worse for me. Maybe he perceived it as a far, far better thing that for my sake our paths never cross again.

* * *

In the heat of that summer of 1968, the pipes connecting to the toilet in my bathroom burst. The doorknob had been fixed the first week of our stay at the Harbor, so from that day I no longer had to go through the bedroom next door to use the other bath, but there was no exceptional advantage in that. Bathroom vs. bathroom, there was nothing to choose between them: both were filthy, with fixtures that seemed to date back to the turn of the century; if anything, the bath next door was preferable because it had fewer insects. Attracted by food and electric light, a horde of horror-movie creatures had taken over my bathroom, complete with a huge black spider at the bottom of my bathtub. I tried to drown him one day with a sudden gush of water. The minute the water hit him he shot up five feet in the air, his fur and feelers striking my chin.

The day the toilet burst, with an indescribable sound and a gush of water that flowed into the bedroom, I disobeyed all orders and simply barged out of the door, yelling and charging my way down the stairs.

At the foot of the stairs was Mr. Wang.

"Go see what's happened!" I shouted at him.

He gave me a look and mounted the stairs. I followed

him slowly. He was inside my room, surveying the damage. Then he turned and met me at the door.

"Well," he said, "a repair will be made."

"What do I do in the meantime?"

"In the meantime," he said, "you have a mop."

"Yes," I said. "I have a mop. The strings keep falling out. It turns everything to mud. It was black to begin with. It's filthier than the bathroom. And that's saying a lot."

He said, "Chairman Mao tells us—"

"If you're going to tell me what Chairman Mao says about a busted toilet—"

He seemed strangely subdued, for him. "Chairman Mao says a good comrade is one who is more eager to go where the difficulties are greater."

"That's not going to make me go into that bathroom," I said.

"I told you," he said, "a repair will be made. The greater the difficulty, the more eager you will find us. In the meantime, I was coming to see you about something else."

"There is no something else."

"Yes, there is." He beamed. "How would you like to listen to the radio?"

"I already listen to the radio. Everybody for ten miles around listens to it."

"No, no," he said. "A radio of your own."

I looked at him narrowly. "Why do you offer me this?"

"Equality," he said. "We are playing Radio Peking for your friend Muckaluckding. You should be entitled to the same."

"I don't want to hear Radio Peking. I want to hear Radio Hong Kong."

The old Wang began to re-appear: "No!"

"Why not?"

"It will corrupt us. We'll lose our military spirit."

"I'm corrupted already. I won't turn it up."

"You will have your radio," he said, "but of course there will always be somebody with you when you listen. If it happens otherwise, the radio will be removed and you will be reported." By now he was hissing again.

"And which will come first?" I said. "The new radio or the new plumbing?"

"Plumbing?"

"My bathroom."

"I've already told you repairs will be made. It was my duty also to tell you about the radio and the rules for its use."

"Then you've done your duty," I said. "And now why don't you go away?"

He surveyed me. "I'm going," he said. "And my report will be about your refusal to mop your floor, and your unauthorized coming out of your room and down the stairs, and your insistence that you must have Hong Kong radio."

"While you're at it, include the toilet in your report," I said, and slammed the door. But even in my anger I feared I'd committed a costly loss of discretion. From below I could hear Wang's voice, in loud and furious counterpoint to other voices. A tremendous argument was going on. Within that argument there could be only two possible things in my favor, and neither could be called all that promising. One of the things was Wang himself, his bizarre and volatile temperament, which had to be as known to others as it was to me. The other was the simple fact that not even a saying of Chairman Mao's could obliterate the fact (even the possible local embarrassment) of collapsed plumbing.

I can only guess that those two factors, tenuous though they seemed, performed their function. For the next morning he left the Harbor, and I never saw him again.

* * *

That left the bathroom, which was fixed, and its insects, which remained. Just as the Chinese had prepared a daily timetable for me, so I prepared a timetable for the insects. Some of what they did, I could not prevent. There were lizards as much as two feet long who crawled through my room, at times even getting into bed with me. At night, I would go to the bathroom and find an entire wall filled with them. There would be a praying mantis five inches long, dragonflies as big as sparrows, generations of spiders, hordes of cockroaches.

The instant I turned on the bathroom light, there would be a great scattering and skittering as they disappeared. But the sound of them was as bad as the sight of them, for they conducted full-scale wars, and the bathroom was their battleground.

At intervals, war would occur. Lying in my bed at night, I could hear the sounds of battle, and the next morning the bathroom would be littered with the bodies of the dead. The night following the battle, a new sound—an eerie, secret, slithering sound—would come to my ears. It was the sound of the victors carrying the dead away. And the next morning, when I went into the bathroom, there would be no insects there at all. So I would have the place to myself for a few days, but then a new population of warriors would begin to build up, and the story of battle would repeat itself.

My "timetable" was to use the bathroom in the morning. It had sunlight, and sunlight attracted the insects, but my bedroom had sunlight too, so they would not concentrate in any one place. They could enter almost at will, for there were no screens on my windows, but I had a kind of "shower curtain" mosquito netting over my bed that I could let fall down around me for protection. At night, I would turn on the bathroom light, and let the insects congregate there. In this manner, and with the knowledge of their war habits, I was able to "reserve" the bathroom at certain optimum times for myself.

One lizard, however, was incorrigible. He was a big one—a foot and a half long at least, I'd judge—and he had an incurable boldness about him. He also had an insatiable appetite for bananas. Any time I was given a banana to eat, he was there, waiting, watching, moving and climbing toward me on what seemed to be giant gunmetal-colored casters, his eyes set and bright, his scales pointed and sharp, his tongue flickering in and out.

I decided to speak to one of the interpreters about the situation. The one on duty was the timid man I'd taught to smoke.

"I have a serious problem," I said to him. "Sit down. I want to tell you about it."

He looked frightened. "If it's about the interrogation, maybe you discuss it with someone else."

"It isn't about the interrogation."

"I'm not useful in those areas," he said. "A personal problem—if it was a personal problem, maybe I could be of help. We could discuss it."

"That's exactly it," I said. "It's personal. Terribly, terribly personal."

A look of comprehension came over his face. He blushed beet red and jumped up and left the room.

Soon he was back, my door just slightly ajar, his hand thrusting through the opening an oblong wad of what would seem to be many layers of slick-magazine paper glued together: the Chinese version of a sanitary napkin.

In the fall, they came to me. *They* were the interpreters. They came and went, and varied in number at any given time, but from the beginning with Lee at the Harbor, they always included at least one woman, assigned exclusively to me.

Lee had been reassigned elsewhere. In her place was another girl, this one from the north of China, who brought me a ruler that I could use in making designs and sketches, and saw to it I got a couch with softer cushions, and gave me a can of condensed milk and a box of pepper. And I got a new broom for sweeping, and my room was sprayed for insects, and the new girl introduced me to an army officer who handed me a bag of walnuts: they were old and moldy, but a big treat nonetheless.

The new girl meant to be kind, I think, but she had little of Lee's tolerance, and my private name for her was Miss Fanatic. Like the others, her grammar was better than her vocabulary, but unlike several of the others I believe she had never been exposed to a foreigner before—by foreigner, I mean even an *Asian* foreigner: anyone from another place with other views, and this tended to make her relentless and dogmatic, not only in her espousal of Marxism but in her refusal to concede that anything anywhere else could be superior to the way things were in China.

With her, as with almost all the interpreters, the idea that they must teach me to speak Chinese would begin reversing itself in practice, and in the end it was I who would be teaching them English. ("I would like to spend six months out of China, to improve my English," the he-man smoker told me at one point. I asked him where he would go. "Maybe India," he said, and it startled me: it was Pakistan, not India, that was the friend of China.)

One of the interpreters, whose English was perhaps the poorest of all, was a tall, heavy-built man who had been in the Korean war, and had worked in a prison camp there. He was thoughtful, and brought me a teapot and toothpaste and coffee. When Lee still was there, from time to time on a summer afternoon he would pick the fruit from a litchi tree and bring it to my room, and the three of us would talk together.

Sometimes you could account for the comings and the goings of the translators—the goings, at least. In Mr.

Wang's case, for example, it was fairly obvious the authorities saw no further need for his rantings, particularly since my formal interrogation sessions had come to an end. In the case of the man who had been in Korea, an equally good surmise could be made.

"Why don't you tell me what it was like in Korea?" I asked him one night.

"Maybe," he replied. "Maybe."

The next day he was transferred away.

Of course I had more to do with some translators than others. One tall, thin translator was at the Harbor for many weeks and ignored me the entire time. Another one, who looked as though he was in the last stages of consumption, used to peer at me through yellowed eyeglasses and say, "Remember, I can understand you. These others can't."

"Understand me?" I said.

"Your use of English," he said. "It's strange."

I think he was more right than wrong in that. My "Lebanese" accent would be there just enough on certain words to throw them off, especially since their experience in listening was so limited to begin with. To have it sound like "chalk" when you say "choke" can be disconcerting. And so the translator with the yellowed eyeglasses may well have had a point—yet at the same time, he was the last one who had the right to make that point, for he had trouble understanding *anybody's* spoken English, even the perfect British style of the other translators.

At any rate, the translators came and they went, but this one time in the fall a deputation of three or four of them at once came to my room. It had been raining steadily, terribly, and great open cracks had formed in the concrete walls of our building. I thought perhaps we were going to have a conference about that; but what they wanted to tell me instead was that it had been decided I should see Jerry and talk to him.

* * *

When I saw him, lying on his bed in his room, one simple thought came at once to my mind:

He's dying.

It was the way he looked, sunken-eyed and hollow-cheeked; and also the way he moved: his fingers, his head, even his eyes moved very slowly, when they moved at all.

When he spoke, his voice was low, and there was a new note to its tone: disinterest.

"Here she is," he said. "Comrade X. Have you come for the secret military plans? They're under the bed. Get the broom and poke them out."

I said, "Jerry, why aren't you eating? Why aren't you letting them help you?"

"First the broom," he said.

I looked at him. Then I went and got his broom and swept a pile of papers out from under the bed.

When I picked them up and looked at them, I gasped. The papers consisted of a series of architectural drawings: house plans. The astounding thing was that while Jerry had been at work creating them in his room, I had been drawing house plans of my own in *my* room! *Is this some universal?* I wondered *Does everybody who's been captured far from home start drawing house plans at the same point in time?*

Jerry's, though, were far more meticulous than mine. This was the professional cartographer at work. Perversely, I said to myself, *He can't be dying and do this kind of job.*

"They're beautiful," I said. "How did you do it? How could you make these arcs and circles?"

In reply, something of a smile came to his lips, and his fingers fumbled slowly underneath his quilt, then brought out a startling draftsman's instrument: a pair of calipers. He had made them himself out of the set of ivory chopsticks the builder of the *Menehune* had given him as a farewell present.

"You see," he said to me, mockingly, "they're easier to draw with than eat with."

I said, "Have you seen a doctor?"

"I'm not sick."

"They say you are."

"Who told them? I certainly didn't."

"You don't tell them anything."

"I tell them everything. Miles and miles of it on tape, Miss Harbert."

"But you don't tell them what you *need.* If it hurts, you don't tell them where it hurts."

"It doesn't hurt," he said.

"Then why won't you eat?"

"This food?"

"Didn't the doctor give you a special diet?"

"Oh, yes," he said. "No fatty foods. Nothing fried."

"And?"

"And the doctor went away," Jerry said.

"Look," I said, "why don't you do what I do? Eat *parts* of it. Enough to keep you going."

"Going?" he said. "Where?"

"Jerry," I said, "they're not going to keep us here forever. You signed your confession. And now the interrogation's over."

"Maybe it's over for you," he said. "In fact, they tell me you're in pretty good shape. Favorable treatment. Sounds great, kid. Whatever you're doing, keep it up."

I said, "I've been trying to get them to let me see you."

"It wasn't necessary," he said.

His eyes told me that some of what he was saying was not meant seriously, that it was some kind of a private joke. But I didn't know where the joking took up or left off. And I wasn't sure he knew either.

A week or so earlier I had come down with a virulent case of flu (they gave me a large pill to take; I think it was nothing more than aspirin, but the equivalent perhaps of three or four aspirin tablets back home), and in my weakness as I lay in bed, alternating between fever and teeth-chattering chills, I wondered what sort of makeup went into different people that came down to the will to survive. I thought of all the people I knew, of their different points of vulnerability. Captivity like this, I thought, would be hardest on someone like my mother. And in Jerry's case, it had to be hard too, but for a complex of added reasons—*new* reasons. *Responsibility . . . guilt . . . despair.* The last had to be the worst. One question kept recurring: that arm infection he'd had just before I arrived in Hong Kong. Obviously it had made inroads on his physical condition. *If he'd felt better physically, would his outlook have been better? The fall from seventy percent is thirty points closer to zero than the fall from one hundred percent.*

Our time together, in his room that day, lasted not over an hour.

"You *have* to get your strength back," I said to him. "You're no different from anyone else."

"No," he said, "except I'm tired. And I march to the beat of a different drummer. Who said that? Was it Emerson?"

Always there was the sound of boat whistles from the docks that must be nearby—one in particular that cut like a blade through the air, with the sound of some prehistoric monster crying out in pain—and then one day it became a chorus. Twenty-five hundred miles away, somewhere on the border separating Outer Mongolia from the U.S.S.R., Soviet troops had driven Chinese fishermen from their island outpost in some unknown freshwater stream. But all China was to know of it. The twin loudspeakers at the Harbor, often broadcasting different radio programs simultaneously, blared out the news. There was the playing of patriotic music and then one new and incredible sound. For what seemed like forever, every ship in that ocean inlet so near and yet so hidden from view tied down its whistle, and the air was rent by a great, bleeding cacophony of mourning.

The intent was in China what the intent of a protest march would be in the U.S. But the effect of course was far more overwhelming. For in China it was the government that was doing the protesting, adding to the voice of its 750 million people even the voices of its ships.

With the approach of winter the air became tight and biting and cold. They had given me new pants and blouses for the hot, sticky summer, and now I was given winter clothing too. The new wardrobe included sweat pants, designed to be worn underneath my outer clothing, but in all good faith the translators who ordered the clothes for me made something of a mistake. They gave my measurements in terms of my height, five-foot-five, which in China is the indicator of a large, fat person. The sweat pants that arrived were, as a result, so voluminous that I wore them over everything else, then wrapped the overhang of the legs around my feet.

I had found an innovative use too for the hand-fan they gave me during the summer. Now, instead of using it to create a breeze in front of my face, I used it as a metronome instead, clicking it back and forth in the closed position while I sang in my room.

The songs I sang were not their songs and that, I think, troubled the interpreters and, I know, infuriated the guards outside. Someone had asked me if I liked music, and I said I did. It was an extremely unwise thing to say. Straightaway they fetched me a record player and some records, the same music I could hear played over the loudspeakers, in between transcriptions of firecrackers and propaganda exhortations dealing with the Ninth Party Congress.

There was the music from eight operas, two ballets, and ten revolutionary songs, and that was all the music there was. Some of it wasn't too bad, some was interesting, some was terrible. The initial impression was that it had been stolen almost intact from classical Western composers. You could pick out the phrases of Chopin, Beethoven, Handel.

I was to learn that many Chinese have an active dislike for music, ballet, dancing. More important, I was to learn that it was perfectly all right to say so. If you said you didn't like music, it wouldn't be forced on you. If you said you *did* like music, then all you were permitted to hear would be those eight operas, two ballets, and ten revolutionary songs. To like music was to like that music and that music only.

Instead, what the guards and interpreters could hear coming from my room was strange music indeed. Not pop, not mod, not the show tunes like "Some Enchanted Evening" that Jerry had whistled, but the standard songs of my young girlhood instead: "Red River Valley," "Poor Wayfaring Stranger," "Joshua Fit the Battle of Jericho," "There Is a Tavern in the Town," "Clementine," "When Johnny Comes Marching Home." With a little variety mixed in: perhaps "Red Sails in the Sunset" and "Blue Moon."

And there was a tune of my own composition—a simple melody line, simple words, much influenced by Bob Dylan. I kept adding words to it. It was to have perhaps twenty or twenty-five verses; I can remember perhaps a dozen of them.

Well I was born at the bottom of a wishing well
But I ended up goin' thru the gates of hell
Well I saw a little good and a little bad
But I ended up goin' thru the gates of hell

Well I met a few good ones and a few bad
But I gotta get goin' for the road is long
Well the grass is high and the water's sweet
But I passed them all by for to see some more

Well some people are good and some people are bad
But the people I met were all alike
Well I met some men and a few girls
But they all spoke to me just the same

Outside the building the guards would put up a chatter when they heard me singing, and the interpreters would burst into my room and find me fanning myself in time to the song. It was particularly distressing to Miss Fanatic. It was counter-revolutionary to sing these songs, she said.

Miss Fanatic was extremely intelligent. Her English was self-taught, her basic vocabulary extra-limited: I would teach her words like "glass" and "chair." But the extraordinary thing was, she only had to hear such words once, and automatically she would know them from then on.

Her presence was complicated by the appearance of yet another translator assigned to me. He was slightly taller than I, with a scar on his left temple that looked like a vaccination mark. He liked to joke and have fun and was not a very serious communist. Most of all he preferred to avoid trouble. Like so many of the rest, he was unwilling to tell me his name, so here again I brewed a private nickname for him: Don't Make Waves.

My songs and my drawings and sketches triggered a drawing of battle lines between Don't Make Waves and Miss Fanatic. She had the Wang viewpoint, that such things were not proletarian, but bourgeois instead (which it was) and therefore dangerous (which I couldn't understand—dangerous to whom?). No matter what I drew—from Walter Keane-type faces with big eyes to house plans to geometric designs—Miss Fanatic would threaten me with the dire consequences of taking the bourgeois approach vs. the proletarian (those words she knew! *chair* or *glass,* no). Once, when I drew a picture of an imagined soldier of the People's Liberation

Army, loosely based on the dress and equipment of the guards beneath my balcony, she ripped it from my sketch pad.

"Who is this?" she demanded.

"Nobody in particular," I said.

She turned to Don't Make Waves.

"How can you stand there and permit her to draw like this?" (I am offering my own guess here as to what it was she said, for it was spoken in Chinese. But in conversations of this kind, you could tell from the tone of voice, the facial expression, and the subject at hand, what it was that was being said. The longer I was to remain there, as I was to discover, the more frighteningly accurate my "translations" of such exchanges would be.)

It was Miss Fanatic's private opinion, I thought, that she should report my "works of art"—deviationist or revisionist at best, outright espionage at worst—to her superiors: not because she disliked me personally, but because this was her view of her "duty."

On the other hand, Don't Make Waves not only saw nothing dangerous or terrible in what I was doing, he even liked some of it and asked for more.

Thus the flare-up of words between the two of them. Don't Make Waves may have been successful to the point of talking Miss Fanatic out of turning me in to Black Fan or whatever other official may have been on the scene at the moment. But if it came to a showdown with the officials, he certainly was not prepared to praise before them the things he had praised to me personally. Trouble, he did not want, in any way, shape or form.

"I could suggest," he said, one day, "that a safe and enjoyable practice would be for you to draw pictures of these." And he showed me the inevitable Thermos bottle of hot water, each of which had flowers painted on the sides. To sketch or paint flowers might be in and of itself a bourgeois deed, but at least the model would have been provided by my hosts themselves.

Furthermore, the acts of painting, drawing, and sketching were things that kept me sedentary and in one place. And that would keep the guards outside at peace. What made them nervous was to see me pacing up and down in my room, singing or, even worse, talking to myself.

I began doing a lot of that. In my mind's eye, I was a movie director, a television director, issuing instructions, working over scripts, talking to the actors and technicians. I concocted whole plots, then translated them to the screen, even went to the premiere and, of course, the Academy Awards night. Of the several "credits" I produced, my best, I think, may have been a story about a girl alone at sea, sailing. She is captured by the Chinese, but then they get mad at her, put her back on the boat, and let her go. But she knows nothing about sailing.

The guards could hear the sound of my voice as I set forth this story line. Worse than that, they could hear my laughter. For the story was a comedy.

From the ceiling in my room at the Harbor, dangling uncertainly from its connecting wires, was a naked fluorescent bulb. It provided the light for the room. When Miss Fanatic came, she occupied the bedroom next to mine, and there was no light at all in that room. An army man came, strung a loose wire through her window, and hung a bulb-and-socket from it. Miss Fanatic was proud to show me the result.

"You see how the soldiers love the people?" she said. "They don't do this for you in America."

Before she came there, the room was empty, as I've said, but for a few days during the summer a group of soldiers came and used it as a place to sleep. At night, one by one, they would come onto the balcony and over to my windows, which had neither curtains nor screens, and shine a flashlight in on me as I slept. Another time, during the summer, I was lying on my bed, wearing underpants but no top—there was a towel beside me, but I think it did not cover me—and I think what I was doing was waiting for them to bring supper. It was around twilight, I remember that, and in the uneven light it took me a while to realize there was a soldier standing on the balcony outside my window, staring in at me. How long he had been there, I had no way of knowing. I reached for the towel and yelled at the top of my lungs, but even then he took his time about moving away.

This was not to be the last episode of that kind, but unlike the visiting soldiers, the regular guards at the Harbor kept their distance and their rectitude as well. Obviously they were under threat of severe punishment if they tried it any other way, and there was the added physical factor of separation between my second-floor room and their station outside the front of the building.

So when they stared at me, it was not a man-woman stare; and besides, I stared back. We developed a series of staring contests. I won them. This may sound like a rather small triumph, but it's surprising what you'll settle for when there are no big ones.

And there's another reason why I could out-stare them: I had nothing else to do. That is not to say some of the contests were all that easily won, for my boredom could not have been all that much greater than theirs. From time to time, one or another of them would actually fall asleep on duty.

They were very young, most of them, and they can not have taken with great eagerness to an assignment that consisted of guarding someone who (a) obviously wasn't going anywhere and (b) occupied quarters which, wretched though they were by our standards, must have been far more luxurious than anything they could have been accustomed to. Wall-to-wall lizards, broken and antiquated plumbing, hot water for washing or bathing delivered in a pot still reeking from kitchen use, cracked masonry, a single light bulb dangling by its exposed weight from an exposed wire, a perpetual pool of water stagnating on the bedroom floor, insects and rodents of every description, no radiator—a report such as that could only come from an indignant description of the worst ghetto conditions in the United States. But to the Chinese, I had a private room and bath.

Worse than that, I had it for free, and all I could eat besides. My landlord (slumlord, by U. S. standards) was the commune, and, I was to learn, the government paid the commune for my keep. Maybe to some of the guards I was an elite assignment, but others obviously resented the job of guarding me and resented me even more than the job. Their method of showing it was almost childish at times, but I suppose it was the only way they had. Their orders said I would be quiet in my room, studying. The only exception could be for my exercise period. Thus, when they saw me pacing back and forth, singing, talking to myself, even laughing, it infuriated them—obviously I was having a good time—and one of them would come into the building to report me. They knew also that my light was on during the daylight hours, a shameless extravagance, and they reported that, too. Time and again my interpreters would tell me there had been complaints, that I must stop doing these things, but at this stage they were lenient about enforcement: why, I'm not totally sure; it could have been for a number of reasons. I'm sure they realized that because I had to wear dark glasses, the light had to be on. I think several of them genuinely liked me. And perhaps it meant something to them that Jerry was sicker than I—if not because it could signal that "my" interpreters were doing a better job than "his," then maybe simply because their purposes in detaining us, paying for our food, shelter, clothing, medical care (such as they were), were not going to be served if we both died.

I believe that what I just put together is an excellent

theory. The trouble with such excellent theories is that they can be the product of American thinking, not Chinese. The Foolish Old Man Who Removed the Mountains, in the fable recounted in the sayings of Chairman Mao, illustrated the precise opposite of my theory. For to him, if somebody died, somebody else just started digging where he left off.

Under this consideration, it seemed to me the best thing to do was fight fire with fire. "Fire with fire" is too glorious a way to put it—better the lighting of one of the toothpick-like Chinese matches, creating a brief and tiny flame. But I took steps nonetheless. One day, as the guards and I were in the process of one of our staring contests, one of them called another one over, began talking about me and gesturing about me, finally aiming his gun at me. Instantly I put up a fit of screaming and hollering. Interpreters hammered up the stairs to my door to see what was wrong.

"He's pointing a gun at me!" I said. "You know Chairman Mao says this isn't the way you treat the people you've detained."

They began to soothe me. "It's a new soldier," they said.

"He's not new," I said. "He's been here before."

"Okay, okay," they said. *Simmer down, Miss Harbert.* "We'll see about it."

The result was on the plus side. From then on, the guards were not so quick to report me if they saw me singing or waving my arms while talking to myself and pacing my room. If my light was on, they said little if anything about it.

Their approach was interesting. They began paying helpful attention to Miss Fanatic, who had moved in next door. Just as one of them had helped string a light bulb into her room, now any time she washed her laundry, her mosquito net, her quilt cover, the guards would come to help her hang it on the line to dry . . . all the while ignoring me.

"It shows you," Miss Fanatic said to me, "how in China everybody helps everybody."

"I'm part of everybody," I said. "They don't help me. Besides, it's common courtesy."

She said, "Courtesy?"

I explained the meaning of the word to her. As she did with all the other new words, she grasped it immediately.

"But you see," she said, "the things that you do in America because of courtesy, we do here in China because of the revolution."

At a later point, I was to repeat that curious assertion to another interpreter, whose thinking I had come to respect.

"I understand what she was saying," he said. "But I don't think *you* understand it. You see, the spirit of the revolution is more important than the spirit of courtesy."

I said, "Not if you've been brought up to be courteous to begin with—"

"That's just it," he said. "You're talking about one person. Courtesy is something that's suggested to you, and if you have it, you think nothing of it. But revolution is *demanded.* It's not a question of just one person. *Everybody* will show it."

In my remaining time at the Harbor, there was only one other incident when I had a gun pointed at me. It came during a staring contest, and a young guard—he couldn't have been more than eighteen—leveled his rifle at me, as I stood at my window. Then he made a great show of squinting along the line of the sights. All that was left was to pull the trigger.

All right, I said to myself, *and what will happen now?*

What happened now was that the bullets fell out of the back end of his gun and plopped in a silly shower to the ground.

* * *

The rains in the fall were not unpleasant. Not to me, at any rate. They were more than rains, they were the inland residues of full-scale typhoons at sea, and there was the rolling of thunder and great washes of water driving down from the sky; enough, they said, to ruin the stand of crops being readied for harvest. But they brought cool weather with them, to end what they told me had been the hottest summer they could remember.

They were also to tell me it was the wettest autumn they could remember.

And the coldest winter.

In the autumn they brought our clothing and blankets from the Island, and almost overnight the wind-whipped, biting chill and cold of winter set in. It never got to the point of snowing, but it never had to. With always a renewed stand of cold water on the floor of my room, with no heat, I became a hibernating animal, burrowing under mounds of quilts and blankets. My feet began to swell from the cold (this was not unusual: Miss Fanatic had been hospitalized three months because of feet swollen by the cold), and my ears hurt from the way I tried to press my head against the surface of the bed.

I gave up exercises, and reading, and singing, and play-acting. I ate less than ever. I began to be sick, with colds and flu in never-ending progression. I had lost thirty pounds since my arrival in Hong Kong the previous spring.

And I began to hatch a private plan to escape.

It would be no problem, I knew, to sneak past the guards. The plan then would be to reach Hong Kong—it could not be more than one hundred miles away.

The weaker I became, the more the plan took shape. At full strength, I would have had to solve the problem of negotiating those one hundred miles, with my American face, and the associated problem of having to ask directions as I went. For if I had a sense of how far freedom lay, I had little if any sense of which direction.

What astonishes me now is that I thought of it at all. In fact at the time, the one greatest barrier to the great escape would have been the effort to get out of bed to begin with.

In my weakness then, I hit upon a substitute plan. I would volunteer a confession of my own. And so I began, painfully, to write it out. It was brief and to the point: I was in China through no fault of mine. I suppose this could sound cold and hard where Jerry was concerned, but the fact was that his own "confession," signed months before on the Island, was one in which he took the total blame upon himself. If that had not been so, then even in my shattered state of mind of the following winter, I think I would never had written what I did. But it was so, and I could recall the summer's interrogation:

Q. When you took your nap on the boat, what time did you wake up?
A. Three o'clock.
Q. Two weeks ago, you said two o'clock.
A. I can't keep track of time that closely.
Q. Two weeks ago you could.
A. Why is it that important?
Q. Because it tells us something. Did he take navigational readings before you napped?
A. I don't remember.
Q. Five weeks ago you said he did. Did he take navigational readings after you napped?
A. I guess so.
Q. Three weeks ago you said he didn't.
A. But when I woke up, we were surrounded by the fishing junks.
Q. Then how could he have been taking navigational readings?
A. I didn't say he was.
Q. Of course you did. You just said it.
A. What I meant was, *while* I was waking up he could

have been taking some navigational readings. But when I finally sat up, I saw we were surrounded.

Q. That's not what you said three weeks ago.

A. It's what I *meant* three weeks ago.

And so the strange extra added attraction: if I wrote out a confession now it could help both of us. For to say the fault was his rather than mine would give them the one thing they had lacked so far and prized the most—a single agreed story offered separately by two different people.

I talked it over with Don't Make Waves. He was sympathetic. He understood what it was I had in mind. "But you should not make it a confession of your own," he said.

I said, "I don't understand."

"Make it a letter to the government," he said.

I drafted it again. *To whom it concerns:* I wrote, *You should not blame me for my companion*'s *actions. I trusted my companion to chart a legal and safe course. My trust was misfounded."*

Don't Make Waves was unhappy as he read it. I asked him why. He shrugged, and took the confession downstairs.

A day or two later he brought it back. "They don't understand some things: *To whom it concerns?* What does that mean, they want to know: *My trust was misfounded?* They have never heard the word *misfounded."*

Somehow, in my weakness, I laughed. "I guess I never heard it either," I said. "It means *un*founded, misplaced. Why don't you change it?"

He recoiled. "No!"

"No?"

"Any changes must be in your handwriting," he said.

"Then hand it over," I said. "I'll fix it."

"Fix it?"

"Yes. Fix it."

Almost sadly, he handed the paper back to me, and what he said then was in its way a direct confirmation that what I had written here could not hurt Jerry. In fact, what he said went beyond that and out the other end: "You think you're saving yourself? There is no saving here. If you help anyone, you help your companion, because you back up his story. Now for the first time they'll know he was telling the truth."

It was wild. The one way to save Jerry was to accuse him. Yet had I not had the sense of that in our own relationship those times we were together on the *Menehune* at the Island? To confront Jerry McLaughlin with the truth then was no different from confronting the Chinese with the truth now.

Except for one thing.

"I very much fear," Don't Make Waves said, "that he is dying."

My "confession" was never responded to, never reacted to. Racked with the cold and with illness, I put a stop to all things in my usual everyday life. The simplest things: brushing my teeth, washing my face—became burdensome chores.

And as the winter of 1968–69 phased on, a new translator appeared on the scene. He was short, and babyfaced; serious and literal-minded. In all ways he reminded me of a limerick I had heard at the University of Utah:

There once was a man so benighted
He never knew when he was slighted
And once at a party
He ate just as hearty
As if he'd been really invited.

For the first time in months, the cold had receded; they had brought me hot water and with it, for the first time in months, I had washed my hair. And in that moment, this new interpreter presented himself at my door for the first time.

I wouldn't let him in. "Wet hair," I explained.

Two hours later there was a tentative, tiny tapping on my door. I opened it, and there he was.

I said, "Have you been standing there all this time?"

He nodded eagerly.

"Why?"

"Because you said: *Wait Here.*"

He came into my room. I asked him his name. As part of the regular chorus, he refused to give it. But he said to me, "I know a great deal about you."

"You do?"

"Yes. I have studied."

"And what did they tell you?"

"They told me you are not responsible."

"Why?"

"Because you aren't one of *them.*"

"Who's *them?*"

"The ruling classes of America. The repressionists. I know you instead as one of the people, struggling against the imperialist masters. Why don't you eat more than you do?"

The sequence of statements and questions was unnerving. I said, "I eat as much as I can."

"But we let you order your own food."

"Then, after I do, you bring me the same thing anyway."

"I will try to memorize what you just said. What is that water doing on the floor?"

"I wish I knew."

"Don't be angry at water," he said. "Chairman Mao says, *When drinking water do not fail to remember the man who dug the well.*"

"I'm not prepared to oppose the sayings of your great leader Chairman Mao," I said, "but I'm not about to drink it off the floor either."

"Of course not," he said. "We are in agreement. You are not angry at water, but you are angry at water on your floor. So that much is settled. Now. You say you don't want to drink the water from your floor. Why?"

"Look at it," I said.

"I have already looked at it. You can't drink it. Therefore you mop it up. But you haven't mopped it up."

"My mop was so bad, they finally agreed to take it away."

"And left you nothing to sweep with?"

"Sweeping is one thing. Mopping's another."

"Chairman Mao says there's no difference."

"Chairman Mao hasn't been sleeping here."

"There are many places Chairman Mao doesn't sleep. That doesn't mean his sayings are any less valid. You stay here. I'll be back."

Less than an hour later he returned, this time outfitted in a slicker and the most earnest set of rubber boots I ever saw. He looked like that statue in the U.S.—where is it? Gloucester?—erected in tribute to Those Who Go Down to the Sea in Ships.

He brought with him a mop and a bucket. Assiduously, he began to mop the water in my room, hand-wringing it into the bucket, taking the bucket to the bathroom to empty it, then returning to begin all over again. In the time period of his trips to the bathroom, a new trickle would have begun once again to add to the basic pool of water in my room. But he kept at it. He was inordinately proud of those boots. And as he was at it, he kept up a single chant, one word repeated three times, that became my nickname for him.

He said it with great and fastidious distaste:

"Dirty, dirty, dirty."

And so that was the name I gave him: Dirty Dirty Dirty.

It would become even stranger than that, but at the moment I didn't see how. For the three people closest to you to be named Miss Fanatic, Don't Make Waves, and Dirty Dirty Dirty is a sort of *Catch-22* incarnate.

The winter wore on, and Dirty Dirty Dirty came to me: "Your companion is sick. It's very terrible. He won't read the magazines we gave him."

In any other setting, that would be ridiculous: for a man's health to be reasoned against his willingness to read forced propaganda. But I knew that with Jerry it was real, and just as terrible as Dirty Dirty Dirty said.

I said, "Then let me talk to him."

"No!" he said, and then, softening, "He has said he will not see you."

"But what's being done for him?"

"Everything he will permit."

I believed that, and yet at the same time doubted it. If he was that sick, and if they cared that much about him, why didn't they hospitalize him?

"He went on a new hunger strike. Twenty days this time." All you could see were the whites of Dirty Dirty Dirty's eyes. "Tell me, what shall we do?"

"If you won't let me see him, I don't know," I said.

"But you did see him. Last fall."

"Maybe it could be different this time."

"But he won't permit that."

As we were talking, a car drove up—you could hear the sound of the engine and the churning of gravel on the unpaved road that ran between the trees beyond my front window. Each time a car arrived, the sensation welled within me: *I'm free—they're here for me.* I went to the window. Dirty Dirty Dirty said, "What are you looking for?"

"I heard a car."

"Yesterday you heard a helicopter." He was very proud of that word, *helicopter.* "Are cars and helicopters so strange to you?"

"Never mind," I said. "I want to know if I can see my companion."

"If it will be permitted," Dirty Dirty Dirty said earnestly, "then I myself certainly see no reason why not."

As the winter turned into spring, in March of 1969, I did see Jerry again. He didn't know I saw him. I came out of my balcony, to hang some washing, and beneath me and to my right I could see him seated in a chair outside his room. The day was chill, but there was a thin sunlight. He was bundled in some kind of a parka, with his feet propped up on a set of books on top of a sort of orange crate. The sight of his feet caught my attention: they were swollen, just as mine had been over the winter. In semiprofile, I could see the look on his face. It was a *What-can-you-do-to-me?* look. He was totally motionless. Then his face turned slightly, and I saw that it had a tight smile.

Two days after that, there was the sound of a truck arriving out front. As always, the sensation—*I'm free*—came upon me, and I went to the window to see what it was.

It was an ambulance. It backed up to the front door downstairs, next to Jerry's room. Some guards gathered around; and some people got out of the ambulance, and they opened the back doors of the vehicle and started taking out a number of white Styrofoam-type boxes. They were like cake boxes from the candy store in my daydreams. What they were for, I didn't know then and don't know now. I know only that they cast the sense of dread into me.

I turned away from my window and went and buried myself in my bed, and stayed that way till the sounds from the outside told me the ambulance had left.

He's dead, I told myself, and I needed no documentary evidence to confirm the feeling. Some of the thoughts that now assembled in my mind were what you might call "prisoner thoughts": a prisoner under such circumstances becomes self-centered by the very nature of his captivity. And so it was a "natural" part of my reaction at this point to wonder what kind of treatment I would now receive, to want to believe it would be better than before. But in knowing what I thought, I know too what I did *not* think: I did *not* think: *He's better off dead.*

Very few people are.

It could readily be acknowledged that Jerry was sick in body and spirit, but neither his physical condition nor his outlook were terminal in the sense that they would not have been reversed. Did Jerry bear as much responsibility for this as the Chinese? The answer would have to be no. He was sick, they were well. He was the captive, they were the captors. If it was his failure not to cooperate with their doctors, it was their greater failure not to provide better doctors. What he may have failed to do within the means at his disposal can not be separated from what they failed to do within the means at theirs.

What had started out with its adventurous side had come down to its sad side: I had never known Jerry that well. I say this in terms of detail—he had mentioned his father to me, for example, and a brother who at the time was in Hawaii, but that was all I knew of his family. I could remember the "old" Jerry—the man I had known in my teens now some six years and more ago—and the flashes of wit and satire and expertise, and of knowledge and pride, that I had seen since my arrival in Hong Kong, all of them further reminders of years before. But events had conspired to make him more, not less, of a stranger, and what we shared in common was that these events were beyond our control.

What I had to assume was that by now his family and friends had stopped looking for him, accepting that he must by now no longer be alive. I assumed that about him because I assumed the same thing about me.

But this was a man who was liked by the children at the Island, and feared by the dialectitians at the Harbor. And his fate could have been prevented.

His fate—I had assumed it, yet without corroboration.

That night, I said to Don't Make Waves: "He's dead, isn't he?"

"No," he said. "It's my opinion he was taken some place else."

"In that ambulance?"

"Ambulance?"

"The truck that came for him."

"I don't know if that was for him or not."

"And what were those white boxes?"

"What white boxes?"

I don't accuse Don't Make Waves. Perhaps he didn't know. But I knew. I could tell from what happened now. For if Jerry were still alive, and the ambulance had come, say, to take him to a hospital for more concentrated medical care, there would have been no reason for any change in my life at the Harbor.

Instead, all kinds of things began to happen.

To begin with, a fat army officer, accompanied by a big smile and a translator, appeared in my room. He wanted, he said, to have a "heart-to-heart talk" (a favorite expression of Mao's). I had nothing to worry about, he said. Was I comfortable? Was I warm enough?

He might have asked in December or January if I was warm enough: now it was the end of March. Suddenly, as in some climactic moment in a Greek play, a Chinese woman began to shriek in counterpoint. I had seen her a time or two, knew that from time to time she had occupied the room across the hall from mine on the second floor at the Harbor. Now all at once she appeared, shrieking in Chinese. The plan, I gathered, was that she intended to move into the room directly next to mine, the one occupied by Miss Fanatic. But in strident tones, it turned out she wanted more than that. She wanted my bedding, my furniture. "I live here!" she shouted in Chinese. "*I* live here!"

All my bedding, except for my own blanket that had

been brought to me from the *Menehune* in the fall was folded at the bottom of my bed. All my windows were flung wide open. Then everybody left. I went and closed the windows, then went and huddled against the one remaining blanket on my bed.

In the morning, Miss Fanatic said, "We need all the bedding and your clothes for laundering. And there are some changes to be made." The changes involved the furniture. Out went my "new" couch with its softer cushions. Back came another couch, this one with bloodstains on it. I sat on the side of the bed, and as I did there was a rap at my door, and in came someone with a flat tin box.

Inside the box was my lunch. I sniffed and stared and didn't believe it. It was a gorgeous, magnificent hamburger, flanked by a stand of beautiful mashed potatoes drenched in fresh butter.

I sensed the upset for what it had to be: further proof that Jerry was dead, and a concerted drive to get my mind away from it. Now things piled in on me one after the other. In the morning one day just after the ambulance came, Don't Make Waves was at my door. "Come," he said. "The car is here."

Miss Fanatic came up the stairs behind him. "You'll forget this place," she said. "You're going to the Commune of the Happy People."

I said, "What is that? It sounds like the Ingrid Bergman picture I saw—*The Inn of the Sixth Happiness.*"

"I don't know about your Ingrid," Miss Fanatic said.

"Ingrid Bergman," I said. "You mean you've never heard of the Inn of the Sixth Happiness?"

Miss Fanatic exchanged a private look with Don't Make Waves. Then she said, "The Inn of the Sixth Happiness, of course. We know what that means."

"I don't," I said.

"It's not important," she said.

"If it's not important, then tell me."

"It's the legend of the old China," she said. "It has nothing to do with today."

Then Don't Make Waves said an unusual thing to her, "How did you learn English?"

Suddenly Miss Fanatic seemed a woman transformed, and I understood at once: this was how she had taught English to herself—through English translations of ancient Chinese legends. When she spoke now, it was by rote, like the hypnotized man in *The 39 Steps:*

"The Inn of the First Happiness," she recited tonelessly, "concerns itself with longevity. The Inn of the Second Happiness concerns itself with wealth. The Inn of the Third Happiness concerns itself with health."

"So far," I said, "I'm batting zero."

But it was as though she had not heard me. "The Inn of the Fouth Happiness concerns itself with virtue. The Inn of the Fifth Happiness concerns itself with peaceful departure. The Inn of the Sixth Happiness concerns itself with the joy of living."

"Then this is the Inn of the Fifth Happiness," I said to Don't Make Waves. "The car is here. We're leaving. Right?"

He looked away. As tonelessly as ever, Miss Fanatic said: "The Inn of the Fifth Happiness is Death."

4

Crossing the Pearl

Well I was born at the bottom of a wishing well
But I ended up goin' thru the gates of hell
Well I walked a few miles and learned a few tales
But I ended up goin' thru the gates of hell

Well the sea is far and the land is near
But I crossed the ocean for to see the world
Well the sky is light and the clouds are red
But I passed them all by for to find the day

Well the rain is wet and the ground is cold
But I slept there for to feel the earth
Well the spring is nice and the summer's warm
But I see the winter all the time

Dirty Dirty Dirty had gone on before us from the Harbor to the Commune of the Happy People, and Miss Fanatic and Don't Make Waves rode together with me and an army driver when I made the trip. We drove in what appeared to be a British car of fairly new make, a nicer automobile, I suspected, than Miss Fanatic had ever been in before. Once when I reached out to push the cigarette lighter on the dashboard, she quickly pulled my hand away. "Don't touch anything," she said. She was not about to have any damage to the car caused by someone in her charge.

It was a warm sunny day. They had given me peanut candy and oranges, and we were to have a long and pleasant drive—northwesterly in direction, by my best guess—in an ever-ascending course amid hills and mini-mountains. The air became less humid and salty, more crisp and fine. Along the partly paved roads we saw water buffalo, rice paddies, one giant field that I remember, totally unoccupied except for one small square patch, perhaps ten feet on a side—no bigger than a smallish bedroom in a typical American home—where perhaps two dozen peasants, men and women both, were busily chopping at the earth with hoes and other ground-breaking tools. It was like a great glob of ants swarming over the one dropped morsel at a picnic. How half a dozen feet remained intact in such close quarters, I'll never know.

I turned to Don't Make Waves in the back seat.

He smiled.

"Collective farming," he said.

Along the way, we passed people and vehicles who in combination seemed almost a treadmill history of ground transportation. Here would be an ancient peasant woman, bearing water in twin buckets balanced from a bamboo pole slung over her shoulders. Here would be a wheezing, ancient bus, crammed beyond belief by standees. (Once, when Don't Make Waves and

Lee were returning to the Harbor on the same bus, he brought me paints, she brought me brushes and newsprint paper to paint on, so thin it blotted and distorted even the finest stroke of a watercolor brush. But I wound up only with the paints and the paper, for Lee said she had lost the brushes "in the crush of the bus." Now I could see what she meant.)

And we passed many bicycles, and cargo-carrying bicycles, with two-wheel and three-wheel "trailers" hooked on behind them like outsize shopping carts. And trucks of all shapes and sizes and description, both old and new. The variety was even greater than what I've just depicted, for time and again we would see "homemade" trucks, an automobile or tractor with its top and sides stripped away and the cargo bed of a truck welded on behind.

What struck me most of all was the sight of old men patiently walking their trailer-bicycles, loaded with goods, up long, seemingly endless slopes. You could see the sweat running and the muscles straining as we passed them, going in the same direction. It would have been the easiest thing in the world for us to stop and help them, to give them a tow up the hill, but we never did. Every once in a while they'd look at us, almost expectantly. I thought, but did not say aloud, of what Miss Fanatic had said at the Harbor: *The things that you do in America because of courtesy, we do here in China because of revolution. It shows you how in China everybody helps everybody.* I still think of those straining old men, skeletons of legs and arms and rib-cage, fighting the weight of their loads and the pull of gravity itself while a new automobile moved slowly, smoothly, continuously past them.

In a fresh mountain setting, verdant with spring, lay the vacation hotel of the Commune of the Happy People. You did not have to be told it was a hotel. It said so even on the chinaware: *hotel,* in Chinese, said the lettering.

The building was split-level, its long side nestled into the up-grade of a hillside that had pathways meandering among pine, flowering trees, and bamboo. My first night there, a mouse ran over my face, but it was a refined and accidental mouse, I think, for my room seemed well put together and there were screens on the windows.

It was the nicest room yet. The building itself was quite new, constructed during the 1950s, I would say, with only a few initial outward signs of deterioration, and my room had a hexagonal-patterned tile floor, old velvet green curtains, furniture in varnished stained wood—a nice desk, a nice bed with a seersucker spread, two arm chairs separated by a table. There were desk and table lamps, their bases of porcelain filigreed with bas-reliefs of goldfish, birds, and dragons.

At the end of the hallway off my room were two public rooms: a lounge, and a sort of half-lounge, set up with a dining table, where my meals were brought, first by a waiter, later by a waitress, from a kitchen building which lay a short walk away at the end of a pleasant outside breezeway. At the Harbor, the "cook"—whoever he or she was at the moment—was reputed to be a specialist in Cantonese cuisine. This was amusing, if only for one reason: my friend Lee, who was from Canton, hated Cantonese cooking. "The duck is awful," she used to say. "And they don't know what to do with vegetables." But here, at the Commune of the Happy People, I was told the cook was a specialist in "Western" food. And the menu was more familiar: more meat dishes, more mashed potatoes. Apparently, too, they had here what they lacked at the Harbor: an oven for baking. And so I would be served fresh bread. It was of very uncertain quality, more chaff than wheat, but at least it was fresh.

There were other amenities: washing machines, (but

only for sheets and linens, not personal clothing) for example, and radiators in the rooms (I wondered idly if, come winter, they actually worked). And close by the building there was a broad, shallow river—as the weather grew warmer I could hear the voices of children swimming there, and gathering firewood beside its banks—and, in between, a pretty yard, even though it was mostly weeds and nobody ever mowed the grass.

Most of all, there was a new degree of freedom. Guards still were in evidence, but they kept mainly to themselves, most of the time in the downstairs laundry wing, and, in the company of various interpreters, I would go for walks in the hills and play badminton in the yard area. They gave me back the nailfile and other things they had taken away at the Harbor, and I began keeping up my appearance, using lipstick, caring for my hair.

"I'll show you how to put it in a pigtail," Miss Fanatic said to me.

"No you won't," I said.

"This is China," she said. "Anyone with hair as long as yours must wear it in pigtails."

"It may be your country," I said to her, "but it's my hair."

"You're setting yourself against the government," she said. "No citizen should do that."

"When did you make me a citizen?"

But if, in the feel of youth and springtime and the up-beat change from the Harbor, I was emboldened to talk that way, still I knew an undercurrent of apprehension. A rash of little things had happened, not all of them good. My first lunch at the Commune of the Happy People, for example—served by a waiter in the little dining lounge—had been my old favorite: eggs; but beautifully prepared, first in the form of a delicate egg-drop soup, then in a plate of strange but marvelous-tasting preserved eggs. What impressed me even more was the shiny new table cloth, and the handsome cloth napkin, and the silverware—knife, fork, and spoon—that was to be my personal silverware from that time on.

But after a couple of days, the cloth napkin was replaced by a paper one—the size of the largest paper napkins available at any American supermarket, but cut in half—and after several days of those paper napkins, there then were no napkins at all. As for the tablecoth, it stayed where it was, draped over the table, and stayed and stayed and stayed; never removed, never laundered, never replaced.

It may be that this was all more or less intentional: that the best foot be forward in my first days there, when they must have realized I could guess that Jerry was no longer alive. And not all the best foot was best to begin with: they gave me the best cups and saucers they had, but practically all of them were gouged and chipped from repeated use.

Still and all, I had the firm feeling that very few out of 750 million Chinese ever got to vacation at a spot as elegant as this one, ever knew what it was to be waited upon at dinner, ever encountered the "little touches" that even by American standards—and by all other American standards this would be at best a third-rate mountain lodge—would be an astonishing delight.

Of course other people had been there before me and others would come after me, for this *was* a resort, and *some* Chinese obviously *were* fortunate enough to vacation here. I had interesting evidence of this, for the day I first moved into my room I found objects that I took to have been overlooked by the previous occupants when they moved out.

There were a pair of old shoes, a fan, a cup, and a comb.

I went to the door of my room and called out to Don't Make Waves. He came and I said, "Somebody left these," and showed him the articles.

He smiled. "They're ordinary."

I looked at him, perplexed. "They may be ordinary, but the point is, they're not mine."

"Oh, but they *are* yours," he said. "That's what I mean: ordinary. It's ordinary that every new guest receives them."

My memory is absolute that I went from the Harbor to the Commune of the Happy People at the very end of March, 1969, give or take no more than three days either way. That I do not have the exact date in my mind is not important—what date, really, *was* important?—but I know I am close enough, and in this one case "close enough" is going to have later meaning in my story. A point of equal significance that I want to make is that if I may fail to remember an exact date now, it is because of the erosion of time since then, rather than because at any time while I was in China I was reduced to chalking up days on the wall of a prison cell. I knew what day of the year it was every day I was in that country. But more often than not it didn't seem important.

In fact, they *wanted* me to know what day it was. Learning to read the date as written in Chinese in their newspapers, learning to pick it out from the announcer's voice on a nightly radio news broadcast, was considered an elementary part of my education

More than that, they flooded me with English-language literature. At first, the flood began as a trickle, with a month-old issue of *China Pictorial*—a magazine published in several languages, mine of course in English—that was handed to me when I was on the Island. The only thing I remember from it was a picture story of Chinese surveyors on a glacier below Mt. Everest. Whatever their mission of the moment was, they first counseled each other with the sayings of Mao Tse-tung.

At the Harbor there were more copies of *China Pictorial,* plus copies of *Peking Review,* a weekly—also printed in many languages, the one they gave me being in English—and once my formal "interrogation" was over, it seemed of a sudden that I was being bombarded with literature, all of it in English: pamphlets about Chinese heroes (no Chinese hero ever died, always it was that he sacrificed himself), and volumes of *Das Kapital,* four huge books of the sayings of Chairman Mao, from which the little red book ultimately became the distilled condensation, not to mention current editions of Maoist papers in Australia, New Zealand and, to be sure, the United States.

"You see?" Miss Fanatic said one day, as she passed me my newest copy of *The Guardian,* which is printed in the U.S. "Even your own people hate the government."

"If some of them do," I said, "they hate a government that lets them print anti-government material to begin with. Do you have any anti-government newspapers in China?"

She bridled. "No one has a need to hate the government in China."

"If anyone did have such a need, how would you find out about it?"

She eyed me closely. "Confession of error is a policy with our government. Therefore, no such need can exist."

"But if it did exist, who would remind your government?"

"In our country, the government and the people are one and the same," she said. "Therefore the reminders are everywhere."

"They pop up here and there in my country, too," I said, and waved *The Guardian* at her. "In print."

"But who in your country reads it?"

She had a point. I myself had never seen *The Guardian* before my stay in China. I said, "I suppose very few."

"While the masses are distracted by bread and circuses."

I was going to tell her that her bread wasn't very good

and I hadn't seen a circus in a year's stay in China, but instead, I said, "And we also vote. We vote our leaders into office and out of office. You have the saying: *While at sea, place your trust in the helmsman; in government, place your trust in Mao Tse-tung.* You operate on blind faith. In my country, we don't. We make changes. People have the right to strike, and redress their grievances. Your pride in confessing error may be necessary to you, but in my country we have a Constitutional amendment that says the opposite: that no one has to testify against himself."

She shook her head. "What a curious country you have. How then do you detect error if it may not be confessed?"

"By many ways," I said, "including the very newspaper you're holding in your hand."

"But you and I both know the authorities suppress papers like these."

"If they do, how did you get a hold of this one to begin with?"

It was a conversation that nobody won on points, and far from my own point in bringing it up, in the context of this narrative. My larger point is that I was kept current not only on dates but on news events, in unusual ways, perhaps, but current nonetheless. An attack in one paper on the U.S. as a lawless country would be what told me that Senator Robert Kennedy had been shot . . . a violent diatribe against the policies of President Nixon would tell me that Nixon had been elected . . . I even learned the United States had put men on the moon—or maybe I didn't learn it. "How can a country that can put a man on the moon," raged the New Zealand *People's Voice,* "be guilty of such atrocities here on earth?" You had to think that one out. Did it mean we were *capable* of putting a man on the moon, or that we had actually done so?

What was of particular fascination was that the commentary in Chinese publications was at least as anti-Russian as it was anti-American. It clocked, one after another, the failures, and only the failures, of the Soviet space program. The lone exception was a note in *Peking Review* that China had sent condolences to the U.S.S.R. upon the death of three cosmonauts killed while their spacecraft was reentering the Earth's atmosphere.

But far more fun to read than the predictable political harangues were the stories of moral uplift, the object lessons, the tales of heroism, frequently illustrated with photographs, that showed not only the courage and virtue of the people, but always the benign wisdom of Chairman Mao. Many times too they offered the premise that anybody can do anything, that the meanest peasant can find a solution to a problem that somehow escapes the expert.

One such tale was unforgettable: I found myself reading it time and again. It dealt with a Chinese peasant woman, who on account of exposure to "counter-revolutionary revisionists" had developed a giant tumor in her abdomen. Her "class brothers and sisters," including the cooks in the village where they lived, held meetings to discuss the "ten what-to-do's" that would permit them to perform the delicate surgery necessary to save the woman's life.

> A hard struggle lasting more than twenty days and nights produced altogether some 120 concrete measures to solve the "ten what-to-do's". Thus, a plan which represented the wisdom of many revolutionary fighters was drawn up for the operation.
>
> At 7:30 a.m. on March 23, all of the members of the health section solemnly pledged in front of Chairman Mao's portrait: "We will follow your teaching, 'Heal the wounded, rescue the dying, practise revolutionary humanitarianism.' We will do everything possible to remove this giant tumour and enable the patient to recover so that she can live and work happily in the great

> epoch of Mao Tse-tung." Chang Chiu-chu [the ill woman] herself recited Chairman Mao's quotation: "Be resolute, fear no sacrifice and surmount every difficulty to win victory." Her mind completely at ease, she lay calmly on the operating table.
>
> The operation began. Just as expected, critical situations developed one after another. No more than five minutes after the anaesthetic was given, Chang found it difficult to breathe. Her blood pressure and her heartbeat quickened and her face was bathed in cold sweat. The leader of the army unit of which the health section was a part immediately encouraged the medical workers with Chairman Mao's teaching: "What we need is an enthusiastic but calm state of mind and intense but orderly work."
>
> A new difficulty arose as soon as the abdomen was opened. The tumour was covered with a membrane. Was this the tumour membrane or the permanent? They could not clearly judge at that moment. Guided by Chairman Mao's instruction, "Our duty is to hold ourselves responsible to the people. Every word, every action, every policy must conform to the people's interests . . ." they made up their minds to find out what the membrane was whatever the difficulties . . .*

Needless to say, some hours and several quotations later the surgery ended successfully, and the convalescing Chang Chiu-chu was photographed admiring her tumor. Even stories with less happy endings had the element of moral victory in the people's cause, though some of it might seem strange to people from the outside world. Take the case, for instance, of The Hero Who Conquered the Flood. This was a man who left his wife

*Collaborator's Note: This extract appears here verbatim as an authentic example of the popular magazine literature of the People's Republic of China. Mary Ann Harbert's memory of what she had read while there—and where and when—made it possible to locate this and the many other items she has cited in the back-issues stacks of the Asian collection in the Sinclair Library at the University of Hawaii—C.E.

and children during a driving rainstorm to help shore up a dam threatened by rising waters. The dam began to give way and he knew his family would be drowned in the torrent. Selflessly, he kept working on the dam, while two other workers went instead to save his loved ones.

Speaking for myself, I found it easy to understand why the Chinese would consider this heroic behavior on the husband's part. What was less easy for me to understand was what purpose was served by his staying to work on the dam if the price of his sacrifice was that two other workers had to leave.

My favorite of all, however, was a translation of the works of Lu Hsün, which Lee had given me at the Harbor. A writer of parables, short stories, and essays, he had gained an international reputation before his death in 1936. His wit and satire spared no one, left- and right-winger alike, but so beloved are his works that to this day both Taiwan and Peking claim him as their own.

"How good Chinese food is!" he wrote at one point. "Foreigners love it! It is so sanitary!" Then a new paragraph which begins: "What food are these people eating?"

In a way, Lu Hsün could be called, I suppose, the Aesop of China, although, just as in the case of Aesop himself, perhaps there is no telling whether his fables of ancient folklore were stories of his own invention or brilliantly told recreations of age-old legends.

I remember most of all in this connection Lu Hsün's tale of two spirits, a brother and sister, who in truth were chrysanthemums who had taken human form. The sister had taken a mortal for a husband, and the three of them lived together in genial harmony, except for one small thing: the brother liked to drink.

One night he got really drunk—his sister's husband had never seen him so bad off before—and he reeled out of the house, tore off his clothes, and stood there naked, his arms flung outward and upward. He was posing as a flower, and before the husband's startled eyes his feet seemed to begin to take root, his hands to blossom.

Rushing from the house, the wife cried sharply to her husband: "Don't look!" He turned away, and she uprooted her brother, threw his clothes back on him. With that, he returned to human form, and when the husband next looked, his wife was screaming at her brother. "How could you get so drunk?" she cried.

Time went by, and the brother took to drinking again. Once again he became violently drunk, and this time the husband, more curious and not so afraid as before, followed him out of the house. Once more the brother threw off his clothes and posed as a flower. This time the husband tried to uproot him, but at his touch the chrysanthemum started to die.

Too late, the wife came rushing out of the house. "You weren't supposed to watch!" she wailed to her husband. All that remained of her brother was a dying chrysanthemum. Tenderly, she took a cutting from the plant, replanted it in a flower pot, and took it in the house to care for it. Faithfully, she watered it each day, but nothing happened: it was as withered as ever.

Then an idea came to her. One day, instead of watering the chrysanthemum, she poured a little wine over it instead. Instantly the flower opened and bloomed into life. From that day to this, the potted chrysanthemum is given a little wine each day, and if visitors become curious, the husband says: "My brother-in-law drinks. Smell the chrysanthemum if you don't believe me."

Dirty Dirty Dirty had a small round voice that fit his small round body. His English pronunciation was the worst of any translator's I had heard. He was the kind of man who should have been anything but what he was.

"Imagine!" he cried. He was seated in my room, reading from one of the English-language magazines he had brought me. "Worker productivity in Albania increased thirty-two percent last year."

"I read it," I said. I would be lying on the bed, with my arm over my eyes.

"But thirty-two percent!" he said.

"I know."

"Isn't it fascinating?"

"I don't know about you," I said, "but I'm going to go to sleep."

He didn't understand. "But if something is fascinating, why can't we discuss it?"

"I already read it," I said again. "I know every word."

"Then you know about the increase? An increase of thirty-two percent in worker productivity in Albania?"

"I'm going to sleep."

"It isn't as if I invented it," he said. "It says it here, in this article."

My eyes would be closed, my breathing deep and regular. I might even try a snore or two at him.

Finally he would give up and go away. I could make him sad, but never angry. Among other things, he was the only interpreter I met who couldn't memorize the sayings of Chairman Mao. He tried and tried, but to no avail. The closest he came was with respect to the saying about the need to be self-critical. If I went to sleep while he was quoting the statistics on Albanian workers, the fault had to lie with him, on account of some failure on his part to sustain my interest. And so he would come back the next day and try again, as eager as ever. "Yes, yes!" he would say, in response to anything you said, as though you had just reported the discovery of plutonium. (Actually, he was the only one who used "Yes, yes" in that way. By now I had learned that "Yes, yes" was simply verbal punctuation, signifying nothing. If you said merely "Yes," that meant merely, "I heard you." As for "No," you never said it.)

The other translators laughed at him behind his back, even Miss Fanatic, who seldom laughed at anything. And by now the other translators included a newcomer, a young, short, fat girl, with eyeglasses down on her nose. Miss Fanatic, Don't Make Waves, and I had met her on one of our walks in the hillside behind the hotel of the Commune of the Happy People. She had, I think, just moved in that day. I think she was there on vacation: there is no evidence she ever had been assigned to me. Among other things, she had just started to learn English.

We saw her the next day, and the day after that. By the third day, she was wearing exactly the same kind of clothes that Miss Fanatic wore. Her message was simple and clear: she wanted Miss Fanatic to like her. She wanted to be friends. For if she were friends with Miss Fanatic, she could spend more time with me, and if she spent more time with me, that meant more time with Don't Make Waves. As for getting Don't Makes Waves to like her, that was no problem. From the moment we met her on the hillside pathway, he had flipped for her.

I knew this, and Miss Fanatic knew it, and it began to grow into a kind of silent contest between us, much more enjoyable for me, I should say, than those repeated sessions in which I found myself retreating into American Legion language in order to defend my country. It was not that I minded defending the U.S., but I resented the need for it under such circumstances.

The contest was simply laid out: Miss Fanatic disapproved of the attraction between Don't Make Waves and the new girl. I didn't. Far from it, I thought it was delightful. Shades of *Hello, Dolly,* I found myself hatching plans to promote the courtship.

The Chinese have a saying, far more meaningful, I was to discover, than anything in the works of Mao Tsetung. It is indeed a very simple saying. What it says is: *Don't borrow other people's towels.*

At the Commune of the Happy People, I had no choice. Towels would be taken away. Other towels would come back. It happens in hotels everywhere.

What also happens at hotels everywhere is that the guests may do pretty much as they please, and so it was at the Commune of the Happy People. In this atmosphere of holiday, of freedom, of being waited on, I took it on myself to do my own thing—to nap when I felt like it, to add verses to my song, to walk in the woods with Don't Make Waves and his girlfriend—even one day, at nap time, to sneak outside by myself to wrest a piece of forbidden fruit from a litchi tree. No one was watching. I plucked at the fruit and felt a terrible stab of pain. I had been bitten by a huge beetle. Instantly, two fingers on my right hand swelled far beyond their normal size. *This is what comes from stealing in China,* I told myself. I thought I would have to call a doctor. If that happened, it would give the whole thing away. Instead, for two days I plunged my hand in running water. The swelling receded. *If this is the worst that happens to you here,* I said to myself, *then count your blessings.* The blessings were rapidly counted. I had been in the hotel no more than six weeks when Miss Fanatic barged into my room. It was quite late at night.

"Get up! Get up!" she ordered.

I sat up in bed. "Get up? Why should I get up?"

"The master wants his house back."

"The master wants his house back? I thought you didn't have masters in China."

"We don't."

"Then the house doesn't belong to him."

"No, but he belongs to the house. You're being moved. Get up!"

Well I was born at the bottom of a wishing well
But I ended up goin' thru the gates of hell
Well I tried a few oranges and a little wine
But I ended up goin' thru the gates of hell

Well the stars are far and the earth is here
But men seek the truth from distant worlds
Well the truth they know is all around
But the truth ain't so and they know that too

Well the world is new and the life is strong
But the air is heavy with life's worn song
Well distant worlds may sing another
But the air they breathe is just as heavy

Maoist philosophy imposes a ritual privilege upon old people in China. Periodically, they are required "to recall past bitterness." Interestingly, such obligation is not imposed on younger people, perhaps on the assumption that, under Mao Tse-Tung, they don't have that much bitterness to recall.

Where that would classify me, I'm not that certain. I do know that the trip by night from the hotel of the Commune of the Happy People to my next place—which was *another* hotel of the Commune of the Happy People—was, as I was to discover the next day, almost literally just that: the difference between night and day.

The trip from one to the other was made in a beat-up old car—always, it seemed, my next destination would be forecast by the kind of vehicle that took me there—and in describing the new hotel, it strikes me that possibly I ought to describe "hotel", the word itself. These places *were* hotels, but in the rustic sense we all associate with a country inn, for they had in common that they were *small:* maybe two other bedrooms besides mine, or three. Something else ought to be said: with the possible exception of Don't Make Waves's girlfriend at the first hotel, and I'm not even sure about her, I was always the only guest.

This time there was no peanut candy, no oranges. When we reached the new place—the trip took barely half an hour—we were greeted by an array of guards. "We" included Miss Fanatic and Don't Make Waves.

The first thing they did was take away my razor, fingernail file, tweezers, even the crochet needle Lee had given me at the Harbor.Then they started searching my luggage.

"Why?" I railed at Don't Make Waves. "Haven't you already searched me enough times?"

He shrugged. "We're under a different system now."

"How can you have a different system? What happened to your centralization?"

Don't Make Waves laughed at that. He was conceding I had a point, but I didn't think it was funny. It became even less funny when now they took away my scissors and thread, even my nail clipper.

"We'll try to get them back for you if you need them," Don't Make Waves promised me, uncertainly.

"What I need is to be where I was yesterday," I said. "What did I do to deserve this?"

But of course it wasn't a question of what I'd done. I'd had six weeks in what passed for a fancy hotel, to get over what they must have known I knew was the death of my friend, and six weeks was enough. Now it was time to remind me of my status again.

And remind me they did. But meanwhile, subtly, the brainwashing process was at work. Look at what I had just said: it wasn't that I wanted to be out of China; it was simply that I wanted to be back where I had been *in* China.

The new place lay to the south of the first hotel, and the building that housed me was a close but inferior copy. The furniture was of poor quality—here again I had a desk, but with a big crack in it. You could tell from the condition of the walls that the roof leaked. And there were insects everywhere.

In the bathroom, the plumbing was older-style than at the northern hotel, and the hot water was delivered only at certain times of the day, generated by a thermal spring. The tub had an outlet at the top that passed for a shower-head—actually, it was no more than the open

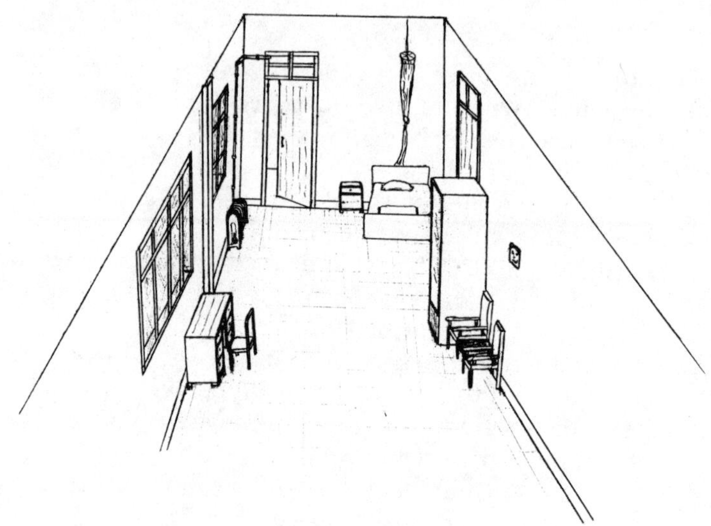

My room at the second Commune of the Happy People.

end of a pipe—but just as I could not share the Chinese passion for hot drinking water, I could not share their love for cold baths, and the tub itself was useless, for it was in the shape of a tiny square with the highest possible sides.

"I prefer showers," Miss Fanatic said to me.

"Under the circumstances," I said, "so do I."

The bath connected with my room, as had been true at the Harbor and the first hotel. My room led onto a central hall where there were dishes in cupboards, chairs of all descriptions—wicker chairs, carved chairs, straight chairs—and a dining table where, once again, a waitress brought my meals. Once again here, the kitchen was in another building, and if I had any remaining doubts that I was in for a rough time, the opposite "proof" appeared the first breakfast of the first day I was there: an absolutely unbelievable set of pastries—light, fluffy, delicately sugared, flaking just where they should flake. With them came a demi-tasse of strong coffee, not hard to take either.

By now, I was totally aware of the rule of thumb: the better the first meal, the better to expect the worst from then on. And the worst arrived. At this second hotel, a typical lunch might consist of a dish of sweet potatoes, a bowl of rice, two dishes of white potatoes (one french fried, one boiled). From time to time there could be a vegetable. From time to time, too, there could be meat, but it was usually rancid. The exceptions, when they came, would coincide with Chinese holidays. Then one might expect an edible dish of fish, chicken, or goose. A dish with three slices of cucumber was a treat. From the pack-every-other-day of cigarettes that I was supplied with, I had developed a genuine cigarette cough, and the Chinese had a prescription for this: raw olives steeped in brine, which would arrive periodically with one or another of my meals. "Olives are good for your cough," they told me, but I noticed nobody else ate them.

The egg dishes were perhaps the strangest of all. "Old" or "preserved" eggs were served here, just as they were at the first hotel—on the menu at a Chinese restaurant in the U.S. they're called "thousand-year-old eggs" —and these can be tasty indeed. But to be so, they'd better be old to begin with. What was offered me at the new place was the horrible inter-stage in between: an egg that was, say, twenty days old. A twenty-day-old egg is a rotten egg.

There was sweet-and-sour pork too, and when it was offered it tasted good, but the rest of the pork was terrible. I found myself yearning peculiarly for the food the way it used to be at the Harbor.

They had no oven for baking there, and the sanitary conditions were hardly of the highest order, but at least the soup was full-bodied, and I had come to learn the meaning of a phrase my parents had related to me only vaguely from the time of the Great Depression, that soup can sustain life.

Here at the second hotel in the Commune of the Happy People, they had ovens. Once again here too they had washing machines. So once again my towels would go out to be replaced by other towels. The significance of this had not occurred to me at the first hotel, nor as yet at this second one. But it was going to come, and with frightening impact.

For the moment I had other things to worry about. My movements here were far more restricted. The same river that ran past the first hotel ran past this one, too, and to the side of the building there was a steep mountainside. Once again here I would be permitted to go for walks, but for a much shorter distance. There were poisonous snakes here, I was told. I wasn't afraid of snakes, but Miss Fanatic was, just as I was afraid of insects. Each of us knew the other's weakness. Once she captured a cricket, brought it to my room in cupped hands, then let it fly up in my face. When I yelled she laughed.

Directly outside the hotel on the mountain side was a brief, steep climb up a bluff, then a brief level area, then the mountain itself. It was on that level area that it was decided we should play badminton. With my cough, I couldn't play it for more than five minutes at a time, but it was a diversion, and outside of *Alice in Wonderland* you could not imagine a more marvelous place to play badminton. There was a drop on one side, a rising mountain on the other. There was no net. Just off center, in the imaginary cross-line where the net should have been, was a large tree. And there we played badminton —but not before the guards came and built a fence of matting to shield us from the river and the people beyond the rear court.

For the first time it occurred to me why the guards were there at all.

They were not to protect me. They were to protect others from me.

* * *

If that was all the guards were for, it would have been one thing. But here and now they began actively to harass me. They were everywhere. They stared into my bathroom. "Get me curtains!" I said to Miss Fanatic. "Why?" she said. "They can't see in."

I would shake my head and look at her. "How do you know they can't see in?"

"Because I have a room and bath next to yours, and they can't see in mine."

"Because you have curtains."

"Who told you I have curtains?"

"I've seen your room," I said. "I've seen the curtains."

"You are getting curtains for yourself," she said. "What you don't understand is that these things take time."

"Like the man who dug away at the mountain?" I said. "How much time do you think I have?"

"Oh," she said, "you have a lot of time, Miss Harbert. You have a lot of time."

The guards stared at me, and from time to time one of them would come and scratch his hand across the screen of my bedroom window. One night at twilight, the guard outside my bedroom—totally equipped with hand grenades, automatic sub-machine gun, bayonet—tried staring me into the ground. I stared back. Now his relief came, another soldier equally equipped with arms. The rule was that when the new man came, the first man left. But instead, this time, the two of them, fully armed, stood together, both of them staring at me.

I charged out of my room and into the hall, beating on the door of the room across the hall where I thought the interpreters were. What I didn't know was that the interpreters had moved to a room at the very end of the hall. So I was beating on a door that didn't answer, and as I did so something like fifteen armed guards poured into the area from the outside. It was a great comedy of errors. The new guards were there not for me, but to see a movie that was to be shown within the building that evening. But seeing me, in my hysterical knocking, they tried to force me back into my room.

I was entitled to cross the hall to see my translators. And they were not entitled to gang up on me. Even the outside guard, staying on after his relief man arrived, violated the rules thereby.

In the bedlam there was an outpouring of interpreters from the back room. They backed me up. I *was* entitled to be outside my room in the hall. The rule *was* that as soon as the outside guard was replaced, he had to leave.

There was a barrage of conversation in Chinese, and soon all the soldiers disappeared, all except the one who had replaced the guard outside. He stayed, and he had no business within the building. I challenged him on it.

"Ask him what he's doing standing where he is," I said to one of the interpreters.

A violent exchange of talk. Then back came the answer:

"He says he doesn't know anything. He just got here."

The black fan moved slowly back and forth before the dark rims of his eyeglasses. Black Fan was back. Through an interpreter, he said:

"You are dissatisfied with the people who have been appointed to guard you?"

"That's not all I'm dissatisfied with," I said.

"I see. Then there's something else besides?"

"Yes."

"And what could that be?"

"What happened to my companion?"

"Who?"

"Jerry McLaughlin."

"Oh, him."

(This being through an interpreter, certain things must be understood: not all interpreters chose to interpret exactly what was said, if only for the sake of not unduly inflaming the exchange; by the same token, a facial expression or a tone of voice could give away what was being said in the other tongue even before, or if, the translator chose to set it in the opposite language. In this one case I *knew* Black Fan knew who I was talking about, and I said so. The interpreter readily confessed it. "I was just asking for my own information," he said.)

Now, Black Fan said: "Don't worry about him. Worry about yourself."

"First give me an answer about my companion."

"There is no answer to give."

Our eyes met, and what was perhaps the one most memorable single memory I have of my time in China was in that look that passed between us. It was a look of pure antagonism, yet at the same time one of perfect understanding. *I am doing my job,* Black Fan's eyes told me, *and I am a professional. I show up only from time to time, because I have other things to do. And you comprehend this, do you not?*

And my look told him, *I comprehend it. But you aren't dealing with one of your automatic textbook subjects. You're dealing with an American citizen and you know it. More than that, you know it's something a little different than anything you've ever dealt with before, because otherwise you wouldn't even be here, would you? You wouldn't have put me up at your nicest mountain hotel. You grabbed two people and you're stuck with the one that lived . . .*

In that moment, we both smiled at each other.

But that's all it was: a moment. "If you insist on opposing the prevailing security provisions," Black Fan said, "we will have no choice but to bring charges against you."

I said, "You should have brought them against me long before now."

"You think we do not know how to bring charges?"

"I think you know how to do anything. You can bring me to trial. Why don't you do that? You can beat me. Why don't you do that?"

"Do you know what you risk, talking like this?"

"I risk nothing worse than what I am now, a monkey in a cage."

That last was translated to Black Fan, and for a moment he looked away. Then he fixed his eyes on mine once again.

"You are leaving something out."

"I'm leaving nothing out."

"You are leaving out," he said, "the confession of error."

This was translated to me. I said, "What confession of error did I leave out? That we trespassed? I've already confessed it. My companion confessed it. He confessed it and you let him die."

Back came the answer, sharp: "You have no knowledge he's dead."

I said, "I know he's dead and you know he's dead."

Back came the answer, turning the point around: "Then is there any reason, if you trespassed, why you should not be held in detention?"

Back came my answer: "You just said it yourself: *IF* you trespassed. I've said we did because there was no way to say it otherwise."

"But your companion confessed to it."

"The same way I did. And because he was physically sick. You knew he was sick. You could have saved him."

"And saved you at the same time?"

I had to ask the interpreter what that meant. It went back and forth a time or two, and then it became clear what Black Fan was saying:

"By *confession of error,* I meant nothing relating to your boat. The confession of error I had in mind had to do with your decision that you now believe the People's

Republic of China states the proper political philosophy, whereas the United States does not."

Do you know what you risk, talking like this? Black Fan had said.

Or had he said it? Was it instead a kind of "code" meant for me? When I had said *Why don't you beat me?*, did the interpreter actually translate that to Black Fan? Or was the interpreter, in solicitude for me, trying to "cool it" instead? As I've already said, they did that from time to time. As I've said too, tone of voice and facial expression would give it away anyway, on some occasions. But as to the words themselves, you could never be totally sure.

I would ask the interpreters afterward but, whether they liked me or not, they would be very cautious in their replies, if they replied at all. The ones who liked me were especially caught up in the private politics of the situation. Their bond with me was that we spoke English. They felt superior to the soldiers on that account, but at the same time loyal to the government. But the soldiers *were* the government.

"You have it better than most prisoners," one of the interpretors said to me at one point. "That's why it might be best to cooperate."

"You just said it," I said.

"Said it?"

"Prisoner. You called me a prisoner."

She shook her head, embarrassed. "No, I used the wrong word! You're a *detainee, not* a prisoner!"

From the look on her face, I saw she was terrified I might put in a complaint against her: that she had called me a prisoner.

"It's all right," I said to her. "I know it was a mistake."

"I didn't mean it," she said.

"I know you didn't."

It put my thoughts back to the summer of 1967, when

my field work at college consisted of driving from Salt Lake City to a place called Point of the Mountain. I'd hitch a ride with a boy and girl who were in my class, and the girl and I would go together to the women's section of the Utah State prison there, to learn how a social worker works. The project lasted eight weeks; two days a week. The women's section was modern: no bars on the windows, carpets on the floor, nice new plumbing.

The other girl and I were supposed to hold "group therapy" sessions with the prisoners. We met with four or five of them at a time in a kind of "classroom." The prisoners had been through it all before. We hadn't.

"We don't have any pencil or paper," the other girl announced, the first day we met with them. The reason she said this was to assure the inmates we did not intend to make a written record of anything they had to say. Thus we would gain their confidence.

So much for that theory. "Look," one of the prisoners said, "grab the piece of chalk and take us one at a time and just put our histories on the blackboard. That's how it's done."

It took until I was a prisoner in China—no, not a prisoner: a *detainee*—before the impact of those sessions set in. We had said "please" and "thank you" to the inmates at Point of the Mountain, perhaps because courtesy costs nothing, but perhaps also a little bit because we were frightened at being cast so new among prisoners who so obviously knew more about our work than we did. And I was to receive that same politeness from most of the interpreters assigned to me in China. Seldom if ever did I hear an order from them. Instead, it would be, "Why don't we . . . ?" or "Wouldn't it be better if we . . . ?"

I learned not one lesson but two. In China at first I resented the polite approach. *Why pretend it?* I asked myself. *It doesn't exist in this situation. So why do they do it?*

But lesson number one was there. It was there in my "staring contests" with the guards, not because staring at somebody was important but because human dignity is important, and you hold on to whatever you have. But it was there too in the politeness of the translators, not only in ordinary conversation but in the way I now know they sought to divert and blunt verbal exchanges between me and officials who only spoke Chinese. From a factor of zero, this came to have more and more significance for me, for in actuality it was a mark of human respect. And that answered my question: *Why do they do it?*

I don't mean to be naive—of course I had the sense of it. But it was never really driven home to me until my captivity in mainland China. It is not hard to comprehend the importance of simple courtesy downward, from jailer to prisoner. What I came to appreciate was the importance of simple courtesy in the opposite direction: upward, from prisoner to jailer. It was not merely a question of *If I'm nice to them, they'll be nicer to me:* if that were true, I still might have been at the paradise of the first hotel in the Commune of the Happy People, instead of here in the paradise lost of the second.

They valued dignity, too, and I was in a position to supply it. I felt good when the inmates of the Utah prison were kind to me. No less did my "social workers" feel good if I were kind to them.

There was of course one difference. The women I worked with at the Utah prison had been sentenced. But nobody had ever sentenced me. A sentence carried with it a time factor: you are sentenced for one year, or five, or ten, or whatever. And beyond the sentence therefore is the factor of release.

And when you foresee release, you can make concessions, particularly because they can speed the time of release itself. This is, in effect, the basis of the "good behavior" parole system as we know it.

Now the Chinese had "offered" me the same thing. If

I would tell them the United States was wrong, they would release me—that was what Black Fan had said. (But had he actually said it, or was this a translator's inducement, to hush an angry exchange between us and make things easier on me?)

But it was all wrong. One reason why it was wrong was that I had done nothing wrong myself, had committed no offense, that is, against the People's Republic of China, other than having been a passenger aboard a boat that trespassed in her waters (if that's what our boat did). Repentance comes easier, I suppose, when you have something to repent.

Under those circumstances, something else was equally wrong. The theory that the captured airman or soldier will turn against his country in order to gain his release is long cherished, I know, particularly in the Far East. What he says is: *My government ordered me to do it . . . I didn't want to do it.* Not all of them say that, I know, but it is there to be said if they so elect.

I don't know if the Chinese expected the same thing of me. If there were some things I had not yet learned about them, then there were also some things they had not yet learned about me. On one level, it did dishonor to common sense—was I about to take pencil to paper and write that my imperialist, reactionary, militaristic government had ordered me to go sailing in a sloop with a man I'd never even had a date with before?

On another level, it did dishonor to me. In fact, it backfired. I found myself approaching a near-jingoistic level of patriotism I'd never known before. I confess, indeed, that secretly it pleased me that I could vex them with it. I would tell Miss Fanatic about the typical American home, with its carpeting and television and two cars in the garage, and its dishwashers and toasters and air conditioning, and so forth and so on, and I could see it driving her to a fury. If she heard of a Communist living that way, she wouldn't have resented it—that was the curious part—but the more she knew about how the imperialistic Americans lived, the more she refused to accept it.

In this manner, the Chinese blundered in their approach to me. Yet that was no victory on my part, because they owned me and I didn't own them. They could keep me as long as they wanted. If they held out the carrot on the stick and I didn't bite, so what? They'd wait two weeks and hold it out again. If I screamed at their officials, so what? The interpreters wouldn't translate what I said. One great lesson I learned was that when a man says to you, "Do this or I'll kill you," it's very easy to say, "Kill me." But when they don't threaten it to begin with, you sound a little stupid.

The most horrifying thing of all was that I discovered, in little bits and pieces, that I was becoming "Chinese". Day after day I would have the sayings of Chairman Mao drilled into me, and of course it did not take much repetition, unless you were somebody like Dirty Dirty Dirty, before you began to know them by rote. It had surprised me, at the Island and the Harbor, that I found myself beginning to memorize the sayings and the other things—the same songs played over the loudspeaker, for instance. It surprised me because they were new, and because they were new I paid attention to them—much more attention (this was the surprise) than the Chinese seemed to. It took me a while to realize they had no need to pay attention to them. They were going to hear them day in and day out in any event. So what I took to be a sign of their being slow to learn, began to dawn on me instead for the fact it was: they didn't learn in a hurry because they had no need to learn in a hurry. It made great good sense, and I found myself following their example.

I fought it. Once I had my own silverware, I would not use chopsticks. I would not dress my hair in pigtails. I would sing western songs. I would be *me:* Mary Ann Harbert, and I would *stay* me.

Some of this was the result of determination, but a lot

of it was habit: I'd never learned to eat a fried egg with chopsticks, and with a knife and fork available I wasn't about to start now. And some of it, in truth, was accident: I might have wanted to try to learn to speak and write Chinese, but I had always found foreign languages difficult, and in this case my interpreters were so anxious to improve their English they seldom if ever pressed their own language on me.

The net effect of all this, nevertheless, was one of resistance: an adherence to my ways which had to be, by implication, a rejection of theirs. My captors knew this, and they tested it. Time and again they would act simply to see how I would react. When I reached the second hotel of the Commune of the Happy People, after the brief but easy time I'd had of it at the first one, they took away all my personal belongings. That had to be a test, a way of separating me from the familiar. I don't know what they expected—maybe that I'd dissolve into tears. And I didn't dissolve into tears.

"I thought you were going to cry last night," Don't Make Waves said to me the next morning. "We all thought so."

I looked at him. "Would you have cried?"

"If I had been you?"

"Yes."

"I can't answer," he said. "I'm not a woman."

"But you would have expected a woman to cry."

"Maybe."

"You just said so—you thought I was going to cry."

"Yes," he said. "But they call you the girl who doesn't cry."

Don't Make Waves seemed sad. I said to him, "Where is your friend?"

"My friend?" he said.

"The girl you met at the last hotel."

His face lit up. "Ah," he said. "Do you know that she's

educated in management and bookkeeping? This qualifies her for anything!"

He was right. In China, it does. Anyone with a formal education is regarded with a sort of awe and elevated to the highest positions, so that an accountant can find himself in charge of an agricultural project, a music major in charge of machinery (I've heard it said the U.S. army operates the same way with its draftees, but in China it happens all over—thus a cook, if he has any education, can take charge of abdominal surgery, as happened in an episode already recounted here. And, as also recounted, the Chinese are quick to celebrate the innovative work of the "non-expert" as opposed to the expert. It is almost as if the country is one large suggestion box. But by the same token this has its reasons and its limits. Any country that can "turn over" 750 million people as fast as China's cultural revolution "turned over" its population must have vast pockets where non-experts are given free rein simply because experts do not, at that place at that time, exist. But in the great hospitals, it is not a cook who performs surgery upon you—it is a doctor. And in the great restaurants, it is not a doctor who prepares the meal—it is the cook.

Now I said to Don't Make Waves, "But where is she? Your friend?"

"At the place where you last were," he said.

Miss Fanatic came into my room. She said, impatiently, "What are you talking about?"

I said, "We left the last hotel so fast, I left some books behind."

She said, "What books? Your sketches? Your poems? Your songs? The dictionary you ruined by tracing the flowers?"

"No," I said. "The books you gave me. The Story of the Long March. Some one must bring this to me."

"Ah," she said. "Suddenly you are interested in the Long March."

I said, "I am trying to learn about China, which is what you want me to do. I understand you have no way of getting in touch with the previous place without sending a letter or making the trip back there yourself."

"We have telephones in China," she said coldly. "If you want books, you can have them within an hour."

"How?" I asked.

She jerked a thumb toward Don't Make Waves. "We will telephone that friend of his. She'll bring them."

"I don't believe it," I said. "In the United States, yes. But not here in China."

"No?" she said. "That girl will be here before today is over. This is my guarantee to you. You just watch."

Don't Make Waves was sitting there, blinking. His girlfriend was coming to be with him again, on orders of the one person most dedicated to breaking up their romance.

And before nightfall, she was there.

"Did you bring the books?" Miss Fanatic said to her.

"What books?" Don't Make Waves's girl said. "All you told me was to be here as fast as possible."

"With the account of the Long March."

"I couldn't find the account of the Long March. She must have taken it with her."

All this had taken place in Chinese—Don't Make Waves translated it for me later. All I was aware of at the time was that Don't Make Waves's girl was there, and that suddenly Miss Fanatic began tearing through the titles of the books on top of the desk in my room. Inevitably, she ran across the book that contained the account of the Long March.

She leveled a finger at me. "You had this book all the time."

"Is the Long March in it?"

"Of course the Long March is in it! I'll find you the place." She riffled the pages, then flung the book at me.

I said, "But it's called *From the Masses, to the Masses.*

How was I supposed to remember the Long March was in it?"

"It's not what *you're* supposed to remember," Miss Fanatic said, and she turned on Don't Make Waves's girl. "If you had no book to bring, why did you come?"

"The officials made me," Don't Make Waves's girl said. "They transferred me."

"Why?"

"Because they wanted to make sure Miss Harbert had an account of the Long March. You told them on the telephone she didn't. You told them to send me."

More important than the Long March was, to me, the short march, the little distance I was allowed to walk up the mountainside each afternoon. Don't Make Waves and his girl would go with me, and Miss Fanatic too, looking for snakes.

"Do you dance?" Don't Make Waves asked me one day, as we were returning from our walk.

"Yes," I said. "I like to dance."

"Then we'll all dance when we get back to the building," he said.

"No," Miss Fanatic said.

Don't Make Waves said to her, "You're embarrassed to dance."

"No," Miss Fanatic said again. Don't Make Waves may have been right, perhaps it would embarrass someone as up-tight as Miss Fanatic to dance. What probably influenced her even more, though, was the prospect that somebody might catch her dancing in the presence of her American captive.

Now she said, "I think there should be no dancing. By anyone."

"But why?" Don't Make Waves said. "Dancing is an honored part of Chairman Mao's cultural scheme."

"Not the kind of dancing Miss Harbert does," Miss Fanatic said.

And so we wound up in the large hall area outside my room, Miss Fanatic and I sitting in chairs while Don't Make Waves and Don't Make Waves's girl danced in front of us. Their zest for it, and for each other, was infectious, albeit it was not dancing in any familiar Western sense of the word (though the music they sang, while Miss Fanatic and I sat there and clapped our hands to the rhythm, had the same odd "Western" touch to it that was common to all the music I heard in China). What they did resemble more than anything was the old American game of "statues," where you take several steps, then suddenly freeze in a pose. "It is a loyalty dance in praise of Chairman Mao," Miss Fanatic told me, and I'm sure she believed it, but to me it told a story as old as dancing itself, the story of the pursuit within courtship. And obviously it had extra meaning for Don't Make Waves and his girl.

A few days later, I said to him, "Why do you suppose we can't take longer walks up the mountain?"

"It isn't safe," he explained.

"Maybe if you explored it, it would prove to be safe," I said. "You and your friend could explore it together."

His face lit up. "We could try it, certainly."

"It would be official business," I said. "You're doing it in connection with me."

"Of course," he said. "And to be successful, it would have to be a complete exploration."

"Yes," I said. "Very thorough. You can't be sure if you just make one trip."

And so Don't Make Waves and his girl began to go off together. One time when they came back, they brought me flowers. Another time they came to my room after one of their walks, and the thin summer trousers of Don't Make Waves showed an unmistakable sign of male arousal. He knew I had noticed it, and to cover his embarrassment he moved across the room with little high steps, like the wolf whipping from behind one tree to another in a Looney Tunes cartoon—and busied himself at my desk. "I have to find something in one of your books," he said.

He and his girl were in a room down the hall one day when a little bird flew in the window and injured itself —I think it had a broken wing. They brought the bird to me, and together we made a little tether-and-stake arrangement for it outside, tying string to its foot.

Miss Fanatic came upon the scene and said, "Why are you doing that?"

"So we can take care of it and feed it till it gets better," I said.

"It won't get better," she said.

"Somebody has to take care of it," I said.

"What will you feed it?"

"Worms."

"Where will you get worms?"

"They crawl up out of the drain of my sink," I said. "Finding a worm is the smallest problem I've had since I came to China."

"They don't crawl up out of the drain of *my* sink," Miss Fanatic said.

I shrugged. "Obviously they prefer the company of an imperialistic capitalist. We enemies of the people stick together."

But Don't Make Waves had already dug up a worm from the earth, and now he brought it and set it before the bird, who took a couple of tentative pecks at it.

"You see?" Miss Fanatic said. "It doesn't even like worms."

I said, "How can you say that?"

"It's supposed to eat the whole thing all at once," she said.

Her dogmatism carried over into all fields, but it was in her political attitude that I could bait her most. Like a fool, I did just that. Not that I invited such discussions, but when she started them, which inevitably she would, it was impossible for me not to seize the advantage that had to be mine, and I confess I made the most of it. This advantage was not that I was smarter than Miss Fanatic, not that I was any better at debate, certainly not that I was better-prepared in the way of statistics and indoctrination. My control lay instead simply in the fact that the discussions had to take place in English, and I had the vocabulary; she didn't.

One night we had a typical argument, which as usual I won. The problem was that I won it too well. I had been getting stomach pains, and my eyes hurt, and I was beginning to find I needed a stronger light to read by. Miss Fanatic told me she would talk to the guards about it, and she did, and the result was that the reading lightbulb in my room became weaker, while a stronger bulb was transferred to the ceiling fixture in the hall outside, so that it shone in upon me, over the transom of my door, all night long while I was trying to sleep. There was a double switch for that hall light, one in my room, the other in the hall outside. Every time I got out of bed to switch the light off, somebody on the outside would switch it back on again. (I'm not saying that by speaking to the guards, Miss Fanatic had *ordered* this new form of harassment—they could think up plenty on their own: they needed only, as Chairman Mao puts it, to "seize the moment," which of course in this and so many other cases they did.)

But in my physical and mental state of the moment, I was not geared to be accommodating during a political discussion, and this one night, when Miss Fanatic started up with it, I turned on her almost in fury.

"If you make only one of anything," I said to her, "what guarantee do you have it'll be any good? All I see here in China is one kind of toothpaste. If you don't have competition, how do you know it's any good?"

"No no no!" she replied. "Just because you only see one kind of toothpaste doesn't mean it's the only kind we make. We have many factories, the same as you."

"You have many factories?"

"Of course."

"Putting out competing brands?"

"Brands?"

"Kinds."

"Yes. Competing kinds. Competing means different?"

"That's right."

"Of course," she said, and nodded vigorously. "Competing kinds. That's exactly what we have."

"The same as we do in America?"

"Of course the same."

"Well," I said, "then you just said it yourself."

"What did I say myself?"

"You start out by telling me the difference between socialism and capitalism," I said, "and you wind up proving there is no difference. You have competing brands. We have competing brands."

She said, sullenly, "It's not just a question of toothpaste."

"I know it's not," I said. "It's a question of automobile tires, and cups and dishes, and television sets . . ." (That last was a sore point: Miss Fanatic was very proud, as was everyone else, of the new television transmission in Canton; unfortunately, because of the intervening mountains, the signal could not be received at the Commune of the Happy People.) "But," I said, "if you have different factories putting out the same kind of thing, why do you say this is something that sets your country apart from mine? All you're doing is copying us."

That tore it. "*You* oppress the workers!" she shrieked.

I said, "Who says so?"

"Chairman Mao. You have the Negro in your country. Your reactionary government, and only your reactionary government, suppresses the Negro."

I said, "That's not true."

"Chairman Mao says it's true. And Chairman Mao is right."

"Who told you he's right?"

"Chairman Mao."

Chairman Mao is right because Chairman Mao says so. There were, I know, people assigned to me who didn't really believe that, but if I say I "know" this it is because I could sense it in things they said and did, not because any of them ever chose to confide such an opinion to me outright. But whatever else Miss Fanatic was, she was not one of the doubters.

She showed it to me in the book of the Sayings:

Among the whites in the United States it is only the reactionary ruling circles who oppress the black people.

"You think that is wrong?" she said.

"I object to the word 'only,' " I said.

"Are you telling me *everybody* oppresses the Negro in your country?"

"Do you believe that?" I answered—a stupid thing for me to say: of course she didn't believe it, for Mao hadn't said it. "The point is," I said, "I know people who are against Negroes, and companies that aren't."

The shrill voice of Miss Fanatic had attracted others into the dining hall outside my room. "You have just read it for yourself! I've just shown it to you!"

"I object to the word 'only,' " I said again, and that was all I would say, and that made her even more furious. She went bursting out into the hall, slamming the door behind her, and I could hear her picking up the telephone and starting to scream in Chinese at whoever was on the other end. Intermingled with this were the voices of the others in the hall, trying to calm her down. *You've done it this time,* I said to myself. *You've really done it.* I got into bed, my knees pulled up against the pain in my stomach, to sleep and wait for what the morning would bring.

The morning brought Miss Fanatic back to my room. She was very calm. She gave me a book in which the entirety of last night's disputed Mao quotation appeared in English.

"We'll both read this together," she said. "Then we'll discuss it."

"No we won't," I said.

Non-cooperative? No doubt of it. But it seemed to me the risk was minimal. If her furious phone call last night had resulted in nothing more than this invitation to further discussion, it could mean that whoever she talked to had already decided on some form of punishment for me, and if that were so, then it was too late to do anything about it. If this session today, on the other hand, were supposed to be some sort of "second chance" for me, what good would it do me to take it? There was no way I could deny something last night only to agree with it today—not the way that quote from Mao ran—and to get into a discussion of it now might provoke another one of Miss Fanatic's outbursts. Two in a row could sign my death warrant.

Thus it seemed to me the best course was literally to do with Miss Fanatic what I had done with Mr. Wang at the Harbor—refuse to have anything more to do with her. It had worked before. It might work again. *In a way,* I told myself, *she's more vulnerable than you are. You're arguing over what something means in English, and the more she carries on, the more it can be claimed her faulty language education is what's really causing the trouble.*

And there was one other thing in my favor: the voices I had heard outside in the hall last night while she was screaming into the telephone. Maybe they were telling her she was wrong; maybe they were telling her she was making too much out of it. But either way, she evidently had not received full support from the others around us.

I don't mean by any of this that I had myself talked into the outlook that last night's blow-up had done me any good. What I do mean is that I saw, as I've said, minimal risk in refusing to "discuss it calmly" the next day. For what would happen if I did? What would the next session be like? And the one after that?

Miss Fanatic didn't press me on it. When I refused to talk with her, she stood up and left my room. I stayed where I was. I still had the stomach ache, and perhaps there is not too much nobility, actually, in taking a stand against your jailers when you're feeling physically rotten to begin with.

Very soon—it could have been the next day—Don't Make Waves came to my room and told me Miss Fanatic had asked for a transfer.

"I'll be leaving, too," he said.

"Why?" I said. "Because of the trouble the other night? You had nothing to do with that."

"No, no," he said hastily. "It is a reassignment. But—what do you call it?—an *ordinary* reassignment."

"You mean routine," I said.

"Yes," he said. "We have a routine reassignment."

"We?"

"My friend and I."

"She's going with you?"

"Oh yes."

"That should be very nice for you."

"Very nice," he agreed.

Don't Make Waves and his girl came to say their final goodbyes, and we had a little ceremony: we let the bird go. I don't know what kind of bird it was, but it was a beautiful thing, with brilliant colors, and whatever damage it had done to itself, hitting against the window screen in an effort to escape into the room, must have been more of fright than anything else, for on release it flew strongly and joyfully away.

New interpreters now were assigned to me, beginning with two girls, both in their thirties, I'd judge. Their names—*my* names for them—were Short Pigtails and Long Pigtails. Short Pigtails was big-boned, and her hair was thick but sparse, so that in places you could see her scalp. Long Pigtails had beautiful hair and was in fact a beauty in every respect. She laughed a lot, and had talent for making animals and objects out of long, thick pieces of straw, much as is done with pipe cleaners in the U.S.

One of the first things that happened when the two of them came was a formal meeting in the dining hall. Short Pigtails and Long Pigtails were there, with Short Pigtails doing most of the translating. Attending the meeting also was a man I had seen several times—he was identified to me as the "master of the house," just as the first hotel in the Commune of the Happy People also had its "master." And there were two men, attired in open sports shirts and sandals, who had come from someplace else simply to be at the meeting. Obviously they were civilian government officials.

The object of the meeting was to review my complaints.

I had them: the food, the guards, the badminton, delivery of hot water to my bathroom during the morning hours so I could do my laundry, the rules about hanging out my clothes, the light bulbs, curtains for my bathroom, the insects, the rule that said it was unnecessary to launder the bottom sheet of your bed, my right to privacy by rolling down the mosquito netting around my bed any time I chose.

I reminded them I had already had a meeting with Black Fan and had complained then about the guards. I didn't have to know Chinese to know they were insulting in the way they talked to me. I didn't like the time I swept a huge jumping spider out of my room and it tried to jump back in at me. "The guards are here to protect me," I said, knowing that wasn't strictly true. "But all they did was laugh." And there had been the time when two friends of one of the guards boosted themselves up on my windowsill and looked in on me as

I lay undressed on my bed. (Black Fan had had a great answer to that complaint: "They're only doing their duty," he'd said. "You have to be under supervision by the guards." "But they weren't guards to begin with," I replied.)

Most of all, I insisted, I had to have my fingernail file, my tweezers, and my scissors. One of the visiting officials wanted to know why I carried on so about a pair of tweezers. "Because I attach great civilization to them," I said.

The list went on and on. One recent morning, I told them, I had awakened to find plaster fallen all around me. Above the thin sheet-board ceiling of my room, rodents coursed and played—"rats in the attic," was the way I put it—and I wanted something done about it.

I suppose it is unusual for a prisoner to list demands in this manner, but it must be unusual too to stage a formal meeting to review the complaints to begin with. I decided to make the most of it. If ten percent of my complaints were listened to and I had one hundred complaints, that meant ten things would be fixed.

I didn't have one hundred complaints (though it must have seemed that way), and ten things weren't fixed, but I did get the curtains, and they did give back my cosmetic things. Even the food improved for a while.

They seemed ready to make concessions, and I tried to reason why that would be. The answer, when it came, would be one I had not expected, but by now I took favors as they occurred. And if they were ready to make concessions, I would meet them with a good spirit. I didn't even object when one of the guards, fascinated by my little vials of contact-lens fluid, experimented in unscrewing their tops. In doing so he held the vials not right-side up, as you or I would do, but sideways, actually pointed somewhat downward, so that each time the top came off the fluid ran out onto the floor. Ever since the Island, the lenses had been no good to me anyway.

Short Pigtails and Long Pigtails were my constant companions. They wanted to watch me put on my western make-up—something that would have horrified Miss Fanatic—and they took particular interest when I used my scissors on sheets of paper, cutting them up into little quadrants, then drawing symbols on each of them.

I was doing here what I had first done at the Harbor: making myself a deck of cards. I don't know how many games of solitaire I must have played since then, but with one exception—Don't Make Waves; and even then, only once—no one was anxious to play cards with me. The one time Don't Make Waves did it, Miss Fanatic had reported him.

"What do you call those?" Long Pigtails asked me, pointing to one set of symbols I had drawn.

"Diamonds."

She nodded. She knew the symbol—Chinese playing cards are the same as our own—but she didn't know the English word. "Those are funny diamonds," she said.

"They're good enough," I said.

"No," she said. "Why hasn't somebody given you real cards?"

"I never asked for them."

"You should have," she said. "The only way to get something is to ask for it."

I asked for my release, I thought, *and I didn't get that. It never occurred to me to ask for a deck of cards.*

That night the waitress brought me a bottle of Chinese beer with my dinner—it wasn't cold, but it wasn't bad—and the next day Long Pigtails and Short Pigtails presented me with a deck of playing cards.

We began to teach each other games. They liked Go Fish, but thought Gin Rummy and Canasta were too complicated. But mostly we played their games—simple games, called Seven, Red, and things like that—all of them basically variants of Old Maid or Go Fish, whose themes depended on "borrowing" cards from other players' hands.

They also brought a chess board, whose playing pieces resembled checkers. On one side of each piece was the symbol of an international chess piece as we know it. On the other side would be a different symbol for the game of "Elephant Chess" played in China.

The chess board itself was identical to the 64-square board we all know, and both girls knew how to play the game as we know it. When you turned the pieces over to play the Chinese version, not only were the symbols and moves different, but the pieces themselves operated along the lines instead of the squares. But if the Chinese version was different, it was not that hard to learn. To me the most striking difference between the two games was the broad stripe in the middle of the dividing line between the two camps on the board itself. In the Chinese version, once any piece has crossed that line it cannot return to the home side of the board. In general explanation, it is called "crossing the river," but in each section of China the river always has a name. Where we were, advancing a piece across the dividing line was called "crossing the Pearl"—for the Pearl River, the great waterway of commerce that splits the city of Canton.

Soon two new male interpreters came to stay in our building, and they liked to play cards and chess, too. One of them preferred cards—he not only preferred cards, he preferred to win. He was tall and good-looking, and he liked to flex his biceps. He also had a definitely married look about him.

By contrast, his associate, who spoke very little English, was an effeminate type. He wore girl-style sandals, with little heels. When he saw me looking at them, he would pull them back, trying to hide them. He was in his late twenties, I would judge, with a pitted, yellow complexion. He had bug eyes and buck teeth, and a brush cut. My private name for him was Quilt Brother—actually, an honorable phrase in Chinese to describe soldiers who pair off and share the same bedding. In truth, I think this has no more significance by itself than the fact that troop trains in the United States, as I've been told from the days of World War II, used to assign one man to an upper berth, two men to a lower. If any allusion to homosexuality were involved in the use of the term of "quilt brother," it might be nothing more or less than testimony to the probability that China has a more advanced and relaxed view of the subject than the countries of the West. I never saw signs of its being flaunted, but of all the places I was taken, one seeming constant would be the presence of at least one guard who was distinctly effeminate—almost always with the same physical characteristics: young, obese, high-voiced—and in fact this type is widely enjoyed in Chinese theater. And when I was being moved from one place to another at night, time and again the headlights would pick up, among the people walking along the road, couples—both men—with their arms around each other's waists.

But the one I am talking about here, the one with the brush cut and the sandals, I remember most not for his effeminacy but for his skill at chess: not Chinese chess, *our* chess. If I beat him, which I did about half the time, it was because, as frequently happens in the game, he played in a way that could only make me improve.

As I look back, it is astonishing, in a way, how many interpreters came and went. Some were reassigned, like Don't Make Waves, for reasons having nothing to do with me. Others were reassigned, like Mr. Wang, because of me. Still others were reassigned because they asked to be, and their reasons were mixed. Some of them couldn't take any more of me. Others couldn't stand being "in the middle," between me and the government. In at least one case, a girl asked to be reassigned because she was jealous of another girl who she thought was more my friend. Still others would leave me at one place, only to show up a year or more later at another. At least one—Don't Make Waves's girl—was literally assigned to me by me. And a few, most mysteriously of all, would come for no more than a week or two, then go away forever.

This last was true of Quilt Brother and his card-playing friend. One day, while Quilt Brother and I were playing chess, Short Pigtails came into my room and began caulking the cracks in the walls—where the insects came through—with paper.

My own prison is being sealed, I thought to myself.

But Quilt Brother was interested. As she later translated back to me, he asked her what she was doing, and she told him she was insect-proofing the room. He asked why she would do this for a prisoner, and she said it was because I had demanded it.

At that point in our chess game, I moved a pawn to the eighth row and exchanged it for a queen.

Quilt Brother stared sadly at the board. "There's some times," he said to me in English, "when the pawn turns into power."

The next day he and his friend were gone.

The river already was swollen that year because of the heavy seasonal rains of late spring and early summer, but there was more of it to come. Some nights I would win strange relief from the glare of the light bulb shining onto my bed through the transom, for during a thunderstorm, all the electricity would be turned off. I supposed this was because of a fear that lightning striking defective wiring might start a fire, but I never asked about it. I never asked about a lot of things. I was curious. But spies are curious, and that was an identification I was just as glad to avoid.

I had never seen such electrical storms as struck the

Commune of the Happy People. The thunder didn't roll, and it didn't clap. It pealed. I know the thunder comes after the lightning because light travels faster than sound, and I know you're supposed to be able to measure the nearness of the lightning by how short a time it takes for the thunder to follow it, but this was something else. It was a light show. As the heat of the day went down and night came on, there would be a great holding sheet of lightning, making the area outside my window brighter than bright daylight. Then before the thunder had a chance to come the area would light up again, hold itself that way, and when the thunder finally did come another sheet of lightning would be hanging white-yellow, and in the driving rain that came with it there could be periods of three and four minutes at a time of continuous stroboscopic sight and sound.

Then at the very end of the summer, there was a day when the sky was gray and the air had a thin, almost reverse feel to it, as if there were really no air at all. The interpreters told me a great typhoon was boiling over the South China Sea. But such storms, they said, followed the classic pattern, the same, I knew, that was true of the North American continent, coming off the sea from the southeast to batter and spend themselves against the eastern shore of the land mass, then circling north, then northeast and finally out to sea again. We would get some rain, they said, but we were far enough inland so that it would not affect us all that much. We might even get some thunder and lightning—but not in any appreciable amount.

And so the lights were left on that time. But then they went off, and not because any official had ordered it. Instead, the rain came, and with it a keening wind, a wind that sang the B flat above middle C, then dropped to the G, then back to the B flat again: a wind that sang, time and again, the first two notes of "Joey" from *The Most Happy Fella.* The rain drove almost horizontally against the windows of my room—my walls and ceiling spilled water—and above everything, in a curious inner vacuum of sound that covered great distances, I could hear the cries of human despair as houses along the riverbank gave way and were washed into the torrent.

In the morning the storm had passed, and you could hear most sharply a strange counterpoint of sounds. Outside my window, a guard worked away with a handsaw at the trees that had fallen during the night. From the river, I could hear the shouts of people as they dove repeatedly into the water, trying to locate and retrieve their personal belongings, and from somewhere on the riverbank the indescribably desolate sound of a man's voice, calling for . . . what? . . . his water buffalo . . . a lost child . . . who could know?

They brought buckets to my room and set them under the leaks in the ceiling. It took them a while to notice the leaks were there but given the ruined state of things, I didn't even care that much.

What's your opinion of Nixon's policies?

Note the contraction: *what's,* not *what is.* Not only frequently in speech, but *always,* it seemed, in writing, the Chinese seemed schooled for this lapse into informality. And the question about Nixon was in writing. Not only was it in writing, it had been prepared elsewhere, at some higher-up official source, and obviously the wording was chosen with great care.

I wrote:

He's been elected since I've been here—how would I know what his policies are?

A day went by. Back came another question:

What's your opinion of the Johnson-Kennedy clique?

I looked up at Short Pigtails, the messenger in this new form of quiz-by-mail.

I said to her, "Do you know what 'clique' means?"

It was a foolish question. Of course she knew. She

might not know what *plum* meant, but she would, like all the others, know what *clique* meant, for as I've said the translators had the most sophisticated words of Marxist English at their instant command. (More and more, I would hold informal "classes" for the interpreters, to drill them in vocabulary, and my most basic textbook was *Quotations from Chairman Mao.* If I tried to describe a plum or even draw one, there would be no sign of comprehension. But if Mao referred to the plum tree in my English copy of his works, I would simply point to the word *plum* and wait for them to find it in their own Chinese edition. And then they would know and nod happily. "Plum, plum, plum," they would repeat to one another.)

Right now, nobody was saying "Plum, plum, plum."

We were talking about the Johnson-Kennedy "clique," and she knew what "clique" meant.

"Why did you ask me that question?" I said.

Short Pigtails was not happy with her role as intermediary here. She said, "I think they asked you about Johnson and Kennedy because you explained you couldn't answer about Nixon."

"But *clique,"* I said. "You're asking me to admit there *was* such a thing as a clique. You want me to write an anti-U.S. statement."

Of course they wanted me to write an anti-U.S. statement. They wanted me to write a whole series of them. I don't know why it came as a surprise to me: Black Fan had already hinted at it; indeed he had more than hinted, if the translators were to be believed—my very liberty, he had suggested, could depend on this.

But in a manner of speaking, their credibility factor was worse than mine. They had tried two techniques with me: interrogation head-on, so to speak, as conducted by Mr. Wang and Miss Fanatic; and formal questioning, as in the sessions at the Harbor, where the officials did the talking and the interpreters' sole job was to translate back and forth. In both those cases, one factor served to frustrate them: the factor of spoken English. (I'm sure that in other cases they found it worked very well, but those would have to be cases where they had something to catch ahold of. My "crime" didn't really lie within their experience. Surely they had intercepted small boats before, and then released them, but these would be cases where western authorities obviously knew the boats were where they were and would come looking for them at once.) Now therefore, they had begun to use me to experiment in a new technique, interrogation in writing. And why should this lead to my release any faster than the other ways?

On the other hand, why not? I knew now that they would not kill me. I knew this not because of Mao's assurances of how well prisoners are treated, but for another reason: by now, too many interpreters had come and gone. Every one of them, being schooled to speak English, was a threat to come in contact with the western world. One single slip of the tongue in any of those contacts, and the fate of Jerry McLaughin and Mary Ann Harbert might begin to become known. As long as I was alive, and being kept at what in China qualify as vacation resorts with extra-good facilities, I was testament to the careful way they accommodated detainees. One death—and I assumed Jerry was dead—could be attributed to accident. But two out of two, from the same arrest, would be a lot harder to explain.

That was a theory I had, and it was to prove to be a lousy theory—especially the release part, because if you thought it out, release didn't have anything really to do with it—but as I have said, it was one of many reasons why the Chinese, in their effort to break me, actually were driving me into a patriotic stance I had never even been conscious of before.

What I said to Short Pigtails now was: "Tell them they're insulting me with the use of that word—

'clique.' " *(My God,* I said privately to myself, *I'm beginning to sound like them.)*

Short Pigtails didn't want to deliver that kind of message back to the officials. She said, "Perhaps it would be better if you answered it."

"How do I answer it without accepting it?"

"Perhaps by not answering it at the same time you answer it," she suggested, and it was superb advice.

So to the question: *What's your opinion of the Johnson-Kennedy clique?* I now wrote: *I am not qualified to answer this question.*

And back and forth we went. One question after another would load the dice against my country, and one answer after another would parry and dodge. I don't remember how many days it kept up, but it led me to understand one thing: this, of course, was why they had been making "concessions" to me in the weeks just before. They wanted to show how reasonable they were, and would expect me to be just as "reasonable" in return . . . and wind up with a collection of the sayings of Mary Ann Harbert, some anti-U.S., some pro-China, *but all of them in writing!*

From some of the things he had said, I detected the hand of Black Fan in some of the questions, one in particular that asked innocuously enough what my definition was of the difference between the government and the people in the United States. Like the others, I answered this one without answering it, for of course the Chinese wanted me to adopt their view that there *was* a difference between the government and the people in my country. I had a notion to put in there that my taxes paid my tax collector's salary, but I talked myself out of it: they would have taken it as sarcasm, and I was inviting enough trouble without adding more of it.

They even asked me, reasonably enough again, if I had any questions to ask about China. I had no zest for that one—why solicit propaganda?—but Short Pigtails said again it was important for me to respond, so I did. *I would like to know more of your history outside of what Mao says,* I wrote, *and I would like to know how you put to practical use the principle of "each according to his needs." Who determines the needs, and how are the needed things delivered?*

Short Pigtails read that, and then she said, "Do you want to say anything in praise of China?"

"Why not?" I said. Among other things, my stomach had been acting up again, and the business with my eyes, which I could not understand, was getting worse. I couldn't even walk up the mountainside any more, because, after the unusual fall rains, the snakes had come out in force. And so, very carefully, I wrote: *China is a very picturesque country. Her people are very colorful.*

Short Pigtails read that, too, and I think she wanted to say something, but perhaps she believed she had already protested too much. It was deliberate, it was condescending, and because it left out any praise of communism or Chairman Mao it had to be downright insolence to boot.

As I relate it now, it sounds only childish on my part. Not merely what I said, but the whole idea of it. But it wasn't my idea. It was theirs. And what came back in the "mail" was the most childish of all: a diatribe blaming the United States for every problem China ever had dating back to imperialistic American designs during the Boxer rebellion and the opium wars.

That was the end of it. They had no further questions to ask me. I certainly had no further questions to ask them. The only questioning that remained was to come from the teen-age girl who served as my waitress.

If you had been a paying guest at some wayside inn and this girl had been your waitress, you would have complained to the management about her. She was lazy and slow, and saw as one of the chief purposes in serving me the chance to flirt with one of the guards outside (others noticed this, and the guard was replaced). But now she appeared before me with an interpreter and a rare treat: a glass of cold water for me to drink. My hands shook as I took the glass from her, not out of nervous anticipation but simply because, of late, my hands had begun to shake (a normal consequence, I was to learn, of malnutrition and unbalanced diet).

Then, through the interpreter, she asked her question: "Do you have any criticism of me?"

I said no, I had no criticism, but my thoughts were focused on something else. In China, I knew by now, it was polite to ask for criticism. But it was done, as a rule, when the work was finished.

Later that day, Short Pigtails confirmed it.

"You're going to be leaving here," she said.

"When?"

"Tonight."

"Why?"

It was a good question. Every move up till now had had its readily apparent reason: from the Island to the Harbor because of Jerry's physical condition . . . from the Harbor to the nice hotel to get my mind off Jerry's fate . . . from the nice hotel to this hotel because the nice hotel was too nice. But why this move now?

"I don't know why," Short Pigtails said.

I said, "Did it have anything to do with the answers I wrote out to the questions?"

"I don't know," she said again. "But I think I should tell you the next place won't be as nice as this one."

Prison, my mind said to me.

In the next moment, I reasoned that they could not put me in prison without formal charges and a trial.

In the moment after that, I remembered it was normal to put somebody in prison while awaiting trial.

The charge against me would of course be trespassing, plus the failure to explain satisfactorily the circumstances which brought it about, plus the refusal to cooperate in the investigation that followed.

No one, the prosecution would argue, would so trespass, then so fail and so refuse, unless she had something to hide . . . particularly in the face of the concession made by her hosts at every turn, down to and including waitress service at meals.

And yet another part of my mind argued the opposite:

They're fooling you because they want to surprise you. They're not taking you to jail. They're taking you to the border at Hong Kong. They know you were innocent of any wrongdoing. They tried to get you to sign some statements against your country—it didn't cost them anything to try—but if you wouldn't do it, so what? You're a girl in her early twenties. What gain would they get out of serious political dialogue with you in any event?

Why then, if they were going to release me, would they be telling me now to prepare for the worst?

I had the answer for that one, too. They wanted it to come as a surprise because if I knew about it in advance my mind would be adding up all the bad things that had happened . . . the things that the sudden joy and relief of liberation, if it came unexpectedly, would wipe away.

They even wanted me to look nice. For Long Pigtails and Short Pigtails had just recently bought me brand-new clothes: a long-sleeved blouse, a pair of trousers.

And now they returned all my toilet articles: the final proof!

Well I was born at the bottom of a wishing well
But I ended up goin' thru the gates of hell
Well I sought some pleasure and a little pain
But I ended up goin' thru the gates of hell

Well I sought some knowledge throughout the world
But the knowledge I found came all from men
Well men know much about their world
But they know little about themselves

Well I sought some pleasure and a little pain
But they came to me just the same
Well I had a good life and regret it not
But the world knows it not for it passed it all by

They sent a scuffed-up Land-Rover type of military vehicle for me—it was about nine o'clock at night—and there were seven of us in it when we left. Up front were the driver and a fat, sixtyish army officer. In the next seat back, Short Pigtails and me. In the rear seat, Long Pigtails, seated in between two very stout individuals. One of the latter was a new interpreter who had arrived at the hotel only a little while before. She was a university graduate—that was my name for her: University—and she was very short (the Chinese say "not so tall"), and each time I saw her she seemed to have put on weight from the time before. Her English was totally British, and equally formal. "Good ahfternoon," she would say gravely.

And on the other side of Long Pigtails in the back seat was another fat, sixtyish army officer whom I already knew. He was the same man who had brought me cigarettes and was all sweetness and light—the one who wanted to have the "heart-to-heart" talk to make sure I was comfortable—just before I left the Harbor for the Commune of the Happy People . . . a time that now seemed many years ago. Now, though, he was all business as he supervised the stowing of my things in the back of the truck.

We were driving through a heavily forested section. Again, here as before, our headlights would pick up pairs of men walking along the side of the road, their arms entwined, who jumped aside and apart as we approached. My guess, as I've said before, is that their "sin" was not their mutual affection but the inadvertent public display of it, for the Cultural Revolution frowned on *all* such overt manifestations—whether between man and woman, woman and woman, man and man, it made no difference. It reminded me of the line in *My Fair Lady:* "The French don't care what they do, actually, so long as they pronounce it properly." In China, the way to pronounce it properly was not to pronounce it at all.

In the light of the moon, we drove past a silent, circular pond, populated by lily pads. The water rested stagnant up to the very edges, a breeding ground for mosquitoes. And there was a short ride across another stretch of water aboard a ferry. And a steel-truss bridge across a wide river, with large, ocean-going ships, lighted up against the night, resting at anchor in midriver.

The Pearl River. I thought of the rules of the game: once you cross the Pearl, you cannot return.

5

The Hospital

"It will be Hong Kong or prison," I told myself, as the Land Rover moved through the dark wooded countryside. Of course I had theories to support both possibilities. But other theories were possible, too. One of them —expressed, I think, by Clinton Duffy, the long-time warden at San Quentin Prison, and taught to us in our college classes in prison psychology—was that ritual was the only thing that made executions bearable. The definition of ritual was simple enough: that which had come to be expected. The opposite therefore was the unknown. The unknown is what the Chinese had confronted me with now, in taking me suddenly away from the Commune of the Happy People.

I had become the very lab animal I had studied, and when faced suddenly with an unexpected situation, the brain of the lab animal, multiplied many times in the case of a human being, tends to function in strange ways. Two impulses—one of despair, the other of hope—seek to take charge. Either way, the mind works to build a case on a foundation of greatly reasoned detail. Despair gave me all the reasons I was to be jailed. Hope gave me all the reasons for being freed.

Two things are of interest in that connection. One of them is how reasonable each theory made itself seem. But the other, even more interesting, is the way the mental processes of despair and hope not only established the theories but excluded all others!

The last thing in the world I was prepared for was what actually awaited me: another room-with-bath at another place, a doctor waiting to see if I needed pills, two soldiers—well after midnight, when the four-hour drive had ended—to recite the "rules." One way or another, I had seen it all before. They weren't out to kill me, they weren't out to jail me, they weren't out to free me. Instead, after a year and a half of trying to break me, they had hit upon what was of course the most logical, and quite possibly the most effective, solution of all, the one that had never occurred to me: more of the same.

There must have been a dozen different friends—by friends, I mean the interpreters—who at one time or another volunteered the thought that this sort of thing was hardest on someone who was as young as I. In this, they mirrored the reflections of the woman I remembered from TV, who had been imprisoned in China and worked a nail loose from her cell wall so the shaft of light could tell her the time of day. She had said that if she were young she would not have survived. I know that to be true in the sense that one who is young has a harder time withstanding the passage of time. As the song says, *It's a long long time from May to December, but the days grow short as you reach September.* But I know too that one who is young has a certain strength, and if the mind has not given up, it can draw on that vitality and sometimes force an ailing body to do uncommon things. At the Commune of the Happy People, I had played badminton not because my body felt like it but because my mind said it was the thing to do. I had done exercises for the same reason. And the reason itself was very simple. It was one of several ways I had fashioned to make time go by.

Another way was sleep. The first night at this new place, I crawled into bed, with the intention of staying there for at least a week.

And that night, for what in my memory was the first time since I had come to China, I began to dream.

I was to have two kinds of dreams, as we all do: the ones that come once and never repeat, and the ones that come time and again. The recurring dream was always the same: I was released to go home, but I had to return to China, for I had promised the Chinese on my word of honor that I would come back. "I'm home but I have to go back," I would tell my parents.

Of the other kind of dream, I remember only one. I was home in the United States and the Communists had taken over the country. All my friends were chasing me. I met my mother in a department store. She told me my father had just died. We went outside to where our car was, to escape. I was driving. There was an elaborate, frightening chase scene. To avoid our pursuers, I turned suddenly into a parking lot and hit a snowbank. I looked at my mother. As I did, she turned to dust and her head fell off.

The new place was the headquarters area of a commune, the Commune of the Red Star. It was in a cleared area surrounded by forest (well south of the Commune of the Happy People, if I could trust my sense of direction during the trip between the two places: in fact, we had crossed the Pearl). From my window I could see a dining building; also a U-shaped structure that housed the guards. I myself occupied the end room of a long rectagonal building of red brick, with whitewashed walls inside and the thinnest ceiling material I had yet seen: it appeared to be nothing more than strips of cardboard. At the other end of the building was the kitchen. The rooms in between were occupied by interpreters and by the cook, and one of the rooms had a Ping-Pong table in it.

The only way to get from one room to another was by means of a narrow covered porch that ran the length of the front of the building. A back door from my room led to my bathroom, which obviously had just become a bathroom. The signs were evident that before then it had been a kitchen. (I wondered idly: *Did they make it into a bathroom just for me?*) What had been a door opening from this room onto the rear of the building outside had been nailed shut, and I could tell by the worn places on the floor that something else had only recently been where, say, the bathtub now stood. I say the bathtub "stood," because although the bathroom itself was "new", its fixtures, here once again, were out of a 19th-century Sears Roebuck catalogue, particularly the tub with its old-fashioned claw feet.

A yard with a fence, made up of poles and matting, ran alongside the end wall of the building outside my room. It was perhaps twenty by forty feet. The fencing continued for a way beyond the front of the building, then squared back toward the building and past it in front, then back to the building again, so that the area included my portion of the porch. Guards and animals —dogs, pigs, ducks—prowled the enclosure, the former because they were stationed there, the latter moving in and out at will through tears and broken places in the

My yard at Red Star.

fence. In the area in front of the building, after the fence ended, there was a place to play badminton, and beyond it could be seen a stream with a bridge running over it; and beyond the main road, leading out of the trees and into the clearing.

The first night at Red Star, I saw a rat in my room. *It's like the Welcome Wagon,* I thought to myself. *Every place you go, there's a rat waiting to say hello. Now watch: tomorrow they'll start you off with a delicious meal.*

And they did exactly that: a delicious omelette with chicken, good butter, freshly baked bread. (The cook didn't do his own baking, I was told; instead the bread and cake was delivered from elsewhere, presumably from the ovens of a large tuberculosis sanitarium situated, they told me, on a hillside not far away.) But as always the food was to deteriorate, for lack of quality control. The cook was around nineteen, though he had a terribly wrinkled face that made him look three times older, and he was always singing in a loud, beery voice. "He likes to make special things," the interpreters told me, and from time to time that was true. At Christmastime, for example, he prepared me a special sandwich —knowing it was my holiday, though of course it wasn't his. It was a sandwich of sausage—intestines stuffed with fat but without seasoning, from cured pork—with a dish of carrots on the side. It tasted good, very "Western," but there was a guard standing at my open window, watching me eat it and running his fingernails across the windowscreen. "Tomma!" he said mockingly. "Tomma!"

I had heard that word before. I knew it was a bad word, probably a dirty word (I didn't want to cause the interpreters the embarrassment of having to tell me what it meant, so I didn't ask them). I do know too that it ruined my Christmas feast that day. I put the sandwich aside, only half-eaten.

The guards at Red Star probably were the worst of all. They were more sure of their ground, since this was a headquarters compound and many of them lived here instead of having been brought in from the outside. And they had an additional element of familiarity to work with: they were free to come right up to my door and windows and stare inside to their heart's content. There wasn't much point in complaining about it. For one thing, there was nobody to complain to: resident officials who might elsewhere have been "attached" to the case of Miss Harbert just weren't there, and the only outsider who visited was Black Fan. He arrived on two different occasions, but stayed only for the briefest periods of time and never gave me the chance to issue any formal objections against the soldiers.

And on a further practical level, even if the guards didn't have their noses pressed against my windows, they could see into my room just as easily from their assigned stations twenty-five feet away. To preserve what privacy was left, I took to doing all my dressing and undressing in the bathroom.

One final factor was not about the guards at all. It was simply, instead, that I was to be at Red Star for a long, long time; and time invents opportunity. I remember, for instance, a warm day, when I had just finished taking a bath, only to discover I had left my towel in my main room outside. I had two choices: one was to put my clothes on over a wet body; the other to go get the towel, in the hope no guard would be looking. I opted for the second way, and came naked out of the bathroom.

The guard was looking. I had left the towel on a chair at the very front of the room, thus had to get very close to him. And it became too close: not for me; for him. Suddenly he gave a shout, raised his rifle, and pointed it at my bare stomach, at a range of perhaps six feet.

Ordinarily, a man pointing a gun at a naked woman has one purpose in mind: that she submit to his will. But one look at his face and the way the gun shook in his hands told me that this brave soldier of the People's Republic of China had exactly the opposite problem on his mind: that I intended that he submit to *my* will. After all the peeking and looking-from-afar, suddenly we were so close—and in fact so alone—that his mind told him I was going to fling open the door and drag him into my embrace. I didn't know then and don't know now what the punishment might be for a soldier who permitted himself to be seduced by the white woman he was assigned to guard, but it couldn't have been too pleasant. I looked him in the eye, picked up the towel, covered myself with it, and returned to the bathroom. The episode didn't take care of the soldiers who continued to stare in my window. But it took care of *that* soldier. His turns of duty thereafter would see him plastered against the farthest possible corner of the fenced yard, and he looked everyplace except in the direction of my room.

Sometimes, more out of boredom than anything else, I found it actually fun to have the guards close to my window rather than farther away. One little soldier, who wanted my light off in the daytime (when I wanted it on, so I could read), found himself playing peek-a-boo with me. I would flatten myself against the front wall, then hit a drinking glass with a stick. Instantly his face would appear at the window, and suddenly I would swing into view, confronting him head-on. Invariably, he would duck out of sight; whereupon I would get against the wall again, strike the glass with the stick, and repeat the whole thing all over.

But like the cook, the guards were unpredictable. The first day of my stay at Red Star, the food was excellent and the guards seemed extremely human. A small Alaskan husky-type dog came and tapped at my door. The guards enjoyed that, as I did, and they began to play with him. And after that there were a whole procession of dogs who came to make friends with me, and the guards played with all of them. (There was no word in Chinese for "pet," Mr. Wang had said.) There was a dog who used to bang at my door while I was taking a nap. Another one was friendly but not pretty to look at: he had a skin infection, and his fur came off in patches. It was interesting: I knew the names of the dogs where I didn't know the names of the interpreters assigned to me. There was Figi, who was the smartest and most polite; Tanka, who was the most clever: he would come into my room and select certain articles which he would carry away in his mouth; and Tonga, a square, brown-faced puppy who "belonged" to the guards but made friends with me. The soldiers paid great and fond attention to him. At one point they got a supply of red ink and painted his eyes and face with it.

Then one day in the winter, the cook, who prided himself on his speciality dishes, stuck a knife in Tonga's throat and cooked him, and the soldiers ate him.

There were dogs before and after Tonga—I asked one of the interpreters why they had killed and eaten him, and they said it was because after painting his face the guards had decided he was a Soviet revisionist. Actually, they felt sorry about it. Their consensus, long after they ate him, was that he had been the best dog of all. Maybe also the tastiest. Eating dogs was not an unusual custom in the places where I stayed.

And for me, there was little if anything to say about it. After all, he was "their" dog. I make this distinction because in the winter of that year, perhaps two months after my arrival at Red Star, Short Pigtails brought me a cat.

"He caught three mice in one night," she said, "and he's still so young!"

He *was* young—perhaps four or five months old, no more than that—gray-white in color and of a good size: at full growth he would be as large as Frederick, my cat in Salt Lake City. Our eyes met, and it was love at first sight. Short Pigtails held him out to me, and I took him in my arms. "You're a Pussycat," I said to him. "A Boopsie Cat." He looked at me in a way that conveyed that he would love me despite what I had just said, not because of it. *I have enough problems in China,* he seemed to be saying, *without some nut American detainee calling me Boopsie Cat.*

In a way too, which I find impossible to explain, Boopsie Cat "assigned" himself to me, much as an interpreter might have been assigned. He knew I disliked spiders, so he took upon himself the job of chasing them down. There was a pond nearby, so I had frogs in my room, and he went after them as well. But he was to weary of that particular pursuit: the frogs were too small for his tastes, which were in the tradition of the French epicure—he only ate the legs.

Meanwhile, my own tactical approach to my situation had changed. Instead of making complaints, I now was making demands. In a way, this made me less contentious, less "temperamental," than I had been before, because I had learned not to go against the rules, at least not in the form of complaining about them. Part of this was the absence of opportunity to present a list of complaints. But part of it too was a conscious decision to obtain what I wanted, rather than object to what I didn't want.

It started with my insisting that I have coffee every morning—no matter how bad the coffee was, I wanted it. Coffee wasn't listed in the "rules" one way or another. And so, a little to my surprise, they began bringing me coffee.

I also insisted on meat for my cat though of course I pretended it was for me. Here once again, they agreed to supply it, though it only appeared at long intervals. The only problem was Boopsie Cat himself. He preferred chicken to meat, and if they brought chicken for me and meat for him, he would perch beside me as I ate and nab the chicken as I brought it to my mouth.

He also liked fish, and here Long Pigtails proved useful to him. She netted some fish at the pond, little fish, mainly, but a few larger ones, including a pretty gold one with whiskers. It was a supply that had constantly to be replenished. Boopsie Cat would sit beside the fish bowl for hours, making his selection, then scooping up the larger, tastier ones with his paws.

And after a meal of chicken and fish he would curl up and go to sleep.

For one of such selective eating habits, he had some strange moments. He liked to investigate garbage, and used to bring me egg shells as a present, and once he disappeared for three days and came back smelling of raw sewage. But he was extremely thoughtful of me.

One especially cold winter night, as I lay shivering in my bed, he left the room. Shortly he returned, and one of the interpreters was with him. She said, "Your cat came to get me. Do you need an extra blanket?"

Boopsie Cat could come and go through an access flap in my window screen, but that was not always necessary, for many times my door itself was left ajar, particularly in the winter. It was part of the incessant war between me and the soldiers guarding me.

Some of the "rules" were vindictive to the point of being retaliatory. In warm weather, my windows and door were to be shut. In cold weather, they were to be open. An "open-and-shut" case? Not quite. I've expressed it here in the extreme. But the effect was practically the same. In practice, the guards would wait as long as possible during cold weather before shutting the windows; and when it was warm, they would close them as early as possible, sometimes even before supper. Thus they would keep me cold when it was cold, and hot when it was hot, but if any criticism resulted they could get away with a mumbled apology for an occasional slip-up in timing.

Another "rule" allowed them to enter my room for one reason, and one reason only. If the glaring, naked overhead light bulb in my room was on during the day, they were permitted to come in, pull the string-cord that controlled the light, and turn it off. And if I turned it off before going to bed at night, they could come in and turn it on again, for the "rule" was that my room had to be lighted all night long.

For a while I played I-pull-the-string-you-pull-the-string with the guards, just as I would play peek-a-boo and hit the glass with the stick, but it was a game I had to lose. There were more of them than me, and one of them was always awake. And the more I pulled the string at the wrong time, the more frequently they had the right to invade my room.

I took then to placing magazines over the mosquito

netting stretched across the top of my four-poster bed. Then I would bring the blankets up to lock out the light, and put a handkerchief and towel over my eyes. The way my eyes hurt and my head ached, even this was not a solution—*any* light, while I slept, was too much light. If I tried tightening the towel around my eyes, the headache grew worse. If I left it loose, two pinpoints of light would come through and hit me in the eyes.

It was the glare that did it; and one day I hit upon an idea. I still had my set of watercolor paints, left over from my stay at the Harbor, and I stood on a chair, and unscrewed the lightbulb, and started to paint it green.

A guard outside noticed what I was doing, and he put up a cry, and Long Pigtails came running from the room next door.

"What are you doing?" she said to me.

"Painting the lightbulb green," I said.

She gave that some thought. Then she said: "Let me help you." And she took the bulb from me and began to complete the paint job.

With this project, Long Pigtails was being not only friendly but, I think, symbolizing the dislike that existed between the interpreters and the soldiers. But at the same time, she was the one doing the painting. Obviously it was her plan to paint the bulb just enough to show me she was on my side, but not to the point of making the room so dark she could be accused of violating the "rule."

"There," she said at last, and stood on the chair and screwed the bulb back into the ceiling.

There wasn't that much difference, so the next day I painted it green some more. That night it was just about right—but I couldn't read by it. It would have shed just enough additional light to enable me to read during the daytime, but the rule was it had to be off during the daytime.

To the soldiers, the rule made great sense—their instructions were to be able to see in my room at all times. So: light off in the daytime, light on at night.

To me, it was harassment pure and simple, and quite deliberate. Certainly their light bulb regulation was suited to the object of seeing into my room. But what was there to see?

It was not, of course, my first experience with lights-on-lights-off at the various places I'd been in China, but the surrounding circumstances, the situation with my eyes, and the continuing passage of time itself made this one far the worst of all.

Finally, one morning I got out of bed, pulled the string-cord as always to turn off the bulb and kept pulling. The string tore away from the little fixture chain at the ceiling and floated down into my hands. Quickly, I buried it in the quilting of my bed. Then I waited to see what would happen. I figured it wouldn't take long. It didn't.

The guard outside noticed what had occurred. He put up a bellow in Chinese, and Short Pigtails and Long Pigtails came running to my room. Outside on the porch, an officer came, and Short Pigtails went out to talk with him.

I sat on the side of my bed, quaking with fear and hatred. Boopsie Cat jumped into my lap and stayed there protectively, staring malevolently at Long Pigtails.

"This can be very bad for you," Long Pigtails said. "Very bad."

"It's bad enough already," I said.

"But it can get worse," she said.

"You can say that," I said. "They don't stare in on you every night. They don't take your light away from you in the daytime when you need it to read by because you're going blind."

She said, "But I'm not the one being detained. You are."

"That's right," I said. "I'm being detained. Isn't that punishment enough?"

Short Pigtails came in the door. "The officer wants to know why you pulled off the string."

"Because I'm not going to tolerate a light bulb any more, that's why," I said. "I come from a country of free people, but you don't believe that. You tell me *this* is a free country. Is this the way a free country behaves? You know I didn't do anything wrong. If I had, I'd be in prison by now. So if I'm not a prisoner what right do you have to treat me like one?"

"You're not treated like a prisoner," Long Pigtails said.

I waved a hand at the light bulb. "No? What do you call that? What do you call this whole business?"

Short Pigtails came in the door. "The officer is very upset."

"Yes?" I said. "Well, you can tell him something for me." And I said again what I'd just told Long Pigtails. "Go tell him that," I said. "See what he says."

"No," Short Pigtails said. She shook her head. "I won't translate that to him. It will be terrible for you if I did."

Now the officer himself came in, with one of the guards. He spoke in rapid Chinese.

Long Pigtails said, "He wants the string."

"No," I said.

They didn't have to translate that. The officer looked at me speculatively, then said something in Chinese again.

Long Pigtails said, "He says if you don't give him the string, he'll search for it."

"Let him search. Does he want me to take my clothes off? Is that the Chinese way, too?"

Again, no translation needed. The officer may not have known what it was I was saying, but he could see for himself that I had no intention of giving back the string voluntarily. Now he motioned to Short Pigtails.

She cast a look of despair first at him, then at me, and began to look for the string. At one point, she was standing on the bed, taking down the blanket I had draped over the mosquito netting.

I said to her, "Don't you feel foolish?"

It was an automatic thing to say, because it was such a foolish scene—all of this in a hunt for a piece of string: if they insisted on a string, why didn't they just get another one?

Of course, if they did that, they'd be giving up their "right" to search, and obviously it was important to them to confirm that right. But to search for a piece of string?

So there was something to be said on both sides, and I could see this fact mirrored on Short Pigtails' face as she looked for the string. Finally she found it, buried in the quilt where I had hidden it.

The officer nodded in triumph when he saw the string in her hand. He said to me (with Long Pigtails translating), "You want your light on in the daytime?"

"Yes," I said, "and . . ."

But he took my nod for assent and broke in with another barrage: "Then you will have it on in the daytime. You will also have it on in the nighttime. You will have it on every minute of every hour of every day and every night from now on!"

They hung the string from the fixture again, replaced the green bulb with a normal white one, bare and glaring as before, and turned it on.

The following day, Short Pigtails left the Commune of the Red Star. She had taken it from both sides, and had had all she could take. So she put in for a transfer, just as Miss Fanatic had done, though under different circumstances, at the Commune of the Happy People.

I think if I had been more patient with her—especially if I had been less critical of her in front of others during the light bulb showdown—she would have stayed on, and I regretted it, even though not regretting taking the stand I did. The interpreters were giving me patience, and I was not giving it back to them in return. And for all my flaring up, all I had done was to lose the Battle of the Bulb.

The new light bulb shone incessantly, day and night. *You could at least have had a green one,* I told myself. Yet somewhere within me, despite my eyes, and the nausea and stomach pains I was beginning to experience with greater frequency than every, I could not yet manage to put down the spark of rebellion.

One day Long Pigtails brought me some tea that was supposed to calm my stomach. I drank it and threw up. Long Pigtails was mortified. "That wasn't supposed to happen," she said.

I assured her it was all right—I actually felt a little better for it. But the next day the pains were as bad as before. And for the first time, a new thought came to me. I could try to tell it dramatically, I suppose, but in truth there was nothing dramatic about it. It came simply as a matter of common sense:

I was dying.

It wouldn't be a quick death, and there would be periods of remission, when I would feel better, play cards with the interpreters, even play Ping Pong. But by now I had come to know that the sickness and pain was bound to return, and each time it would be a little worse than the time before.

The fat intellectual girl, the one I called "University," asked me at one point, shortly after Long Pigtails gave me the tea, if I would like to hear about a "concession" the government had made. "Everyone realizes it's uneconomical and foolish to have your light on in the daytime," she said. "So they have decided you can have it off during the daytime."

That was their "concession"—to put me back right where I had started.

"All you have to do," University said, "is pull the string."

The spark of rebellion (compounded, doubtless, by my physical condition at the moment: *I'm dying, what difference does it make anyway?)*—here it came:

"No," I said. "I won't be the one to pull the string. If you want to turn it on and off, you'll have to do it yourselves."

University shook her head, sadly. "But you know the rules."

"The rules don't say I have to pull the string."

"But you keep fighting everything," she said.

I said, "What was wrong with the green light bulb? At least it was better than this."

"I suppose it was against the rules," she said.

"But nobody ever said that," I said. "They let me have it and didn't take it away till I pulled the whole string down."

"I'll ask the officer," she said, and went away. She returned just as my lunch had been brought to me.

"The officer says you must keep the bulb you now have."

"Then take the lunch away," I said. "I don't want it. And tell them not to bother with supper either. If they want to kill me, I can't stop them, but they're not going to do it by making me blind first."

Shades of Jerry—a hunger strike! But again, let me not over-dramatize it into something it wasn't. When your stomach is upset, it isn't hard to refuse food. It might even be good for you. But I don't want, either, to make it seem that everything in my war with the guards was a consequence merely of poor physical condition at the time. My reaction to their tactics may have been a part of the way I was feeling, but my mind, I discovered, was objective about it, almost like a cool bystander. If anything, my thinking was sharper now than when I first had reached China, because much of the bewilderment had been stripped away, and the people and conditions had become more familiar to me.

And there was also, of course, one commanding difference between Jerry's hunger strikes at the Harbor and mine at the Commune of the Red Star. Jerry had refused to eat without explanation. *If he'd only tell us what it is he wants.,* they had said to me, time and again.

But in my case they knew exactly what I wanted. I wanted a green light bulb. Maybe it sounds ridiculous, saying it now. But there was nothing ridiculous about it then.

One of their first moves was to turn the "negotiating" over to a male translator. (The females certainly had been making no headway, despite their best efforts.) He was an educated boy—short, thin, small-boned, with little dark-rimmed eyeglasses—whom I had met first in the latter part of my stay at the Commune of the Happy People. Now he had come to Red Star. As with the others, I didn't know his name, and yet I did know it, for I noticed that when somebody said what sounded like "Sally" to him he responded just as you or I might when somebody uses our name. So I called him Sally and he accepted it.

By now I had refused solid food for a week, and at that point Sally came to me and said: "Okay, Miss Harbert. The government has agreed to put in a green light bulb." He smiled. "Will you eat now?"

"Of course I will," I said.

So I began eating again. The food arrived, but the green light bulb didn't. There was a delay in shipment, I was told. The proper bulb was not one to be painted by hand on the spot, but an official pre-manufactured green light bulb.

This went on for two weeks. At the end of that time, I said to Sally, "Did you think I was kidding?"

"Kidding?"

"Fooling. Pretending."

"No, Miss Harbert," he said. "I told you what I was told: they have agreed you can have a green light bulb."

"When?"

He shrugged. "It's coming."

When I first came to Red Star, Sally had said it was his "opinion" that I might be kept in China another two years. By now, I was past all consideration of the possibility of release. I would be kept in China until I died, and we all knew it. So I said to Sally, sarcastically, "Maybe the day they release me they'll give me a green light bulb to carry over the border with me."

"No," he said. "The light bulb is coming."

"All right," I said. "Then if it's coming, I'll wait for it to come."

"Good," he said.

"And I won't eat until it does," I said.

Thus commenced my second hunger strike. This time they went out of their way to tempt me to break it. The food that came to my room, which I refused to touch, was consistently the best I had seen. The plates were arranged attractively. One day they even brought me a little server of salt with a beautiful hard-boiled egg.

Salt is a treat? I said to myself. But of course it was. And back it went untouched.

As the days went by I knew I was losing weight and becoming weaker, but in my physical state my appetite never was over-demanding. The greatest temptation to end the strike—and the most sorrowful anxiety—was my cat. He would examine each meal as it was brought to me, and try not to look concerned when I told them to take it away. I had always shared my food with him before, but I think he understood, somehow, that now this could not happen. He went back to scrounging for fish and frogs and insects, as he had during my earlier one-week hunger strike, and he made daily trips to the kitchen to bring me back eggshells and garbage, more than he had ever brought before. These he would deposit before me gravely. *I know you can't eat the food they bring you,* he almost seemed to be saying, *but it's all right if I bring it.*

Two weeks after it began, my hunger strike ended—perhaps in the strangest way any hunger strike has ended before or since.

Sally came to my room.

In his hand was a green light bulb.

With the coming of spring, the green light bulb blew out. Immediately, it was replaced by another green light bulb, this one, unfortunately, a darker green, so it was almost impossible to read or play cards with the interpreters in my room. Instead the interpreters came up with a new project: we would turn the yard outside my room into a vegetable garden. It was a group project for three of us: Long Pigtails, Sally, and me. (University had left Red Star. "It's my turn to re-educate myself with the peasants," she explained.)

The work was supervised, more or less, by Boopsie Cat and the various dogs. By some private arrangement among them, Boopsie Cat was boss of the yard, and the dogs' place was outside the fence. Of course they could get in, and the cat could get out, through the breaks in the fence, but Boopsie Cat seemed to be accorded the right to chase the dogs if they got in, and they the right to chase him if he wandered out. It never occurred to me to wonder who would chase me if *I* wandered out, because one of the things that had left me by now was any ambition to escape. Not just sickness, but time and the Chinese had taken care of that. My goal by now was not to leave China but to maintain my own identity *in* China, for the rest of my life, if necessary. And even here I had the sense of frustration and gradual failure. You draw a line, and it seems, by itself, such a silly thing, so you retreat and draw a new line, equally silly when viewed all by itself, and it becomes the old story of the camel's nose in the tent. And if you decide to make a stand, and tell yourself *This is it,* then—this is what? Before I pulled the string off the light fixture I had a dark green bulb that would have been all right as it was. Now—two hunger strikes, a period of constant glaring illumination, a humiliated interpreter and a half-starved cat later—what did I have to show for it all?

The same thing I started out with: a dark green bulb.

Sensible? Hardly. And yet perhaps in one direction it did make sense. For one way or another, I still was managing to withhold from my captors the one thing they wanted most of all: acquiescence.

The area we chose for our garden had already been plowed and used for that purpose before, with no better results, I suspect, than we got. We worked hard at it, adding ashes from the kitchen stove for their fertilizing effect, but it was bad, tired soil—more a mixture of sand and clay, really—and when we hoed it we turned up nothing but rocks. We planted corn and sweet potatoes, and a few flowers, but our edible harvest was a total of three ears of corn, each about six inches in length, and three sweet potatoes that were even worse than the corn.

I was in my room one day, directly following this "harvest," when there was a knock at my door. "Miss Harbert," a voice said, "are you at home?"

There was no mistaking that voice, any more than there was any mistaking the insane nature of the question it asked: *Are you at home?*

"Come in," I said, and Dirty Dirty Dirty opened the door and appeared. I had not seen him in over a year, but of course he had not changed. As always, he bubbled over with a blend of self-importance and earnest incompetence.

"I've heard about your garden," he said. "We'll have to arrange a better result next time. Maybe we'll move the garden. Can you think of a better place?"

"Iowa," I said.

"You what?"

"Nothing," I said. "What are you doing here?" I almost bit my tongue off for asking that: of course it was a question that over-stepped the bounds of permissible curiosity.

But of all the translators who dealt with me, Dirty Dirty Dirty would have to be the one most unlikely to notice such a slip. "My duties bring me here" he said importantly, and looked, equally importantly, around me room. "Do you know you have a green light bulb?"

"Yes," I said. "I know."

"Would you like a standard one instead? I can put in a requisition."

"No, thank you," I said. "I prefer the green."

"But how can you read by that light?"

"I do other things. I play Ping Pong."

"Are you as good as the Chinese?"

"Some Chinese."

"Me?"

"I don't know," I said. "I've never played you."

"Come," he said, beckoning with his finger. "You'll find out."

I don't believe this, I said to myself. *Here I am, held captive in deepest China, and here comes the inspector from the government. He doesn't want to rape me, he doesn't want to torture me, he doesn't want to interrogate me, he doesn't even ask me how I feel. Instead, he wants to play Ping Pong.*

So we played Ping Pong, with Dirty Dirty Dirty acting as staccato scorekeeper all the while. "Fifteen for me, four for you!" he would cry. The other interpreters looked on, amused. The Ping Pong rules in China are the same as those everywhere else, but the scorekeeping is done in reverse, with a minus charged to the score of the loser of each point, rather than a plus for the winner. Thus 15 for him, 4 for me, meant I was ahead 15-4. And he was, without much question, the worst Ping Pong player I ever saw.

His visit to Red Star lasted only a little while, but in the summer he was back again. By that time we were trying to grow another crop in our "garden." "You're doing it all wrong," Dirty Dirty Dirty said. "Let me show you. I learned from the peasants how to hand-pollenate." (He had memorized the phrase). He began to "hand pollenate," holding the pollen from the cornstalk directly over the plantings. "You see," he said to me, "this is the way it's done. You do it the wrong way. You waste too much. It all goes on the ground."

But it was too late in the growing season for a new crop anyway, even if we hadn't "wasted" the pollen.

Just as he had at the Harbor, Dirty Dirty Dirty began spending time reading to me: translating news stories in the Chinese press into English. Inevitably he chose to read pieces that were critical of the U.S., and some of his translations were wild. "The strike paralyzed the city" came out, in his translation into the English vocabulary at his command, "The strike gave the city infant paralysis." And a picture of a billboard either advertising or (more probably) identifying a U.S. Cavalry division became proof positive to him that the Americans were employing a dread extra weapon in Vietnam: horses.

A little of that went a long way, and at one point I flared up at him and told him I didn't want to hear any more garbage about American aggressiveness. He went away, but the next day he was back, with another article.

"Leave me alone," I said.

"But you must listen," he said.

"No I mustn't," I said. "Please leave my room."

He rose gravely and left, and I knew that once again I was jeopardizing my good standing, and risking a bad report about my conduct. But once again too, the upset stomach, cramps, and nausea were upon me. And once again too, I underestimated Diry Dirty Dirty's inability to be offended. He was back again the next day. "You were angry with me, weren't you?" he said. "Well. Tonight we'll go to a movie."

So tonight we went to a movie. It wasn't exactly the Bijou down the street. Instead, just beyond my fenced enclosure was a flat area where the soldiers would gather on summer evenings to watch films projected against an outdoor screen. Often the interpreters and I would take chairs into the yard and watch the movies over the fence. I remember one called *Taking Tiger Mountain by Strategy;* another called *Comrade in Arms,* which was about the Korean war. And there was an Albanian picture about underground guerillas which, if it was a typical example, would not make Albania the moviemaking capital of the world, although it was better than China. All of the movies were simplistic. If they showed boy-and-girl love interest at all, it would not be with kissing or touching so much as with a smile or a longing look. The films left Dirty Dirty Dirty entranced. For my benefit, he kept up a running commentary throughout, a blend of propaganda and description of what was taking place on the screen, although it was perfectly obvious without explanation. "Now he puts away his gun," he would say. "Now he goes into the house." I wondered idly at times what he would do with a first grade Reader: *See Spot run. Funny funny Spot . . .*

The movies distributed by the government were part of the cultural revolution's design to separate the young people of China from tradition. The music played during a movie, for example, would make a point of staying away from the folk songs passed from generation to generation, for most of them were love songs. And this was a problem that came to a head during holidays and festivals. There were seasons and reasons for holidays in China, and these were too strong not to be observed. But if you celebrated the same holidays as before, how did you go about overcoming the tradition that generated them?

The government's answer was to frown officially on tradition, and meanwhile try to separate the younger people from it by offering alternatives, in the form of movies, mass singing of new songs and, perhaps most of all, indoctrination in the schools.

Perhaps strange to say, the greatest triumph of the government—assuring three bowls of rice a day for a previously starving populace—served in a way to impede the cultural revolution, for it kept the older people alive where otherwise they would have died off from starvation, and for every grandparent and parent who survived, there were memories and traditions and family ties to be passed on to the children.

And so the holidays that I saw celebrated at Red Star—made possible though they were by the new China—were throwbacks to the old China. Some of the holidays were national, some regional. There were the spring festival, the moon festival in the fall, the dragon festival. People would bake little cakes and relatives would gather to pay homage to their ancestors, just as they had centuries ago.

For me, there would be extra treats at holiday time: beer and candy and cakes. During the spring festival of 1970, the cook at Red Star personally brought me an assortment of dirty crackers and cookies. They had come from Canton. They were boxed for export.

The cook had another gift for me. From a litter of kittens, apparently born in the kitchen, one scrawny, underfed little guy, yellow and white with huge eyes, began to visit me. Or perhaps he was visiting Boopsie Cat. The fact was they liked each other from the start, and finally Boopsie Cat let me know that he thought we had to adopt him. So we did.

The kitten imitated Boopsie Cat in every way, a fact which had its disturbing side, because some of the bigger cat's habits were unique. Boopsie Cat had a dish, for example, filled with water. But he never drank from it.

Instead he preferred the water from the fishbowl; even more, he enjoyed drinking my water from my cup. Seeing Boopsie Cat avoid his own water dish, the new kitten avoided it, too. Seeing Boopsie Cat stand up to drink from the fishbowl, the new kitten tried that too, but he could hardly reach the top of the container with his paws. And so, by process of elimination, my drinking source, my cup, became the kitten's drinking source too.

That was fine, except that when the cats got ringworm, I got what everyone thought was ringworm, too. It was well into the fall by now, and once again there had been a shift in interpreters. University had returned, bringing me three potted plants as a present and looking fatter than ever. Then Long Pigtails became jealous of the amounts of time University seemed eager to spend with me, and put in for a transfer. Then University left again, but by that time two new girls had arrived, and once again I assigned them nicknames. Both had been teachers, one in primary school, the other in middle school, so in my lexicon they became Primary and Middleschool.

Primary was just about my own age. She was short and stocky, with athletic mannerisms. She wore her hair in little side-pigtails tied with ribbon, and in fact was quite good-looking, I thought, and intelligent too, although she seemed to prefer not to apply herself to difficult things. She was an excellent card player, for example, but she chose to play only the simplest of the card games. Yet she struck a sympathetic chord with me, because I recognized in her approach to me the same nervous, uncertain approach I had brought to my prison cases at the penitentiary in Utah. And so, more in her case than anyone else's, I went out of my way to extend the same helpfulness to her that the prisoners in Utah had extended to me.

Middleschool was older. And she was more practical, and more pessimistic, too. "I don't speak good English," she said, when first we met. "I don't even know what I'm doing here." My case of "ringworm" didn't entrance her either. "I'm going to stay away till it's over," she told me.

A female "barefoot doctor" came to treat my ringworm. I was to see many barefoot doctors during my stay at Red Star. They were essential to the distribution of medical care throughout the country under Chairman Mao, and certainly they did more good than harm, even though all many of them had was, essentially, a six-week crash course in basic medicine. The difficulty was that many barefoot doctors, trained by real doctors, in turn trained other barefoot doctors, so that by process of diffusion even the minimum course of instruction would be spread even thinner. In the case of my ringworm, the barefoot doctor brought little bottles of some kind of medicine. I was to paint myself with it, and I was using six bottles a day. When it didn't clear up, University got me some bottles of dark-brown, stronger stuff. Middleschool had agreed to rejoin me when the barefoot doctor assured her the medicine she'd prescribed would avert any question of contagion, but when University brought in the stronger stuff, the smell of it drove Middleschool off once again. She was not good-looking, and her clothes were too large for her, and she obviously was not happy in this line of work.

Some time later another "Middleschool" arrived. She had also been a teacher, and she enjoyed neither the novelty nor the sense of mission that could come with this assignment. But this new Middleschool, who was to be assigned to me from then on, had the broadest command of English, the best vocabulary, of any of the translators, and if she was less than enthusiastic it was because she obviously found little new or challenging in being an interpreter. For that reason, I think, she and I were to become quite close, as any two people might who find a given task mutually unexciting. We talked about many things that had not come up before. It was from Middleschool that I most sensed what I already had detected in others in their attitude about the United States: namely that the thing wrong with having two cars in every garage was not the two cars or the garage but that it was the Americans who had them.

Middleschool herself was not particularly envious or upset about this state of things, but she found some of them hard to believe.

"I heard," she said, "that in America you make clothes for dogs, and even have special stores that sell them."

"Even more than that," I said. "There are cemeteries where people bury animals when they die."

"*Tomma!*" Middleschool said, half to herself. *Tomma*—the same word I had heard the guards shout at me. Now, though, it was not being addressed to me at all, so I dared at last to ask about it.

"'*Tomma*'—What does that mean?" I asked.

Middleschool thought to herself for a time. At last, she said: "I don't know how to translate it."

That served to confirm what I'd already guessed, that *Tomma* was an epithet, maybe just an out-and-out dirty word, which in either case could prove of use to me. If I could report the guards for using that word, then—since bad language was expressly forbidden by the strict Maoist code—who knew what new concessions I might be able to win?

So I pressed Middleschool about it: "But it must mean something. Try."

She shook her head perplexedly. "It's a Chinese word. It may not have meaning in your language. I don't know."

"Then think of something close to it. As close as you can come."

"Well," she said, "to us, 'tomma' means 'too much.' But what would that mean to you?"

"Too much," I said.

* * *

As that autumn ended and became winter, everyone in the commune was sick, and barefoot doctors came and passed out pills and cough medicines. There were no examinations that amounted to anything, no prescriptions. If you knew what to ask for, or perhaps just had a private theory as to what would benefit you the most, then they would dispense it, and that would be that.

Thus, if you sought medical advice, it was as likely as not to come from the nearest bystander. At one point, Sally recommended that I take a certain pill for my stomach pains.

"What makes you think it will do any good? I asked.

"It always works for me," he replied.

It was almost as though he were saying that what for me was an alarming condition was for him and hundreds of millions of others a way of life. This may have been, in fact, a reason why my forms of illness, which would have sent me running to a doctor at home, did not seem to impress the Chinese all that much. Even the doctor who had first awaited me the night I arrived at Red Star had done little more than order a high-protein diet for me, orders that of course were followed to the letter—for the first twenty-four hours. There is a difference, of course, between being bred to stomach distress and having it come upon you for the first time in adulthood and grow worse with each passing month. You live with the one, and I suppose sooner or later you die with the other. But there was no reason to expect the Chinese to appreciate that difference, nor to blame them if they didn't. As far as Sally could tell, I was normal: I had the same stomach he did.

Nor is this to say he was lacking in perception. Far from it, he was, perhaps, the best-educated of anyone I met in China. In learning English, he had read things like Thomas Hardy's *Tess of the D'Urbervilles* and the English version of De Maupassant's *The Necklace,* and discussed them eagerly and at length with me. He had a respect for words and for the great literature of the world, but he had understanding too, and on Christmas Day of 1970 (although officially he was not permitted to observe my holidays) he presented me with something to read. It was in small print, and he knew as well as anyone that small print was the last thing my eyes were capable of handling. But still it was something to read; more than that, it was the very reverse of what ordinarily would be given to me in China. Their whole trust, as I've already said, was to separate me from the familiar: in fact, it was their form of brainwashing. But Sally's gift to me took the opposite form. What he gave me was *Webster's Collegiate Dictionary.*

Sally was to come to the rescue again, in a different way, because my kitten left the room one day and didn't come back. To Boopsie Cat, this was a form of disaster. He waited three days, then took it upon himself to go out and find the kitten and bring him back.

Then I waited three days for Boopsie Cat. I waited more than three days.

But he never returned.

Now I was not only sick but alone, and the interpreters showed their concern. Dirty Dirty Dirty came back from a trip, and they told him, "She needs a cat, we all need a cat."

He said to me, "They tell me you need a cat. You are not acting right without one."

"Go away," I said.

"They also say *they* need a cat," he said. "I ask them for what purpose, and they say to catch mice and because you'll be a nicer person."

I lay in my bed and said nothing.

"You understand the function of my duty as a government official," he said. "Under the circumstances I must fill out a form for the government."

"Then fill out a form," I said. "Anything, so long as you leave me alone."

"It will be an unusual form," he said. "I've never asked the government for a cat before now."

I stared at him. "What are you going to requisition? One pussycat?"

"It may take time," he said.

"I should imagine," I said.

But in the cold of that winter, Sally found a cat somewhere outside on the grounds of the commune. He was a kitten, actually, no more than three months old, scrawny, wild, afflicted with all kinds of ailments including diarrhea. He wanted nothing to do with anyone. Sally tied him to a rope outside my room, but I insisted he be brought inside. "It's too cold for him out there," I said. "We'll have to build a fire for him. (A fire for a cat? None of us had fires.) And then when the coals are warm they can be his bed."

The interpreters said, "He won't let anybody touch him."

"He'll let me touch him," I said. So they brought him into my room in a box. I reached out to pet him, and he leaped from the box and under my bed, climbing in among the springs.

For a week I tried to lure him out. It was a group project. The interpreters and the cook formed an alliance, producing the finest meals in the history of China for a neurotic kitten named (by me) Charley.

Once when I reached for him, he bit my finger so it bled. He would come toward the food, but not to the point of leaving his haven. Finally I found myself under the bed with him, pinning paper onto its underside with tacks to keep him from getting up into the springs, and occasionally, as I engaged in this project, he would nibble at the food I brought with me.

At last he began to place trust in me, though not in any of the Chinese who gathered to observe the project in action. Finally one day he came all the way out from under the bed. We had dishes of food and water waiting for him. "Go away," I said to the interpreters. "Leave us alone. Let's see what he does."

What he did was exactly what I had ceased doing. At every place in China, my room had a wardrobe mirror. By now, at Red Star, I'd stopped looking in mine. My skin was beginning to show sores, and what I had first noticed at the Commune of the Happy People as a "thinning" of my hair was now something far more advanced: my hair was beginning to fall out.

But Charley wanted to look in the mirror. What he saw was another cat. When he reared back, the other cat reared back. I went and stood between him and the mirror. He turned, and when he turned he saw his dishes of food and water, and for the first time he ate a full meal. All the time he was eating and drinking, he was talking to himself.

If Charley's function was supposed to be to catch mice, the result had to be classified as a failure: during the winter and spring, a mouse that needed catching by Charley would have to come to him and request it. His wildness toward others was coupled with a refusal to leave my side.

But catching mice was of course not the interpreters' main reason for wanting me to have him. Charley was there simply to boost my morale, which they knew was dangerously low. And here he succeeded. He wasn't the only medicine I received while at the Commune of the Red Star, but certainly he was the best.

By late spring, however, even this best of medicines was clearly not enough. My skin had become a mass of freckles and liver spots. My cough was no longer a cigarette cough—in fact, smoking or not smoking made no difference. My eyes and stomach had grown worse. My teeth hurt. My ears hurt. And my head ached almost constantly.

One doctor at Red Star gave me some pills which he said would make me sick, and they did. But they may have helped some too, and I asked for more of them. This time Sally brought me different pills. The first had been yellow: these were red. I had had them before.

"No," I said, "they give me a different reaction than the yellow ones."

"A slight difference," he said.

"That's all the difference," I said.

Actually, the yellow pills made me sick to my stomach; the red ones made my throat dry, produced a terrible thirst, and suppressed my cough. It was, among other things, an example of the language barrier at its worst: in the treatment of the sick. What I had tried to tell them was that I needed something to make me cough up the accumulations of phlegm that were making me nauseous: an expectorant. But, misunderstanding, they were treating me by inducing vomiting from the stomach and suppressing the cough. And when it was done the phlegm was still lodged in my chest and throat.

Dirty Dirty Dirty saw practically nothing of these treatments. It wasn't that he was insensitive to the situation: instead, typically, it was that he could be impervious to reality—any reality that did not conform to his own plan of the moment. (Thus, in demonstrating how to "hand-pollenate" corn, he was so taken up by the technique that he remained blissfully unaware that it was too late in the growing season anyway.)

Also he was away from the commune a good deal, in his serious "government business." He returned from one such official tour late in the spring of 1971, and the first thing on his mind, naturally, was to play Ping Pong.

I had it in mind that they could wheel a Ping-Pong table to my deathbed, fit a paddle into my hand, and the last words I heard before dying would be Dirty Dirty Dirty's: "Fifteen for me, four for you!"

But playing Ping Pong was better than lying in bed. To do the latter was to give up totally, to give the mind as well as the body the assignment of deteriorating together. As long as I could stand, I could walk; and as long as I could walk, I could play Ping Pong. And since I could still stand and walk, why not play Ping Pong? All the barefoot doctors agreed: *diet, pills, and exercise.*

But the quality of the food had gone down again, this time alarmingly, sometimes with meat swimming in grease topped by fatty globules. Perhaps it was superior to the noodles swarming with worms at the Harbor, but the worsened condition of my stomach could not accept that distinction.

As for the pills, they didn't work.

That left the exercise, and that was up to me.

So I played Ping Pong with Dirty Dirty Dirty.

But not for long. After only a few minutes, there was a stab of pain in my stomach: yet I hardly felt it; what had come over me at the same time was a sleepy, distant feeling, a sense of falling while knowing, not unpleasantly, that you would land in a great soft downy quilt and lie there and never have to move again.

I said to Dirty Dirty Dirty, "I can't play anymore."

"Why?"

"I'm too sick."

"What is it, all of a sudden?"

"What ever it is, it isn't all of a sudden. I've been sick for months."

"Why didn't you tell somebody?"

"I did. It doesn't do any good. All I get is the same doctors, the same medicine." I moved toward the door. The pain was there, but with it the enormous new lassitude, almost a sense of deliverance.

Dirty Dirty Dirty looked at me as I left the room. He looked at the Ping-Pong table. The ball lay entwined in the net, where he had just hit it. He called after me: "But you're *winning!*"

* * *

I went back to my room. Charley was there, drinking water and talking to himself in the process. I got into my bed and he came and settled down beside me, with his warmth in the curl of my stomach.

I don't know how long we stayed that way. But at some further point in time, I opened my eyes to see Dirty Dirty Dirty standing there. With him was a woman I had never seen before.

"This is a *real* doctor!" Dirty Dirty Dirty said proudly. "She is the head of the clinic. She will treat you with herbs, the most expensive herbs in all China!" He nodded. "And you will have just the right food to make you well. The doctor will see to it."

For once, it was the truth. The food did improve, and with the herbal medicine I was able to eat it, even to enjoy it. But it had come too late. Perhaps a year ago it would have worked, but by now the best it could do was to slow the deterioration, not reverse it.

I had expected Dirty Dirty Dirty to order a new supply of the medicine when it ran out: for although it was not enough to make me well, it was the most effective medicine I had had so far; and besides, the woman doctor who prescribed it was his idea, and whatever he thought of had to be right.

But instead, he came to me and said, "You have no more medicine?"

"That's right," I said.

"Then I have a different plan," he said. "You will be taken to the hospital."

I studied him for a time. I had no reason to doubt that he did believe I should be hospitalized. But obviously that required a decision at a higher government level, and equally obviously Dirty Dirty Dirty was too incompetent to be taken seriously at any higher government level, this despite all his pompous accounts of "official government assignments."

At last, I said, "Are you sure I'm going to the hospital?"

"Certainly I'm sure," he said.

"When?"

"Tomorrow."

"Who ordered this?" Again, a too-curious question for one of my status to ask, but by now I was beyond caring. And again, Dirty Dirty Dirty would be the last to notice it in any case.

"I ordered it," he said.

My mind did not take me into any fancy flights this time. I knew from past experience that the likelihood I would be going anywhere tomorrow was somewhat dim. As for being taken to a hospital, that prospect seemed even dimmer. If anybody else had promised it, that would have been one thing—but a guarantee from Dirty Dirty Dirty was too self-inflated to carry any effect of conviction. Dully, my mind told me that the most that was happening was their preparing me for yet another transfer to yet another place. They had told Dirty Dirty Dirty it would be a hospital, because they knew he'd tell me that, and take credit for it, and that would make me amenable to the new move, so I could go from here to there without making a scene.

I knew the way to thwart that, even in the face of surprise. And the surprise came. The next morning, a very jolly army doctor came to my room, accompanied by a couple of the interpreters. Through them, he said to me:

"We're taking you to the hospital."

Through the interpreters, I said back to him, "No, you're not."

There was conversation now in Chinese. Then the question:

"Why don't you want to go to the hospital?"

"I didn't say I don't want to go to the hospital."

"Then you will go?"

"Only if I can take my cat."

This was the test, and I watched the translation carefully. Then the answer came back:

"Of course we want you to take your cat."

The test was hardly conclusive. It still didn't mean I was being taken to any hospital. But at least it meant that wherever I was being taken, Charley would be with me.

The doctor said something else in Chinese, and the interpreters nodded gladly.

I said, "What does he say?"

"He says you can bring your fish, too."

"My fish, too," I repeated. "Anything else?"

"Only that we have to begin to get ready at once. We'll help you pack your things."

There was an afternoon of packing and an early dinner, and then there came to the door an army man and a nurse.

"The nurse will give you an injection," I was told.

"No she won't," I said.

"It's to make it easier while you travel."

"I'll travel the way I am."

Primary said to me, "Why don't you have the injection?"

"Because I want to stay conscious, that's why."

"Conscious?" she repeated, bewildered. "What does that mean?"

"Alive," I said. "And while we're at it, where's my little friend?"

"Your little friend?"

"The one I always beat at Ping Pong."

"Oh," she said. "He's gone away. I don't believe you'll ever see him again."

Well I was born at the bottom of a wishing well
But I ended up goin' thru the gates of hell
Well I've seen a great deal but not too much
But I ended up goin' thru the gates of hell

We left at sunset: the strangest caravan yet. This time there were two cars. The one in front was a late-model Russian make, with an army officer and driver in front, and Middleschool and the nurse on either side of Charley and me in the back. Behind us was a jeep, with a driver, Primary, the fish, and the luggage.

In the first portion of the trip we re-traced the route that had brought me to Red Star, going north this time, with the same ferry, the same circular lily pond, the same bridge across the same river. But then we made a sweeping right turn, toward the east, and I began to see propeller-driven passenger planes, very low in a landing pattern in the sky.

"The airport of Canton," Middleschool said to me.

We seemed to be circling the airport, driving past acres of rice and other crops, and our final turn led us to a graveled drive leading to what seemed to be an endless compound of rust-colored brick buildings.

"The Hospital of the People's Liberation Army," Middleschool said to me. Our relationship was close but carefully delineated. If she had a choice of lying to me or upsetting me, she would lie.

We drove up to a gate manned by a guard.

"This isn't a hospital," I said.

"Of course it's a hospital," Middleschool said. "You're upset."

I still had difficulty accepting it. Institutions look like institutions. Hospitals look like prisons.

Now the young man at the gate, after talking to our driver, suddenly squeezed into the front seat and started giving directions. We drove—almost endlessly, it seemed—to a long, low bulding, and were led inside to a room that had two hospital-type beds. I looked around the room, then looked back again, and the military men were gone. None of them had had guns to begin with.

"That will be your bed," Primary said pointing. "And the officials say they would like me to have the other bed, if it's satisfactory to you."

There had been two beds in my room at the first hotel in the Commune of the Happy People, too, and there the officials wanted me to share the room with Miss Fanatic. I had refused point blank, and raised such a ruckus that they dropped the notion at once. At that point, they were going out of their way to be nice. But now at the hospital they were being equally solicitous—word had traveled, I suppose, of my earlier insistance upon having a room to myself. The difference between then and now was of course the difference between Miss Fanatic and Primary.

"Of course it's satisfactory to me," I said to her.

It still hadn't come over me completely. At last, I said, "This *is* a hospital."

"Of course," Primary said. "Isn't that what you were told?"

"But—*how?"*

"On direct orders," she said. "From your friend. The one you always defeated in Ping Pong."

* * *

My fourth summer in China, and each had been spent at a different place: first at the Harbor, then the Commune of the Happy People, then Red Star, and now the PLA Hospital just outside Canton.

By now, I was beginning to have a sense of place. Not so much because anybody sat me down with a map—of course they didn't—but because of a progression of little things. I knew the ocean was there: I knew it at the Harbor, from the sounds of the whistles; I knew it at Red Star from the occasional scent, when the wind was right, of salt-water marshes; I knew it at the Commune of the Happy People, because even though you are somewhat inland, a typhoon is still a typhoon. I surmised that all the places I had been were within Kwangtung Province, which is the southernmost coastal province of China. This was interesting: I suppose I could have been held captive in remotest Mongolia and still heard the same party line about America's presence in

Vietnam, but proximity affects everyone, and there was a special quality of virulence to the way I heard it where I was. And why not? Canton is closer to Hanoi than Saigon. Kwangtung Province borders North Vietnam.

Yet each place I had been taken to was different. At the hospital, for example, there were no guards; that is to say, no uniformed men with guns. Two men, civilians, did occupy a room at the other end of the long building where I was housed, and since they weren't sick, I assumed they were there because I was there. I had another reason for assuming this: my room was in the children's section of the hospital. So what were two healthy grown men doing there? Preventing my escape? I no longer thought of escape. Reality here had taken over from desire. Actually, it had taken over long before now. As long ago as the Commune of the Happy People, when they had "insect-proofed" my room by caulking the walls, I knew they had another purpose: to prevent my being able to see out and divine some route of escape. True, they let me walk in the hills behind the hotels, but never by myself, not even when I "stole" the forbidden litchi fruit when the interpreters weren't looking.

But in a sense they were ritualizing it. They sensed I had the ambition to escape, but they also must have known I knew it couldn't be done. Here now at the hospital, the "guards" hardly made their presence known. Once in a while they would come to borrow our playing cards, or to play Ping Pong in the very end room of the building, which was where Middleschool slept. Primary and I were in the room next to hers. Next to us on the other side was the bathroom, but you had to go outside, onto a small porch which faced a large yard area, to reach it.

So the absence of armed guards was different. Yet other things were the same. Before I was allowed to go out into the yard, they had to drape the intervening

The Ping Pong room at the hospital.

areas not bordered by other buildings but by fences: they wrapped the fences in sheets, so nobody could look in on me. It was a worthless pursuit: the children who were there as patients had to exercise too, and they used to cluster around me each time we went out. *"Ay-ya,"* I would say, meaning "Oh, my." *"Samdi,"* I would say, meaning "Oh, dear." By now I was talking Chinese. But only certain easy phrases. I began to wear my hair in pigtails too, but in American Indian style, with the pigtails out to the side, not pulled back close in as the Chinese did.

The children at the hospital, those that I saw, were ambulatory cases, many of them hospitalized for the treatment of great carbuncles and boils and skin disease. It was not uncommon under such circumstances for their parents to come and live at the hospital while they were there. The children themselves were young—an average, I'd say, of no more than five or six years of age—and they were given responsibilities they weren't old enough, or trained enough, to handle. Many of them were too young to use chopsticks. They would eat with their hands off the sidewalk that fronted our building. Then they would wash their own dishes by holding them under a cold-water spigot outside.

I had brought with me my gift set of chopsticks from the builder of the *Menehune,* as well as the knife, fork, and spoon I had been given at the Commune of the Happy People. The children and the interpreters alike were fascinated by the uses I made of them. Primary always ate with chopsticks. Middleschool ate with a big spoon. Neither of them could understand what possible need I had for a fork.

"The spoon can do everything the fork can do," Middleschool said to me.

I said, "But it's what I'm used to. Just the way you're used to chopsticks."

"The only reason I use a spoon," she said stiffly, "is that I left my chopsticks at home." Home, for her, was a small apartment in Canton. She had a husband—I learned that much—and we had talks about marriage in China. Happiness, she said, was not a factor: you worked for communism, and that was that; you got married to have children, not for love. And once you were married, you were married.

Both Short Pigtails and Long Pigtails had been married: Sally told me that. Both of them came from the north of China, and when they left me, both of them returned to their husbands. Gladly so? I had no idea. I said to Middleschool, "What if you can't get along with your husband?"

"We marry comparatively later," she said, as though that explained it.

"But what about a divorce?"

"A divorce?"

I told her about divorce, American style. "Nobody in China would know how to go about it," she said.

I asked her about birth control pills. She had heard of them, but they were not in general use in China. "A married woman might have a reason for them," she said. "An unmarried woman: never."

I've said some things were different, some things were the same. To Middleschool it made no difference either way. One of the things she had brought from Red Star, for use in the room that Primary and I shared, was my green light bulb.

The first night at the hospital, Primary and I found a hot, bright light shining down on us from a ceiling fixture in our room.

Primary said to me, "I can't sleep with that light on."

"Then let's have it turned off," I said.

"I think that's a wonderful idea," she said, and went and switched off the light.

I waited for someboy to come and switch the light back on, but nobody ever did.

That could have been a milestone, that business with the light the first night at the hospital, except that other things happened too. "Go look at the bathroom next door," they told me proudly when I first arrived, and so I stepped onto the porch to open the door and look at it. It was the most modern bathroom I'd seen since I'd come to China.

But while I was gone, something was happening in my room. We all knew Charley was wild—particularly if moved to new surroundings in this way—so they were supposed to have a cage waiting for him, where he could be housed till he got accustomed to the new place.

But no cage was ready. From outside in the hall, I heard awful shouts and screams from my room. Charley had been on a rope-leash for the trip from Red Star, but he had broken the rope, and now he had everyone in the room terrified—interpreters, attendants, doctors, and nurses alike.

Reassured by my return, Charley began to calm down, and I became the one who needed reassuring. The sight of a doctor so frightened he tries to climb a wall is not rewarding for his patient-to-be.

"But the medicine and the people here are excellent," Primary told me that night, after we had got into bed. "The hospital has an excellent reputation."

"Who says so?"

"All the students."

I was dubious. "None of the medicine I've had so far has seemed to do much."

"Here it's different," she promised. "You can have acupuncture."

"No," I said, "they're not going to stick any needles into me."

The next day my treatment began. I would be in the hands principally of two doctors, one an older man who had studied in Russia, then a young one who had been locally trained; and two nurses, one large and fat ("Big Nurse") and the other petite, very young, with a shiny, healthy face and a mania for playing Ping Pong. The younger one seemed to be assigned to me almost on an exclusive basis.

I was examined and fluoroscoped, and herbal medicines and vitamin shots were prescribed. The food was better, including chicken or fish at least once a day and, from time to time, a rather good beer. "What do you think you need?" they asked me. "Fruit," I said, so they brought fresh fruit too. And they took me to another building to visit a dentist.

I say he was a dentist, although he was also the resident optometrist and eye-ear-nose-and-throat man. Once again here there was the matter of breakdown in communication, the language barrier. Once, at the Commune of the Happy People, I had been walking in the hills with some of the interpreters, and we came upon a tree with wild fruit: it had a soft, yellow skin and contained many seeds with a sour taste. I decided to try one; before I did so, I offered it to Short Pigtails. She shook her head and pointed to her mouth. "The teeth," she said. "The teeth." The way she did it, I assumed she had bad teeth, but what she was telling me instead was that this particular fruit was regarded as bad for *any*body's teeth.

With the dentist at the hospital now, a similar problem arose. He was a sallow man who needed a shave, and he wore a face mask that afterwards he would store in a dirty pocket. I had holes in my teeth—he could see them, obviously—and this is what I thought he would fix, but what he decided I wanted was pain killer, so that was what he applied. With my teeth in the shape they were, this had the effect of causing more pain than it alleviated.

There was the sensation, in dealing with *any* doctors in China, that up to a certain point *you* were expected to tell *them* what was wrong with you and also to prescribe the treatment for it. Of course at the hospital level there was more professional diagnosis, but the patient still was accorded unusual leeway. In the U.S., a doctor treating my cough might well have ordered me to give up smoking (even though I smoked no more than half a pack a day); at the PLA Hospital, in contrast, their solution was to let me have filter cigarettes instead of plain.

The vitamin shots administered by the young nurse always were given in the same place—the inside of the calf of my left leg— and they were prolonged and painful. A twisting pain would follow each shot, as I lay on my face on the bed, and within a week or so I began to lose sensation in the leg, and to drag it and stumble when I walked. I couldn't even feel Charley's tail when he sat at the bottom of my bed and flicked it across my toes.

What I suspected proved to be true: the nurse was using the hypodermic needle not only to give me shots but for acupuncture directly afterwards. Having given the shot, she would then hold the needle in place and twist it from side to side. This was why I always got the shot in the same place, a place on my leg that was supposed to relate to my stomach.

But my stomach didn't improve, and the leg got worse. The paralysis lasted for about a month after the acupuncture treatments were stopped, and gradually normal feeling returned. I don't know whether the treatments stopped because I demanded it—which I did—or because the hospital people could see they were having an undesirable effect. Once again, there was the uncertain line that separated medical opinion from the patient's personal wishes in the matter, but from then on I got my vitamin shots in the hip. Acupuncture was an extremely popular form of therapy at the hospital and many patients volunteered to have it done. It was considered a sure remedy for everyday illnesses—rheumatism, headaches, indigestion. Oviously it was neither effective nor painless in every single case; there was also a tendency to credit it with results that most probably would have happened anyway. One day Primary complained to the nurse that she was feeling dizzy, and asked for some pills. The nurse suggested acupuncture instead. She inserted a needle into Primary's left wrist: Primary screamed with pain. The nurse now switched to the right wrist: there was still pain, though not so much as the first time.

"Now lie down for a while," the nurse said to her, "and you'll feel better."

Primary lay down. Two hours later she sat up. "It worked!" she said. "The dizzy feeling is gone."

I said to myself, *If she'd done that in the first place, that would have worked, too. Why did she need the needle?*

* * *

In the summer and early fall at the hospital there were things I had never seen before in China: always the passenger planes overhead, both in take-off and landing patterns from and to the adjacent airport, which I supposed to be the main airport of Canton; popsicles made out of some kind of bean, but cold and very refreshing; hot soup made with a peanut base—and always the children.

I had seen them first in the beginning days of my captivity on the Island, jumping rope, playing basketball, bouncing a badminton bird cleverly with their feet, the boys among them engaging in mock military drills, featuring gestures associated with hand grenades and bayonets. The children at the hospital were no different. They would make chains out of rubber bands, draw them taut, then jump on them, producing a sudden slingshot effect. As they played their games, their parents and other older patients would sit on the sidewalks surrounding the yard, dishing food out of buckets, eating, washing dishes and clothes.

The doctors wanted me to exercise, and each day the loudspeakers played exercise music in the compound, but I was too self-conscious and too stared-at to be willing to exercise when the others did. Instead, the interpreters and I would exercise after dark, in privacy, except that there was never real privacy. Out of the darkness would emerge the children. Some of them would hover on the other side of the fence and peek through and snicker at us. Others joined in the exercises. Some of them had attached themselves to me. The interpreters didn't like this close association, but it was there. Two little three-year-old girls, both hospitalized for skin disease, with swollen necks and carbuncles, would stand beside Primary and me when we played cards out in the yard. Each had hand-fans, and they would fan us gravely while the games went on. At night, when we exercised, they would come to join us again, often in the company of two boys, one very young, the other about twelve, and all of us would line up and solemnly do the exercises together. The children always carried with them little swab-sticks, with tufts of cotton at the tip. They made inventive toys out of them, and each evening they would contrive some new imaginative use for them. It was a satisfied kind of fun for me to watch this, for I was the one who made the swab-sticks. Each morning, when I wasn't reading the works of Lenin, I would wrap dozens of sticks in cotton. Everyone agreed it was a useful exercise.

"If you want to play here, then pull weeds," the nurse would tell the children who came into the yard. Again: a useful exercise. Two other children—I named them Lucy and Linus—would come out in the daytime and be as close to us as they could. Lucy was the Lucy of the Peanuts cartoon strip, both in looks and characteristics. She was perhaps five years of age, but extremely intelligent. She had not yet started school, but she learned and memorized things in an instant, from the rules of the various card games to the libretto of an opera she had heard on the radio.

"Go away," the interpreters would tell her, while we were playing cards or chess, and obediently she would back off, but only for two steps or so. Then she would appear to become fascinated by some nearby object—a post, a clump of weeds—and gradually she would ease back to the exact proximity as before. If she was shouted at again, she would take a new tack. Suddenly, she would be dancing, singing, striking poses and all the while staring at me. I was the one who didn't shout at her. The antics were irresistible. We would laugh, and that of course was the adrenalin she needed.

Her brother "Linus" was three years old, a carbon copy of Linus in the Peanuts strip, except that he lacked a security blanket. Wherever she went, he went. Whatever she did, he copied.

Some of the children deserved to be yelled at. There was one four-year-old boy who thought a stick ought to be a weapon with which to hit anything that moved. He lashed out with it at adults, other children, even my cat Charley, when Charley reached the point of being willing to go outside in the yard by himself.

I would yell at the youngster for this, and so would the gate-boy, the man who had first met us at the gate to the hospital when we arrived at Red Star, and taken the wheel to drive us to the right building. He loved to play cards and chess, and so he joined us time and again on the porch and in the yard. But Lucy and Linus bothered him. Lucy especially, for she wore colorful blouses, some of them bright green and gold ("Clothes show the customs of a nation," Big Nurse had told me, and she knew that Chinese clothes usually were drab and colorless). Together with the blouse, Lucy would wear long skirts topped with elastic ribbing. Sometimes, to draw attention, she would stand before us and take off her skirt. The gate-boy found it furiously embarrassing. Once, she went through the performance repeatedly while another small boy, a four-year-old hospitalized for liver trouble, stood beside her with a look of great concentration on his face. The enraged gate-boy asked her what she thought she was doing. Lucy smiled and pointed to the four-year-old beside her. She said something in Chinese, and Middleschool began to laugh. I asked her what it was about. "She says," Middleschool replied, "that she's teaching him to count."

The gate-boy spoke no English. We might spend afternoons playing cards or Chinese chess (his especial favorite) on the porch, with milk and cookies beside us. Lucy was not the only thing that bothered him. The interpreters and I would talk in English while he frowned at the chess board. We were talking in that fashion at one point when he suddenly erupted into a tirade of Chinese. "He wants you to play faster," Middleschool said to me. "He says you take so long it makes him nervous."

I said, "Tell him if I play fast, I don't think fast." She told him. Then I said to her, "Boys like to win, don't they?" She laughed, but wouldn't translate that part to the gate-boy.

He was, I would judge, seven or eight years older than I, yet I saw in him the reflection of the me that had first come to China in 1968. He was impatient, as I had been. Somewhere over the intervening years, certainly at no one isolated moment in time, the ingredient of survival had come to me: I had learned patience. I accepted this, and was glad because of it, but not really glad. I thought back once more to the old woman I had seen in that television documentary so many yars ago, who said that her age was the reason she managed to survive imprisonment in China. *"If I had been younger," she said, "I would have been more active. If I had been more active, I could never have lived through it. I would have torn myself apart."*

Surely I was more active than this woman had been in her jail cell, even more so now that the medical care and diet I was receiving had slowed down some elements of my physical delcine, arrested others. But now I had what she had: patience.

It was, I knew, an incalculable gain. I knew this except when I looked in the mirror. For the face I saw then was an old woman's face.

Seventeen, I called her, because that was her age. I hesitate to call her just another new interpreter. True, she was newly assigned to me, but among other things she had trouble interpreting.

She came because Primary was leaving for an interval of a month or so, and the authorities obviously wanted me to have two female attendants at all times.

I said to Primary, "Why do you have to go?"

"I'll be back," she promised.

"But *why?*"

"It's practical," she said.

"I don't like your definition of practical," I said.

She laughed. "You were telling me the other day how in America you have machines that smooth the tops of desks and tables by sanding them. Sanding? You know? putting sand on."

"Yes," I said. "So?"

"So," she said, "you think that's practical."

"Of course it's practical," I said. "The alternative is to sand it by hand, with sandpaper. That's what you do in China."

"That's not really what we do," she said. "If we have desks that need to be sanded, we don't use a machine, and we don't use what you tell me is sandpaper."

"Then what do you use?"

"Just sand," she said.

"That's not practical," I said. "It's primitive."

"Well, we will never quite appreciate our separate cultures," she said. "You see, what we do is to put the sand on top of one desk that needs sanding, and then we take another desk that needs sanding, and then with the sand in between we rub the two desks against each other. That way we sand two desks at once. That's what we mean by practical. What do you think?"

"Tomma," I said.

Seventeen bubbled over. She was small, petite, totally vivacious. She brought a radio with her, and no matter what time of day it was—regardless that the hospital loudspeaker was blaring the news at six, noon, two, six, and nine—she could always find music on it, and any time there was music she wanted to dance, and did.

She brought something else with her, too: a box of

chocolate creams. Shades of my daydreams at the Island! She offered me one. I took it. She offered me another. I said yes, I thought I would. Then with a wisdom belying her years she went out of the room and left the box behind. "Come over here, Charley," I said to my cat. "I have something here you're not going to believe." He came and together we finished the box of chocolates.

Middleschool frowned on Seventeen's ebullience, but there was not much she could do about it. Among other things, Seventeen had read famous English stories *in Chinese,* and she insisted on relating their contents to us. She would tell the stories in Chinese, and Middleschool would translate them into English for me. It was a familiar task for Middleschool—she had already translated for me some chinese accounts of the Pentagon papers, of Henry Kissinger's visits to Peking, of the intention of President Nixon to visit China within a year's time.

But what she was translating now was an enthusiastic young girl's excited version of stories she had read. One after another, I recognized them: *The Speckled Band,* one of the adventures of Sherlock Holmes, and Shakespeare's play *The Merchant of Venice.* Even conceding that these were not "controversial," conceding too that in the past year or so the cultural revolution had begun to wane, so that you no longer expected to see a Mao badge on everyone's shirt pocket, the question still remained: how would this western literature have invaded the curriculum of a Chinese teen-ager?

But Seventeen did not want only to tell stories. She wanted to *hear* stories. And so, with Middleschool in the middle as before, the translation process reversed itself, and I told them stories. Some of them were from the Bible. I talked about Adam and Eve, and about Noah and the ark.

"Stop for a minute and tell me," Middleschool said. "Are these folk stories?"

"Some people believe they're true," I said.

Middleschool shook her head. "They must be folk stories," she said. "Do you know any songs?"

"Some."

"Sing them for us."

And so I sang for them. "Home on the Range," and my own song, the one I had been writing all the time I was in China, and some Bob Dylan verses about prison and freedom. My existentialist philosophy, like his, had really nothing to do with freedom in and of itself: it went instead to the freedom that can be found within the bonds of captivity—a concept which undoubtedly had a lot to do with my survival.

Independent of that, with my better physical condition had come a feeling of optimism: perhaps my release was not so far away after all.

I had a reason for thinking this way: most of my medical treatments had run their course, and yet there were still no signs that they intended to move me away from the hospital.

My hopes bounded further in the autumn when Middleschool told me they were getting me some new clothes. It was the same sensation I had had at the Commune of the Happy People, when they brought me a new outfit: *They want me to walk across the border in style.* The same hopes, yet buoyed further by the fact that they were keeping me on at this nice place.

The new clothes came, and they were fine: two corduroy suits made up of pants and blouse; two pairs of shoes, one of leather and one of cloth.

You will walk across the border in style, I repeated to myself, but in the act of saying it I stopped. With half of China still trying to acquire proper clothing, was I going to walk across the border in two blouses, two pairs of trousers, two pairs of shoes?

6

Zack

"Think of what clothes you'll wear tomorrow," Middleschool said to me, one night well into November.

I said, "Why?"

"Because the government says we can go to the Fair."

"The *Fair?*"

"The Fair."

The emphasis was different. I had heard of the Fall Commodities Fair held every year in Canton, and I knew it was a major event; to the Cantonese, it was of course *the* event. But to me, its significance was that for the first time in more than three and a half years I was being allowed to leave a restricted area, to move freely among strangers.

I said to Middleschool, "Tell me more."

"There's no more to tell," she said, then: "Oh, wait. There's one other thing. They said to tell you it's all right for you to have beer with all your meals now. If you want it, all you have to do is ask."

I said to my cat, "Charley, did you hear all this?"

He had heard, and I don't think he thought much of the news. He had come a long way since our arrival at the hospital. Our first week there, he had refused to leave the room at all, and I had a wing-ding of a fight with the hospital people, to provide him with a proper litter box. The logical filling for the box would have been dirt, but the same hospital whose doctors carried instruments and gauze masks in filthy pockets expressed a horror for anything dirty. They offered me coal ashes instead. Charley disliked them because they would be delivered hot; I disliked them because they were dirtier than dirt.

In those first days, I began leaving the window open, even the windowscreen, and Charley began to venture out at night. Because the screen was open, I insisted on mosquito netting. The hospital had other ideas about this too. They sprayed against mosquitoes, and lit fires against them—in fact, that was why the nurse had told the children to pluck the weeds in the yard: the weeds would be the fuel for mosquito fires.

But they could see evidence that mosquitoes were invading my room, so they draped the posts of my bed with a canopy of mosquito netting. That intrigued Charley. He decided that during the summer months he would sleep on top of the mosquito netting stretched over the bed. It was a sight to watch him clamber up the netting to get to the top and a less enjoyable sight when his weight caused the netting to give in and he came plummeting down upon my stomach. I corrected this by spreading a wicker fan as a sort of "cat mat" over the top of the netting. At least that supported his weight, but it was a temporary exercise, for as summer turned into fall and the nights grew crisper, he began to prefer sleeping in my bed rather than over it.

Finally, he would sleep next to me with his face on the pillow but only after I had acquired the kind of pillow he wanted. In China, the pillows come in three varieties (though all the pillowcases look the same: envelope-shaped and embroidered with little flowers). The rarest and most expensive are filled wth goose feathers. Others are stuffed with old rags. Still others are filled with husks, seeds, corn, and rice, round and hard and rolling around under your shifting weight, so that it is like sleeping on marbles. That was the kind of pillow they gave me to begin with at the hospital, and that was the kind of pillow I gave back. I wanted one with the feathers. So did Charley. Somewhat to my surprise, they gave in to the demand and produced one. Maybe they were entranced by the notion that a cat wanted the same thing.

But Charley's progress took time. Slowly he ventured out, first at night, then daytimes during the nap period —noon till two o'clock—that was as much a feature of China as the siesta is a feature of Mexico: a time when everything went silent and stopped.

For Charley it was a case sometimes of one step forward and two steps back, for the outside world was filled with hostility. Other cats, a big yellow one in particular, would chase him, then gobble his food. The four-year-old boy who liked to hit people with sticks took after him. Even a little kitten, no more than six weeks old, who wanted to make friends, proved a frightening adversary. In Charley's world, I was the only friend he had.

"If I go to the Fair tomorrow, I'll be back at night," I promised him.

He gave me the same look Frederick gave me in Salt Lake City when I assured him I wasn't going back to prison.

* * *

In a way, the streets of the giant city of Canton bore the look of home. By "home" I mean the Chinatown of San Francisco, so largely peopled by Cantonese who faithfully reproduced the arcade sidewalks of the mother city. I was struck too by the fact that for a city of its size—a population of over 3,000,000—it gave off a much smaller look. There are a number of reasons to explain this impression. One was that the population crowds itself in, with whole families occupying a tiny flat. Another was that despite the hordes of buses and bicycles—the two main forms of publc transportation—the principle of the commune, practiced in this one respect even back before the time of Chairman Mao, was that cities were cities, outskirts were outskirts, so that you would encounter only very little of the western feel of sprawl. I think that any American city with one-fourth the population of Canton has four times as many suburbs. In their place, Canton has miles of unoccupied open country, some of it leading almost to the very heart of the city itself.

A third possibility is of course that I saw only such segments of the Canton area as would support the conclusions I've just made. It's easy to spend a week in China and come out an expert. The longer you stay, the less easy it becomes.

The Trade Fair that I was taken to was a giant exhibition that ran for six weeks. The first four weeks would be strictly business, for foreign buyers only, with all the goods and machines and manufacture of China on display. Then the last two weeks the Fair would be open to the public, and that is when we went. It was impressive and yet at the same time not impressive: many of the most delightful displays were scale models of factories and farms which would spring into action at the push of a button, but by this time too many of them were no longer in working order. You could admire the model, but when you pushed the button nothing happened.

This is equally true of any exhibition anywhere in the world, I suppose: when it comes to the closing down stage, things don't work the way they used to.

The Chinese have a saying: *In agriculture, learn from Tachai—in industry, learn from Taching.* These are the great farming and oil complexes of Maoist China, and their products dominated the Fair, together with an astonishing variety of ready-made dresses and other clothes, all in western styling.

On our way back to the hospital, Middleschool said to me, "What did you think of the Fair?"

I said, carefully, "There was too much of it to see in one day."

"I agree," she said. "We'll go again tomorrow."

The next day we went to the Fair again, then to two pottery factories. I was exhausted.

"Do you want to see a silk factory tomorrow?" Middleschool asked.

"Yes," I said.

Every day became a new journey to a new place, with Middleschool, Seventeen, and Primary (who by now had returned from wherever her "practical" absence had taken her) shepherding me from one tourist spot to another. Until the visit to the Fair, my only "entertainment" at the hospital had consisted of watching wrong-way movies: in the summer, we would sit on the opposite side of a transparent screen, concealed from the audience, and watch the horses ride in from left to right while everybody else was seeing them ride in from right to left. "This is ridiculous," I said to the interpreters. "It's the only way," they replied. "If we take you out front, they'll stare at you instead of the picture."

They had a point. At the Fair, I looked at the exhibits and everybody else looked at me. At some places we went, this could prove to be an acute embarrassment. At one factory, a man said to me, through one of the interpreters, "Is this your first trip to a commune?"

We all looked at one another. At last the interpreter—I think it was Middleschool—told him something to the effect that she could not translate the word "trip" to me. He nodded in full understanding, and changed the wording of the question.Now it came out: "Is this your first *visit* to a commune?"

"Visit" was legitimate. I nodded my head yes. "Wait," he said, holding up his finger, and ducked under his workshelf. When he re-appeared, he held a bottle containing a strange, blobby object. He spoke in rapid Chinese to the interpeters.

"He wants you to see his bladder stone," they told me. "You should admire it."

"I admire it," I said, and nodded happily at the man, and he nodded back.

There was more of that sort of thing. I was taken to a deaf-mute school, where acupuncture was used to effect extraordinary results, then to a huge hospital, even bigger (if not so spread out) than the PLA Hospital where I was staying. There I was introduced to a man who was about to have a bladder stone removed, and to a woman who had a tumor on her ovary. Both of them were about to undergo surgery with acupuncture as the only anasthetic. The interpreters and I were led to spectator seats overlooking the surgery area, which consisted of two separate rooms with walls but no ceilings, so the action in each could be viewed from the spectator balcony above. (The actual ceiling overhead was a carbon copy of too many places I had already been, thinly covered, with the noise of running rats above.)

I decided to concentrate on just one of the operations: the removal of the tumor from the woman. The doctors gathered around her were dressed the same as any surgeons in the United States might dress, except for one distinction: they were barefoot.

The needles were applied, and then the abdominal incision was made: a huge, deep cut. They drew out the tumor, sewed her up, restored the sheet. She had been conscious all the time. She wanted to hold the tumor in her hands, so one of the surgeons gave it to her. Then she took one of her hands away and looked at her watch.

We went to Fatshan, just outside of Canton—a place world-famous for its porcelain dinnerware—and saw two different factories there: one of them an unbelievable, decrepit sweatshop that seemed five hundred years old (though, even more unbelievably, we were told it had first been built in 1952); the other a lovely place with fountains playing in the center of the rooms where the workers turned out ashtrays and figurines. We visited a reservoir, a shopping center, a pumping station. We went to a hotel for lunch (the second-finest hotel in Canton, for Chinese only: the doorman tried to refuse to let me in; the one better hotel in the city was, perhaps understandably, exclusively for foreigners. The hotel we went to served the first truly decent cup of tea I had tasted since coming to China. It also had a hairdressing parlor, whose proprietor swore he could give me a western hair-do. He was true to his word, but his word was short-lived. The set only held for a few hours and by the time we got back to the hospital my hair was as limp as ever.

We used the same hotel to rent a room where we could nap for a couple of hours in the early afternoon. We went to a basketball game (but I was stared at, and we left very soon). We went to the zoo, where I was not stared at so much. The four of us—Middleschool, Primary, Seventeen, and I—were driven there in a very nice car, apparently of British make, and I saw the famous pandas of China. It was a large zoo, with elephants, fish, lions, tigers, monkeys, and snakes—but also, and for some reason equally attractive to the Chinese, vast caged collections of the most mundane animals: cats, dogs, pigs, horses, and cows.

Everywhere we went, we saw people sweeping the streets, and when we visited the public parks we saw them pulling the weeds. At all places we saw the great traditional, mystical, medicinal, legendary flower of China: the chrysanthemum. Its range of uses, from tea to prayers, defies proper description. But like all the cared-for flowers in China, we saw them not growing out of the ground but cultured as flowering plants in pots.

"It might be a good idea," Middleschool said to me, "if you put down in writing that you entered China by mistake, and that you have been treated well since you came here."

I looked at her. "I did that more than two years ago."

"No," she said. "No, you didn't. What you wrote then was that you were misguided."

"But my companion also gave them a statement."

"Yes," she said. "I have his statement here." We were in her room, where the Ping-Pong table was, and it was late at night following one of our all-day jaunts into Canton. Middleschool was obviously tired, but as long as this remained to be done, she would have to remain awake.

I have his statement here. It was curious: translators would come and translators would go, but the documents seemed to shift hands endlessly and always be current. Middleschool had never met Jerry, but she had in her hand the "confession" he had signed at the Island. I looked at it and recognized it at once, from the draft version he had shown me at the time. In fact, there was no way not to recognize it: my thumbprint and signature both were on it.

"In my opinion," Middleschool said carefully, "it would be the best thing if you see what this says—"

"I already know what it says."

"—and write something that is more or less the same," she said. "It will have to have two parts. One will say that you trespassed. The other will say that you were treated well while in China."

"While in China?" I said.

"Yes," she said, looking up, almost in irritation. "While in China. What other place?"

"But *while in China* means I'm through being in China."

"It could mean that," she said. "If you do it right." She wasn't angry about it. She didn't even espouse her government's point of view. She simply accepted it. On more than one occasion, I had told her I didn't think her government was justified in keeping me captive. "What do you expect when you trespass?" she replied.

"All right," I said now, taking pencil and paper. "What is it exactly you want me to say?"

"I've already told you." She yawned. "It has to take two parts—"

"I know," I said, and began to write. It dawned on me now what they were doing. They wanted to release me. That was part of the Kissinger-Nixon business—a unique part of it, perhaps, because neither Kissinger nor Nixon knew I existed. I'm not guessing at this: I *know* it; for if the Chinese had given them specific word of me, then they could no longer keep me from communicating with the outside world. Nevertheless, I had obviously become a part of whatever plan they had, and that in turn explained a lot of things: why I was being treated so well, why I had suddenly been turned loose on a guided tour of the great city of Canton, as though two and a half weeks could undo the attrition of nearly four years.

While Middleschool lay on her bed and yawned, I sat at the Ping-Pong table, writing and rewriting. I was sure they wanted something abject that they could show on display; some instinct within me refused to give it to them. I finished one draft version, then wrote another one, shorter than the first; then a third one, the shortest of all.

Middleschool was almost asleep. I shook her by the shoulder and asked her to read what I had written.

She read it through. At that point she had one comment, "It doesn't have a title."

"All right," I said, "then write down—"

"I don't write down anything," she cut in. *"You* write it down."

"Very well," I said, and I wrote down a title at the top: STATEMENT.

She nodded, half to herself. "I suggest," she said, "that you do it over. Wake me up when you're through. This time write down CONFESSION, instead of STATEMENT."

I looked at her. "Why?"

"What do you mean, *why?"*

"You want me to call this a confession. I have nothing to confess."

"Do you want me to tell the officials what you just said?"

"Of course I want you to tell them."

"Then you'll be upset. Because I can't translate that."

"Why can't you translate it?"

"Because you're acting the way they've told me you've acted all along. I don't know why you've done this, and I don't want to know. Maybe your mind tells you it was the only way you could stay alive. Whatever it is, don't explain it to me. I tell you they'll accept a confession but they won't accept a statement. You can write whatever you want. But it might be a good idea for you as an American to confess the way we Chinese apologize."

"But I—"

"But you humble yourself," she said. "It's up to you. Write it down on the paper, because after you do I have to translate it into Chinese and show it to the officials. If I get to sleep before the sun comes up, I'll be fortunate."

And so I wrote my "confession." I said I'd trespassed and I said I'd been well-treated. That was all I said. Actually, the document was far less abject than the one I'd written during that bleak time at the Harbor. But it had the magic word at the top: CONFESSION.

And that was, after all and everything, the one thing they wanted.

The next night I was summoned to the administration wing of the hospital. With an interpreter in attendance, an army man stood beside a desk and read to me the contents of an official document.

The document was Jerry's death certificate.

He had died, the official read in a cold voice, on March 12, 1969. Cause of death: suicide. Manner of death: he had hanged himself.

The interpreter raised his eyes and looked at me with a slight smile. What he said in Chinese now, as translated to me, obviously did not appear in the official language on the death certificate. Equally obviously, they wanted me to hear it:

"Everything possible was done to revive him."

If I had been ninety-five percent sure I was going to be released, now I was ninety-eight percent sure. They wanted me to bear witness to the fact that Jerry was an unavoidable suicide. By now, they reasoned, I would have lost track of time and could accept their version of what happened, and their version of course carried wth it a conveyance of sincere but helpless regret.

What they did not know was that, from the balcony of my room at the Harbor, I had seen Jerry alive *after* March 12, 1969. They had used that date—that intentionally moved-up, earlier date—because at the time he still might conceivably have had the physical strength to commit suicide in the "acceptable" manner the death certificate reported. But by the time I last saw him, he no longer had that strength.

In a word, the Chinese were counting on me to confirm to the world their version of Jerry's death: to say, as they claimed, that it was a matter of guilt on his part, rather than neglect on theirs.

"Have you heard everything that was said?" the interpreter said to me now.

"Yes," I said.

"Excellent," she said. "Then we will go back to your room."

The shock wave was beginning to hit me. It was surprising, in a way: as positive as I had been at the time that Jerry was dead, I must have had some vestige of hope. Now this official announcement sealed it off. *He was a good man,* I told myself. *He didn't have to die.*

But also there was the matter of my having been lied to, systematically, by the very interpreters I had regarded as my friends. For weeks and months after March 12, 1969, I had asked about Jerry, and the answer was always the same: *He has been taken someplace else.* It may have been the official line, that they were forbidden to counter. But it was still a lie. And Middleschool was one of the liars. She had come late into my life in China, but too much information had been passed along, from one place and one person to another, to make it unreasonable to suppose she hadn't known it too.

I said to her, "One question first."

"Oh?" she said.

"Where is he buried?"

"He's not buried," she said, without bothering to go through translation. "He was cremated."

"What will happen to his things?"

"They'll be returned to you when you go out of China."

"When will that be?"

"I don't know. But soon, I think. Very soon. Come, we'll go back to the room."

We went back to the room. Charley had been pacing the floor, waiting for me. "We think you will be released the day after tomorrow," one of the interpreters said. "Tomorrow morning, we'll pack your things, and then spend a night in the hotel in Canton."

I wanted to confirm the fact that I was going to be released, and I hit upon the same tactic I had used at Red Star, to confirm that they were in fact bringing me to the hospital.

I said: "No."

Middleschool, Primary, and Seventeen all stared at me. They said: *"No?"*

"Not without my cat," I said.

It had worked at Red Star.

It wasn't going to work here.

"He *can't* go with you," they said to me. "The border officials won't take an animal."

And now it stopped being a question of me and became one of Charley instead. I said, "He can't survive if I leave him here."

"Of course he can," they said. "Look how fat all the other cats are."

"But he's afraid of people."

"No. The nurses love him, and the kitchen help too."

At that moment, Charley himself entered my room. He looked around at all the people. Then he jumped up to where I sat on the bed and pressed the top of his head against my neck. I could feel and hear the steady purring of contentment and security.

And now the number of people in my room increased. As if by mystic message, they came from all parts of the hospital to witness this sight: the captured American girl who in all these years in China had never broken, never cried: now clutching a nondescript cat and crying loud and openly, as though her heart must break.

* * *

In the morning, there were line-ups of people in my room, almost like a cast of a musical review coming onstage for their separate curtain calls. First a group of nurses to shake hands—then the children, each one bringing Charley a special tidbit to eat—and finally the doctors. Of this last group, each member suddenly had become a specialist, and he or she bore an emblem of his or her specialty: one with a stethoscope, another with a little rubber hammer, even a woman doctor who held a filled douchebag against her breast like a teddy bear while my final and cursory "discharge physical" was taking place.

Then Primary, Seventeen, Middleschool, and I were taken to a large hotel downtown and shown to our rooms: Seventeen and I in one of them, Primary and Middleschool in the other. After that to another room in the hotel off the lobby, where an army official sat behind a plain desk. There was one other man in the room with him:

Black Fan.

The same open-necked shirt; the same black fan moving back and forth before his dark-rimmed glasses. The army official spoke in Chinese to the interpreters. I noticed my passport lying on the desk, among other papers. But I was watching Black Fan, and he was watching me. There was no sense of victory for either of us. If my look had said to him *I won,* his look in return would have said *What did you win?* Instead, it was almost as though we were two highly skilled professionals, experts, he at being a captor and I at being a captive, now according each other a final exchanged glance of mutual respect: not so much because we had done our jobs that well, but because we had done them at all. We were like two veteran baseball players who face each other in a big game, do nothing in the game that makes headlines, then walk off the field together afterwards, sharing some private understanding of something that happened not just in that game but over all the times leading up to it.

"All right," Middleschool was saying to me now.

"What does that mean—all right?"

"You've been released. Here's your passport. Why don't we have some lunch?"

We went to lunch, but nobody ordered from a menu.

"On the sea, place your trust in the helmsman," Primary said to me. "In revolution, place your trust in Chairman Mao." It was one of the most revered and often-heard sayings in all China. If it had ironic implications for me, that was nothing to get paranoid about: its application was far too broad for anything like that. Here, Primary was using it to say: "And in this hotel, trust the chef."

"But I wanted to order Cantonese lobster," I said, knowing from as long ago as my talks with Lee at the Harbor that nobody in Canton had ever heard of Cantonese lobster. I'd intended it as a joke, a laugh-line, but I found the interpreters looking at me strangely as I talked. I think they fully expected me to react in some new and excited way because now my release was official.

There were several reasons why I didn't react that way. The first and (I would have supposed) most obvious was that I had been to this well too often before: I knew I had my official release, but I would believe it when I crossed the border into the New Territories north of Hong Kong, and not till then.

Another reason, which I think the interpreters could not have understood, was that in the very process of accepting my release for a fact, my mind had begun to conjure the problems that went with it. Some of them may sound absurd in retrospect, but they didn't seem that way at the time:

Where were my parents? I didn't know. Were they both

still alive? I didn't know. Would the shock of the news that I had been released kill one of them? I didn't know. If they weren't alive, what would I do to live? The Chinese had returned all my money, but that was barely enough to buy my passage back home. My return ticket on Pan Am? That had expired. Would they honor it anyway? I didn't know. Would the British even permit me to cross the border in my physical state, with my cough and eyes still not fixed and with perhaps other forms of disease I didn't even know about? I didn't know. Suppose everything else was all right and I did get back to the United States: would the Americans be mad at me for trespassing? For "confessing"? Would *they* put me in jail? I didn't know. My only contact with State Department policy had been while I was in Saudi Arabia, and that was hardly reassuring. The policy there was openly to avoid any inter-government trouble rather than to be concerned with the individual U.S. citizen. Was it the time now for President Nixon's forthcoming trip to China to be compromised by a girl who had taken off with an older man, confessed to trespassing, certified in writing that she had been well-treated? I didn't know.

But as if those first two reasons for my lack of enthusiasm were not enough, there was still another one: the most absurd of all, if you like. Already I was beginning to hatch a scheme to smuggle out my drawings, my house plans, my songs. Jerry's things, his clothes and his books, had now been delivered to my room. It was up to us—me and the interpreters—to pack them properly for the trip across the border. I restrained myself all day, waiting for the moment at night when Seventeen would fall asleep and I would have the room to myself.

Seventeen was not about to fall asleep. She was more excited than anyone. "Let me do it!" she kept saying. "You're tired," I would say. "Who can be tired at a time like this?" she'd ask.

At some point her ebullience began to force a little

common sense upon me. I was acting nonsensically. Was it worth it—worth what?—another four years or more in China?—to try to sneak out a picture of a flower, a verse of a song?

In a way, it *was* worth it, but the next morning, when we assembled to have breakfast and leave for the train station, I was thinking more logically.

Far more logically. "Be sure to take your sketch pad with you," Middleschool said to me. "They may let you take it across the border."

"No," I said.

"You don't want to have it with you?"

"I want to have it with me, but I don't want to be the one carrying it. *You* carry it."

She looked at me. "You don't seem to be in very high spirits."

"Neither do you."

"You have to understand," she said. "I've been to the border twice before."

My final decision, as we left for the train station in the morning, was to take two items of local manufacture with me.

One of them was an ashtray I had been given as a souvenir of one of my visits to the factories in and around Canton. The other was a tube of Chinese toothpaste.

I said to Middleschool, "Will they be angry at me because I have these things?"

"I don't see why," she said. "They don't make you different from any other tourist."

A car was waiting to take us to the railroad station. We had a waiting room all to ourselves, and sat there for perhaps a quarter of an hour until the train came. Then we got on and found we had our car almost to ourselves.

It was a two-hour trip from Canton to the border—a

distance of perhaps seventy miles, maybe less. We made two stops en route, where vendors came aboard the train selling tea.

Then we were at the border, but had to wait aboard the train till all the other passengers had debarked. I had a lot of luggage, both Jerry's and mine (I thought again of how remarkable it was, how much the *Menehune* could carry). I couldn't possibly handle it myself.

I didn't have to. As if some contrived climax to a play, two old women, wearing shapeless clothes and lampshade hats, came aboard the train. Mirror images, they were, of the two old women who had first rowed Jerry and me from the *Menehune* to the Island.

Somehow the two of them seized all the luggage there was—suitcases, pillowcases, boxes, books, clothes, blankets—and hauled them off the train, while the rest of us followed. The customs building was on one side of the tracks, a hotel on the other. We went to the hotel, then up three flights, where we had lunch: a big fish on a bed

Leaving China—old women baggage carriers.

of rice, the fish complete with fins and staring eyeball.

"How long are we going to be here?" I asked.

Nobody seemed to know. Seventeen said, "I brought a deck of cards. Do you want to play Red?"

"Yes," I said, and we began to play Red. Then one of the other interpreters came with a form. "You have to fill this out," she said. "It's a tourist declaration of how much money you have with you."

I began to fill out the form. I said: "When do we leave?"

"Soon," I was told, and soon we did. Back down to the bottom floor, then out onto the station platform. The train was still there. To get across to the customs station, we had to climb the steps of one of the cars, pass through the vestibule, then down and out through the other side. Ahead of me were the interpreters. Behind me were the two old-women luggage-bearers, pantingly ascending and descending the steps of the railroad car.

The customs inspection was thorough—it lasted at least an hour—but not unpleasant. There was no body search. The customs inspectors smiled all the time. They readily waved through my ashtray and my tube of toothpaste. As for my book of sketches, which I had left in Middleschool's hands—it was confiscated. But they wrote me out a receipt for it, as they did for everything else I had to leave behind. They even seemed annoyed when a photographer, who had accompanied us on the train from Canton, snapping pictures, now tried to invade their sanctum, and they ordered him away.

We went now to a waiting room, where we sat. Then, at some imperceptible signal, we went to another waiting room, where we sat some more. Then an army man came in and said something to Middleschool. She rose. "Say goodbye," she said to me. "In my opinion, that's the best thing to do." She was looking at me, and at Primary and Seventeen. I rose and shook their hands and followed Middleschool and the army man outside.

The border between China and Hong Kong is totally

uninteresting, and yet at the same time it is pure China. Jagged hills rise on either side of it, with the border itself marked by a deep ravine crossed by a single railway bridge. On the Chinese side there was a row of park benches, totally vacant. The five of us—myself, Middleschool, the army man, and the two old women with the luggage—sat by ourselves on one of the closest benches. After a time, at a signal from the army man, we all rose, went to the next bench, and sat down again. The process was repeated another time. And a time after that.

Of all the anti-climactic ways to end my stay in China, this had to be the best. And yet it suited my mood almost perfectly.

"Well," I heard Middleschool saying, at last. "It's time for you and me to shake hands goodbye."

The army man had gone away and come back. When he came back, he brought with him an ancient ox-cart. Silently, the two old women were stacking some of the luggage into the cart. Now Middleschool and I were walking, alone together, to the railroad bridge that crossed the ravine.

I said to her, "Will you take care of Charley for me?"

"He'll be cared for," she answered. "You mustn't worry."

We came to the bridge. She held out her hand. "I wish you success and happiness," she said.

"I wish you the same," I said, and we shook hands. I looked around. "What should I do now?"

"Walk across the bridge," she said. "Do you have your pocketbook with your passport?"

"Yes," I said.

"That's all you need," she said.

I turned and began to walk across the bridge. It was about 2:30 P.M. in the afternoon of what in the Far East was Monday, December 13, 1971. The bridge was narrow, and not more than, say, one hundred feet in length. I walked in the space between the outlapping of the single-track railroad ties and the bridge railing. Behind me were the two old women with the luggage. Ahead of me, at the Hong Kong end of the bridge, stood one man: a husky porter, waiting with a large, iron-wheeled, Railway Express kind of luggage carrier.

I reached the end of the bridge. "Hello," I told him. "I'm Mary Ann Harbert."

He looked at me as though I was crazy.

Now a man in uniform strode out from the building beyond, and came to where I was. He said, "We've been expecting you, miss." His voice was unbelievably British.

I said, "You mean you know who I am?"

"I don't mean that at all," he said. "All they told us was to expect Fecteau and a girl. My inclination is to assume you're the girl."

I said, "Fecteau?"

"He was on the same train you were. He crossed earlier by himself.* They may have held you up on that account, I'm afraid. So that would make you the girl. But who are you?"

"Mary Ann Harbert."

"Mary Ann Harbert."

"That's right."

"Well, you have the advantage of me," he said. "Perhaps you have some identification?"

"I have an American passport."

"That would be excellent."

"It's expired."

"It still might do."

I dug into my pocketbook and pulled out the passport. He stared at it for a long time, than back at me, then back at the picture in the passport again.

"Look," I said at last, "if you don't believe that's who I am, I have other identification."

"Ah," he said, "of course you have other identification.

*See page x.

How stupid of me!" He acted as though he didn't believe a word of it. "And what might that other identification be?"

I dug in my pocketbook again. "A Utah driver's license," I said.

"A Utah driver's license," he repeated.

"Expired," I said.

"Expired," he repeated.

"Do you want to see it?"

"No, I don't think I do." He handed me back my passport. "Will you come with me, please?"

I followed him into the low-lying customs building at the British side of the border.

"I guess this is her," he said to another uniformed man inside.

"But *naturally* it's her!" the other said. He was a young, greatly enthusiastic Scotsman. "Now would you believe we've been waiting for you?" he asked. "Your friend is already here. Would you like a beer, or perhaps a wee drop of something stronger?"

My "friend" of course was Fecteau. The Chinese had released two Americans that day. Fecteau was one of them, I was the other. He had been held for years on formal charges, and the U.S. had known about it. I had been held on no charges, and no one knew about me. We shared in common of course the fact that we were both Americans, but that was all. He had been in China far longer than I, under actual prison sentence, and now he sat off to one side, understandably withdrawn. We were introduced, but there was practically no talk between us. I suppose there are situations in which circumstances bring about "reunions" between people who were never united to begin with, but the release of two strangers from separate detentions in Red China would not, at least in this case, prove to be one of them.

Both of us were offered food, and both of us declined, though Fecteau said he would have a glass of beer.

"We've a doctor here for you, miss," the enthusiastic

Scotsman soldier said to me, and led me over to a tall Britisher who seemed, himself, an extraordinary specimen of excellent physical condition.

"I'm Mary Ann Harbert," I said to him.

"I see," he said.

"I suppose you want to know what diseases I've had."

"Do you? How long were you in China?"

"Almost four years."

"Very well," he said, and turned away.

I said, "Well, what do you want to know? My diseases—"

"My dear young lady," he said, "don't tell me your troubles. Tell them to the Americans. You walked across the room to me. We chatted for a moment. Everything was fine on both counts. I'm just here to tell you you can go home."

Similarly, he certified Fecteau as being well enough to travel, and it occurred to me that the British in fact wanted very little to do with any of this: their job was to turn us over to the Americans and see to it the latter got us out of there.

The latter were just about to do just that. From not far away we could hear the sound of an arriving helicopter, and soon there came through the door a man who had dark, graying hair and was, as the Chinese might say, not so tall. His name was Robert Drexler. I learned later that he was, at the time, chief of the political science department—a specialist on China—of the United States consulate in Hong Kong.

We talked briefly. He said, "Would you like to go home?"

I said, "How soon?"

"How about right now?" he said, and then: "By the way, where *is* home?"

I thought about it. "I guess I don't know," I said. "At least, I can't be sure of it. My parents were in California, but that was nearly four years ago."

Together with Fecteau and a British official, we went outside, and the four of us got into a waiting helicopter, which took us to a large military airport in Hong Kong proper. There we were taken to a special lounge—the "VIP Room," they called it—where an entire meal had been prepared for us, together with a complete layout of bottles: Scotch, bourbon, gin.

Another State Department man—tall, pudgy, wearing eyeglasses—was at the airport to meet us. He had just arrived from Washington, apparently on an unrelated assignment, and now had been instructed to turn around and accompany us back to the U.S.

His name was Robert McGee. He said to me, "I'll bet you've got quite a story to tell."

I said, "Is there anything you want to know?"

"You mean on an official basis? No."

"Is there anything you want me to say—you know, in public?"

"Lord, no," he said. "Say whatever you feel like saying."

I said, "I have a return ticket to San Francisco."

"I'm sure the air line will cash it in for you when you get back," he said. "But the ride's on us. So is the hospital at the other end. You might want to have a check-up."

This was quite a different State Department from the image I had had of it in the Middle East.

I said now, "But if I don't know where I'm going, how will you know where to take me?"

"Because your airplane knows where *it's* going," Mr. McGee said. First Clark Field in the Philippines, then a re-fueling stop at Honolulu, then non-stop to New Jersey."

"New Jersey?"

"McGuire Air Force Base."

"Why there?"

"Because it's closest to the hospital. The hospital's at Valley Forge."

They had selected Valley Forge, apparently, because it was close to the New England homes of Fecteau and a fellow prisoner named Downey, whose release also had been expected but did not take place. Obviously they had made no plans for me. They didn't expect me.

"It's too late to change where the plane's going," Mr. McGee said to me, "but if you feel like it, you can get off at Honolulu and take a commercial flight the rest of the way on your own. By that time we ought to know where your folks are."

He seemed singularly cheerful and alert for a man who had just flown from Washington, D.C., to Hong Kong and now directly was on his way back to New Jersey. "It's the secret way to handle jet lag," he explained to me. "If you do it fast enough, it never catches up with you."

With the food and whiskey offered but untouched, we were taken out now to a giant U.S. Air Force jet, a hinged cargo-type of plane. Inside there were some seats, all of them facing backwards; the rest of the area was given over to sets of chains from which litters could be hung. I asked some one aboard why we were stopping first at the Philippines.

"So you can fix your hair," he said, and grinned.

I'd worn a brown corduroy suit—half-Chinese, half-western in styling—when I walked across the border. At Clark Field they gave me a pair of slacks and two sweaters, one with short sleeves, the other with long. They also gave me a comb, a brush, and a can of hair-spray. I'd come out of China wearing my hair in one pigtail in back. The stopover at Clark Field was brief. But there was time enough for me get rid of that pigtail.

In one of two adjacent homes in the small town of Delta, Utah, on the morning of December 13, 1971, the television was tuned to The Today Show, *fed from the NBC outlet in Salt Lake City, one hundred miles to the north. The occupants of the two houses were not only neighbors but friends—two couples who had come to know each other through the fact that the husband in each case worked for the U.S. Geological Survey.*

In the house where the set was turned on, the husband was watching news. One item told him that a Mary Harbert had been released from Communist China.

The man who heard this shook his head for a moment, then went out and knocked on his neighbor's door. When the other man answered, he told him what he had heard.

They talked for a little bit. There was a tendency to believe that Gene and Polly Harbert, Mary's parents, already had heard the news. There was counter-balancing speculation as to what to do if they hadn't. Nobody wanted to be the one to make a cold phone call to the parents who had given the girl up for dead.

Finally, the second man picked up the phone and dialed a number in Palo Alto, California, the number not of the Harberts, who still lived there, but of yet another mutual friend from the Geological Survey, a man named Jack Minta.

"Jack," the second man said, when Minta answered the phone, "it's Jim Tennant in Utah calling. Russ Curtis just came from next door. He was watching the news —The Today Show—*it says the Harbert girl's alive—she just walked out of Red China."*

"Mary *Harbert?"*

"That's what Russ says."

It was perhaps 7:20 A.M. *in Utah at the time—6:20, an hour earlier, in California.* The Today Show *is staggered across the time zones. It goes on at* 7:00 A.M. *local time. Thus it would not be seen in Palo Alto for still another forty minutes.*

In Palo Alto, Jack Minta hung up the phone slowly. He knew he must call the Harberts. But first he needed to rehearse what it was he wanted to say, in case they hadn't heard.

It was not till after 6:30 that he finally picked up the phone again and dialed the Harberts' number. When it answered, he said, "Gene, this is Jack Minta. I just got a call from Utah. Have you heard anything? Have you got the television or the radio turned on?"

No. Gene Harbert had heard nothing. Minto plunged ahead. He told Gene Harbert what the phone call from Utah had said. "Watch *The Today Show* at seven," he said.

It didn't occur to Gene Harbert to do anything else. Once he had turned to Polly and told her the news, he recalls that there seemed no reason to doubt it. No one could invent such a story. And so the Harberts did not turn on the radio, did not open that morning's San Francisco *Chronicle*. The most important thing seemed for Polly to get dressed. It had a convincing logic all its own.

And then their telephone started jumping off the hook.

Some people were calling them. But others were calling the newspapers, the wire services, the television stations. The problem of the State Department people—to locate the Harberts—was no problem at all. The task was being executed for them instead by the public: caller after caller who not only knew who the Harberts were but where they were. Within an hour, reporters and photographers would be camped at their doorstep.

In logic, Gene Harbert's first order of business was to put in a call to the State Department in Washington, where it was now past 10:00 A.M. The result was predictable. He got an operator who shuffled him to an operator who shuffled him to a department which shuffled him to another department. Perhaps, he shared his daughter's formed impression of U.S. diplomats at work as they both had seen it in Saudi Arabia. Foremost *in his mind at this moment was that if she had been released at the Hong Kong border, he would have to go there to get her.*

Finally, he was put through, in his phone call to Washington, to a special subdivision. The woman's voice at the other end said, "Department of Welfare and Whereabouts."

Gene Harbert found it hard to believe that name, and said so.

"It's a good old name," the voice at the other end said stiffly. "It's been with us a long time."

Surely somewhere at Foggy Bottom there was a record of the missing-person report of forty months ago. Surely somewhere also there was the news of her release. But neither of these things had yet filtered down or up to the Department of Welfare and Whereabouts. It was left that they would call back.

There was another phone call to make, of course: from the Harberts to their other daughter, Mary Ann's sister Sue, as soon as she arrived at work at eight o'clock. The State Department didn't get back to them till ten o'clock, Pacific time, and by then the parents knew from the press everything Welfare and Whereabouts had to tell them: that she was just now about to land in Honolulu; that she had accepted an offer to continue on to the hospital at Valley Forge—no, she was not in any sort of critical condition, but some medical care and tests, undertaken wholly at government expense, could only be beneficial to her.

Stay by the phone, Welfare and Whereabouts said, because we're putting together a radio patch so you can talk to her. And don't say anything about where the plane is going or what route it's taking.

There was nothing cloak-and-dagger about that last part, not even when you consider that Gene Harbert, like many other people, had a subsurface awareness of the fact that in addition to its hospital, Valley Forge housed a CIA installation as well. At the core of it instead was simply an honest effort on the part of the State Department to shield Mary Ann and Fecteau from incursions by the press. In Mary Ann's case, as it was expressed to her father, they estimated in all good sense that she might not want to expend physical energy at this point on a battery of flashbulbs and TV cameras and shouts.

We landed at Hawaii, but there were so many reporters waiting at the ramp that nobody got off. I assume Fecteau wasn't up to a mass press conference at that point; I know I wasn't. We stayed on the plane, and by then I had decided it was the right thing to continue on to Valley Forge to accept the government's offer of free medical treatment and check-out. By now I knew that my parents had been located, alive and well, in Palo Alto. Already a phone patch was being put together—I could talk to them from the flight cabin of the plane almost as soon as we took off from Honolulu. And the stay of a week or so in a hospital, for what immediate care was necessary and a thorough checking-out, seemed to be by far the most logical course to take, even though it meant a delay in our physical reunion. The most important things were what we already knew: I knew they were living, they knew I was living.

The airplane did not have an elegant name but it seemed an elegant place to be: it was an aircraft of the 9th Airomedical Evacuation Group (PACAF), in charge of Col. William Johnson, Jr., a man who had a way of making you happy you were home. There were nurses aboard who served not as nurses but as stewardesses: suddenly I found I was ravenously hungry, and they brought out a steak dinner. They had other things to do, too: they began hanging Christmas decorations within the passenger cabin. Fecteau, the man who had come out of China the same day I did, reacted to this. He still was taken up with his own thoughts, but as he saw the tinsel he began, for the first time, to smile a little bit.

I spent a good measure of the time up front, in the flight cabin, where it was quieter. That was where, three different times as we flew from Honolulu to McGuire Air Force Base in New Jersey, I got the chance to talk via the plane's radio with my parents. Each time the connection was bad—so bad it was limited to shouted *Hello's* and *Can you hear me's?* on both sides—but it established our presence for each other, and that was what it was for.

When we landed at McGuire, there was another helicopter waiting, this one to take us the distance of perhaps forty miles across the northern outskirts of Philadelphia to Valley Forge. It was at McGuire that Mr. McGee, of the State Department, left us. He had flown from Washington to Hong Kong, back with us from Hong Kong to McGuire, and now was off for Hong Kong again, to resume his original assignment. I'm still ahead of the jet lag," he said to me. He smiled, cheerful as ever. "But *you'll* have insomnia."

He was right about me. I did have one or two wakeful nights at Valley Forge. As we went there from McGuire, in the helicopter, I could see the Christmas lights on all the suburban homes beneath us, and for the first time the sense of being back in the U.S. really took hold.

I was to spend the next nine days at Valley Forge. Not for debriefing. Two State Department people had taken over from McGee: at McGuire Air Force Base I was met by Mr. Alan Romberg—tall, bespectacled, gray-haired and correctly dressed—and at Valley Forge, State's man was Larry Davis, bespectacled too but short, well-rounded, the wearer of extra-mod loud clothes and bright-colored figured ties. Romberg's job was to talk to me and Davis' job was to talk to the press, and both of them acted in accordance with the sensible minimum. I had one brief press conference, set up by Davis; and where Romberg was concerned, he interviewed me once, in a session that lasted only two hours, and took hardly any notes.

On the list of my certified diseases, it was decided at Valley Forge that the Chinese, at the PLA Hospital in Canton, had cured me of pleurisy and colitis. My teeth were better, but with cavities still unfilled. The loss of my hair had been checked. At Valley Forge they went to work on my bronchitis, my earaches, and my eyes. I have to think the eyes were the most important. The diagnosis at Valley Forge was that I had trachoma, described in at least one medical text as "the largest single cause of blindness in the world." For the first time I appreciated the basic wisdom of the Chinese saying at the Commune of the Happy People: *Don't use other people's towels.* Trachoma is highly contagious and can be transmitted that way. But it responds to antibiotics.

And so did I. I told them at Valley Forge that I felt well enough to go home. After those broken-up attempted phone calls while my plane was en route, I had called my parents from Valley Forge the next morning, and we had a long and clear conversation. I understood it when my mother said she wanted to be at the hospital the instant I arrived there. But there was governing good sense to doing it the way it was done, and we all knew that.

I flew back to San Francisco, from Philadelphia, on United Airlines, on December 23—two days before Christmas, four days before my twenty-sixth birthday. The discharge date was of my own choosing. I remember thinking *People aren't nice* when I left the U.S. in 1968, but that thinking had changed now. Lots of things had changed. At Valley Forge, I saw Ed Sullivan on television, and he had sideburns! The government didn't pay for my transportation from Philadelphia to San Francisco, practically all by myself in the first-class section of the United passenger jet: my father did. He sent a check to the airline. They didn't say anything about it, one way or the other. Instead, they simply declined to cash the check.

When we arrived at San Francisco, in mid-afternoon, one of the stewardesses asked me to stay on the plane till everyone else had left. As the other passengers moved past me to leave by the front exit almost without exception they turned to me and said things like "Welcome home," or "Good to have you back."

Then I was alone, and my father came into the airplane.

We had a moment together, and then we went out to where my mother and sister were waiting. Then there was the sudden surrounding of television lights, and I was to have a press conference, similar to one I'd had at Valley Forge. The exchanges that stay in my memory are:

Q. Before you were in China, what career did you have in mind?
A. Prison work.
Q. What would you like for Christmas?
A. A cat.

The prison didn't come; the cat did. In the factual outcome, I was flooded by offers of cats; but I put them off, not because I wanted to select one cat against another so much as because my parents lived in an apartment complex where no pets were permitted, and even though the management might have looked the other way in my case, I wanted a place of my own. I found one —a one-bedroom apartment in Santa Clara, with a little patio extending out behind—and at that point I accepted a cat from the Blossom Time Cattery, in Thousand Oaks, California. He was an extremely special kitten. His name is Zack. Such cats as he are known officially as "Ragdoll," but that serves almost to belie their heritage, for they are of a particular Himalayan extract, a near-sacred Burmese-Persian strain. But if Zack was aristocratic, he was playfully so. Time and again I would come home from shopping, and look around for him, and not find him, for he is a believer in camouflage. Sometimes he would be lying inert across the shelf of the end table beside the couch. Other times I would look across the room, and all of a sudden the wastebasket would start moving, as if occupied by a serpent in need of a conjurer's flute.

In this manner he was to become my closest friend. But he had sad eyes—not China eyes, just sad eyes—so I got him a friend, a little white kitten, and then the same thing happened that had happened at the Commune of the Happy People: a bird—a sparrow this time—flew into the yard, and was injured. I kept the cats inside the apartment while I went out to get a bird cage, and I came back and rescued the sparrow and put him in the cage inside, where now he is fed on birdseed and sings all the time.

So many people went out of their way to be nice to me when I came home. At first the publicity was immense, then it started to drop off. The last picture of me in the paper was with Zack when I first got him, perhaps three months after I returned from China.

But the nice people remained. I guess it is fair to say the minority of others remained too. I never heard from them directly, but the feedback was always there. They were a recognizable type: the conspiracy-minded. They preferred the account that Jerry had hanged himself, although of course I had told this for what it really was in public. That was "evidence" against him, they thought. With a little added knowledge, it could become even an added indictment: some who heard he was an expert cartographer concluded that no such expert, even if he were aboard a boat (so long as the boat was within some sight of land) could ever "trespass." So to this day they think he did it intentionally.

The same group takes even a stranger look at me, for I was the one who lived. They see that I was never actually imprisoned, walked out of China after nearly four years in apparently good physical shape, by-passed my parents to spend an immediate nine days at the CIA headquarters in Valley Forge. From all this, they draw the conclusion that I myself must have been the spy. The evidence may leave them troubled in one respect, because of one question they cannot answer. It is one thing to decide that somebody must be a spy.

But for which side?

There is a mosaic of other things that happened after I got home. Upon my father's retirement, he and my mother moved to San Jose from Palo Alto. (When I left in 1968 they were living in Menlo Park; when I returned they were in Palo Alto. Interesting: Menlo Park and Palo Alto are practically side-by-side, but how would I have known about that in China?) For my own part, I took my own apartment in Santa Clara, then in the fall of 1972 moved to another apartment in Burlingame, also a suburb of San Francisco, but closer to the city. With my strength returned I was looking for work. Prison work? No. My sense of mind would not permit that, at least not yet. Secretarial work, yes. Except that people kept looking at you strangely when you told them you had no job experience over the past four years, and there were doors that closed on that account.

I caught up on old news: Frederick, my cat in Salt Lake City, had been taken to live with people in Arizona. He had a wheezing that passed for asthma, though in fact it turned out instead to be an allergy against fleas, but in the end he encountered a dry climate, and eventually in Arizona he died a natural death.

My eyesight was restored one hundred percent. That was interesting too, in its way. At the hospital in Valley Forge, they put through a crash order for new glasses that I could wear when I flew home to San Francisco. I had brought contact lenses and prescription sunglasses to Hong Kong with me, and of course the contacts had become both corroded and warped. At the hospital in Canton, Seventeen showed me how you can use toothpaste on things like contact lenses and the faces of watches to reduce scratch-marks, but my lenses were beyond the point of that kind of repair. Had I ever gone to the Chinese and asked them for new glasses? No. It never occurred to me. One of the reasons it never occurred to me was that it never would have occurred to them. I had prescription sunglasses and I could see through them. Thus why would I need anything new? Also, their "specialists" were not available, any more than their dental care was available. Once I got to the hospital, they did have their version of a dentist, but I saw the work he did, just as earlier I had seen the glasses the Chinese wore. None of it was reassuring. I settled for what I had.

From the Chinese translators, I had picked up a "British" accent. Gradually, after my return to the U.S., I lost it. I wondered whether I would dream of China. I have never dreamed of China. I wondered whether things here would remind me of things there. It didn't happen. If you want to call April 1968-December 1961 the "lost years" of my life, maybe there lies the most realistic proof of all: the shortage of memories.

When I first got home, I went out a lot. I was living on adrenalin, I guess, because there would be bleak and down days of no energy in between, but at least it was fun. When I say I "went out," I mean for evenings with my parents and sister and with friends. At one restaurant we went to, a man at a neighboring table looked to me, then said in a loud voice:

"Look! It's the chick from China!"

The chick from China. All right. Jerry's father, whom I had never met, came to California, and we talked together. I told him the Chinese version of Jerry's death was a lie. That was what I could provide by way of comfort.

It was wrong to make broad statements. One of the Chinese could be capable of saying *When drinking water do not fail to remember the man who dug the well* as though it were an admonition from Chairman Mao himself. And yet it was the most ancient of Chinese sayings: it was written in Chinese on the cup that was one of the marks of hospitality awaiting me in my room at the first hotel of the Commune of the Happy People.

They appreciated the new: I taught the interpreters to play checkers on their most ancient Chinese chessboard just as they had taught me their game of chess. The rules of chess on that same board were that once you crossed the Pearl River you never returned.

There is no point in attaching special significance to that. For I had crossed the river and returned. It had meaning for me. Coming back from Red Star, en route to the hospital and freedom, I turned to one of the interpreters as we went over the bridge.

"The Pearl?" I asked.

"No," she said.